ON LOOKING BACK

Elizabeth Dumpleton

Matador
9 Priory Business Park
Kibworth Beauchamp
Leicestershire LE8 0RX, UK
Tel: (+44) 116 279 2299
Fax: (+44) 116 279 2277
Email: books@troubador.co.uk
Web: www.troubador.co.uk/matador

ISBN 978 1783062 607

British Library Cataloguing in Publication Data.
A catalogue record for this book is available from the British Library.

Typeset in Minion Pro by Troubador Publishing Ltd
Printed and bound in the UK by TJ International, Padstow, Cornwall

Matador is an imprint of Troubador Publishing Ltd

To my good friends:
Annette for getting me started, and Pat (my former neighbour)
for her outstanding patience in the reading and correcting
of this book.

Also thanks to my family for all the laborious manuscripting
the book entailed.

CONTENTS

JOHN

Charlie

Joe

ARTHUR

JIM

FOREWORD

In this modern day and age nobody would bat an eyelid at the ratio of single mothers in our society today. They are mostly women, who, for one reason or another, have decided to take on the formidable task of raising their families alone, with all that entails.

My mother was one such person who chose to take on this struggle, but at what cost?

In making this decision, the gods decreed that she had not much choice, but the difference between now and then is that, in my mother's day, you needed to be very brave and strong in character to take such a step. A woman of her time, during the 1930s era, didn't have the independence that women enjoy today. They had no careers to fall back on and no family allowance to help them survive. In fact they had nothing very much.

Sometimes, of course, a woman who leaves her marriage, usually with very good reason, can look to her own parents for help and support and this is a very fortunate person; to have a family to help her through the darkest days.

My mother had none of this. She survived purely on thrift and the support and friendship of our immediate local Catholic church who gave to her as much assistance as they were able. However, my mother never took their caring for granted; she needed it too much.

Today, the church has become somewhat redundant with the growth of affluence in our society. People, to a large degree, don't seem to find pleasure in the simple things of life as we did then. They are too distracted by all the technology that comes with affluence. But are they any happier? I sometimes think that they are not.

I am not advocating a return to the bleak time that my mother knew, but there was a contentment then in families that doesn't seem to exist today. We accepted our situation in life, and strove to survive what was meted out to us under our own steam so to speak.

Had my father lived up to his responsibilities towards his family, instead of being a feckless waster, he, and my mother, could have lived fairly comfortably in spite of the depression of that era. He was a skilled man in regular employment, whose wages, instead of providing properly for his family, went on drink in the pub where he spent each evening with other wasters like himself. For these men, there was no tomorrow, no sense of responsibility, nothing but the drink.

After a period of time when it had been necessary for my mother to intercept him each Friday as he left his employment with his wages, to cajole money from him before his sojourn to the pub, she at last decided to rebel. She set the wheels in motion for a legal separation from him. There was a limit to what even she was prepared to endure.

Nothing could be worse than this fraught situation, and so, with the limited help from the welfare, she moved lock, stock and barrel with the children, into our drab little house in Kent Street. Our salvation lay in her resilience and the help of the church while she brushed my father to one side and poured scorn on his head. She was determined to make it alone.

This first book tells of the amazing fortitude of my mother in rearing her five boisterous sons, and their younger sister, through immeasurable odds. An East-End family living precariously on the edge in a nondescript three up, two down dwelling, alongside other equally nondescript houses with their own little colony of featureless shops dotted along the extensive street.

The huge church, surrounded by a lovely park, just around the corner at the top of the street, dominated the area and was a major feature in the life of my family. Its stalwart support made life a little more bearable for my mother and others in the street who were in the same predicament as ourselves, even though my brothers were a shameful nuisance to the church with their ridicule and unacceptable derision. Joe, the eldest, was the main culprit, which left my mother at times mortified and embarrassed as she fought a losing battle with him, and his brothers, to conform.

Some of the boys' attempts within the book to earn a little money for themselves are quire hilarious. One memorable encounter with their feckless father, when my mother called on his support in disciplining Joe, proved quite disastrous. But even without this support, her unruly, swearing and forceful brood emerged eventually into stable beings.

But the toll on my mother, in due course, took its effect. She died when I was just nine years of age leaving me to endure a second stage of my life without her or my brothers. This was a life fraught with unhappiness and danger which was to occur during the period of my sudden evacuation to the country; the war with Germany having finally and irrevocably erupted.

The Author and Her Family

PROLOGUE

By the law of averages, I should not be around for the writing of this book, nor the subsequent ones, but it has to be said that in this life, against all the odds, there are the survivors, which is obviously the category into which I fall.

I allow no interference with the presentation of my autobiography, because only I know how it should be told – how to compel the reader to read on.

Those of a fastidious disposition should not attempt to indulge the book because of its initial coarseness and swearing but one could never accuse these indiscretions in the family of being profane. To them, this mode of behaviour was completely intrinsic, with no offence whatsoever intended.

Each chapter that I have written in the book evoked different emotions within me. The one about John, for instance, with it being rather poignant, so that in certain parts a tearfulness overcame me as I intertwined the circumstances of his death with Thomas Hardy, the famous novelist and poet and yet earlier in this chapter I had laughed as I recounted the episode in John's earlier years when he was young, of a bucket of horse manure being tipped over his head during a fierce confrontation with another boy who had tried to muscle in on his endeavour to earn himself some pocket money with the manure venture.

The book goes along in this vein, with the reader chortling one minute but then sinking into a concerned sadness the next.

Whatever the opinion, however, the reader might conclude from this autobiography, I know that no-one could ever deem it to be monotonous. It is a compelling, compassionate read from start to finish; the only problem being the compulsion to not put the book down until the very end! 'ON LOOKING BACK'

PART ONE

THE EARLY YEARS

THE PARK

The church bells rang out loud and clear, as Sister Margaret hurried along the path that led from the front entrance of the church into the adjacent park.

The wailing that she heard was mournful, pitiful, each utterance almost ending in a howl. She had a very good idea from whom this wailing came and had already decided to take the necessary action. This was happening far too often she thought as she thrust herself forward. It would be unfair to ignore the child's distress any longer, and so she continued with a determined step. Yes! This time it would be sorted out once and for all.

There I sat on the log where my brothers had left me, and I was bawling my head off.

"You stay 'ere, Liz," Joe had said to me while holding my protesting body firmly down. "Stay 'ere awright?" I didn't want to stay 'ere, I wanted to be with them, and I continued to wrestle with him to escape from his unyielding grip on me.

"Yer can't come wiv us, yer can't," he told me in his hardened manner.

"Why can't I then?" I persisted.

"We don' wan no girls tagging along, that's why." He had no intention of giving up, but he modulated his voice a little as he said, "You look after the cart fer us though, eh Liz. We'll 'ide it in the bushes 'ere. Don' let no one take it awlright! Don' let no one take it," he emphasised, staring rigidly at me, eyeball to eyeball, as he pressed home the point which left

3

me in no doubt as to the consequences of not guarding the cart, with my life if necessary. Then he was gone as he quickly scampered off with the others leaving me alone there, 'dumped' in the park, just like some old piece of unwanted baggage.

The park surrounded the church where we would come each day to get from under my mother's feet. It was, if you like, a refuge of sorts, and we spent many hours there. It wasn't too far from the house, which we would leave soon after breakfast each morning, weather permitting. If it was raining my mother would almost pull her hair out.

"Oh no!" she would exclaim, looking out of the window as my younger brothers squabbled and rolled around the floor fighting while I just sat and sucked my thumb. "I 'ope this rain won't last fer too long. Get up will yer and be'ave!" she shouted at the boys who needed to be out to get rid of their surplus energy.

But how could she push them out into this? She tried to be reasonable now. "Joe, John, ge' into the kitchen and do some sandwiches," she told the two older boys, "this rain probably won't last fer long."

The school holidays were unbearable for my mother with five boisterous, unruly boys to cope with. What would she do without the park?

Sandwiches done and stacked in a carrier bag with a large bottle of lemonade, the rain having eased to just a drizzle, off we trudged.

"Yer can sit in the shelter at the park and eat yer sandwiches if the rain comes on again, carn't yer?" she threw at us in a guilty tone as we left the house.

"Yer awright," said Joe, resigned to the fact that what my mother was trying to say was, "just don't come home before four o'clock!"

We'd spend many a day just sitting in the shelter reading comics, sorting through flick cards, comparing marbles or just talking; anything to pass the time until the rain stopped. Then we could venture within the bounds of the park. It was just a short walk as we left through the front door. Picking up the cart on the way from behind the garden gate we turned right and walked along the street until we reached the main road which led to our destination. We would turn towards the church, not too far along the road, and take a short cut at the side of it, while

4

looking furtively at the church's front entrance, uncertain if this short cut through the grounds was allowed. Would Father Joseph or one of the Sisters suddenly appear to reproach us for this misdemeanor and reprimand us? But they never did. If they had ever noticed us I think they would have let it go, realising, obviously, that this was a safer route than our taking the weary trek along the main road.

I was being pulled along by my brothers in a home-made wooden cart consisting of a soap box flanked by pram wheels and two long wooden handles attached to either side. They would take turns in getting between the handles, then, tipping the cart up, would stride along like a horse between the shafts of a barrow.

On several occasions I had been shot straight out of the cart when it had been tipped up too abruptly. Of course I would cry bitterly but my brothers would just say impatiently, "Ow shu' up Liz!" It was a real chore for them to have to drag me along all the time wherever they went.

"What's 'appened to 'er now?" my mother would holler later that day when she finally noticed my battered and bruised face. She would automatically turn to Joe, he being the eldest. Last time it had been a split lip, the time before a cut forehead.

"It wasn't my fault," remonstrated Joe. "She came out when Jimmy tipped the cart up. She should 'old on tighter," he finished, looking sullenly at me.

My mother leant forward and swiped him. "Well don't let it 'appen again!" she shouted. "You know 'ow delicate she is."

…Glancing through my tears now, I saw Sister Margaret hurrying along the pathway from the church, her black habit billowing behind her, a look of concern on her lovely face. As I realised she was heading towards me, my wailing became louder and the tears coursed in profusion down my grubby face. The effect on Sister Margaret was immediate and she hastened her stride towards me.

"Now, Liz," she spoke to me in her soft voice. "What are you doing here all alone? Where are your brothers?"

"They've left me," I sobbed, the tears blinding my eyes.

"Are they here in the park?" she asked.

"Yes somewhere," I replied.

"Come along then, Liz," she said gently. "Let's go and find them shall we?"

She drew me up from the log that I sat on, wiping my tears at the same time with a corner of her habit. But as we walked off I suddenly remembered the cart hidden in the bushes. The boys had left me in charge so that no other gang could walk off with it.

"Sister, wait!" I pleaded. "The cart!"

"Where?" she said, looking all confused.

"In the bushes, look!" I said as I attempted to retrieve it. No way could I abandon it. My life wouldn't be worth living. It had taken the boys a whole week to construct, with a lot of squabbling, falling out and swearing at one another.

After a lot of twisting and tugging, a slight look of disdain on her face, Sister at last managed to retrieve the cart. Then, taking me with one hand and one of the handles of the cart with the other, we proceeded to trundle somewhat haphazardly in search of the boys.

The park was a haven for all of the kids in the district, who would spend hours within its confines, out from under their parents' feet with the usual sandwiches and lemonade to sustain them throughout the day. They would play their games of marbles or flick cards and sit comparing, swapping, or just talking the same as us.

The girls would wheel their dolls in rickety prams, bought by their mothers for them from the second-hand shop along the High Street. Or they would skip with their skipping ropes or play hop-scotch with the boys, the chalk having been obtained from the dump on the other side of the park, hidden from view by tall irregular shrubs just left to grow wild.

Now my legs were aching. The park suddenly seemed a very big place and I started to stumble.

"Sister!" I cried.

"Hush, Liz," she said, looking down at me. "I think I can hear them. Stay here a minute."

She sat me down on a small wall, the cart beside me, and proceeded to make her way towards a thicket not far off. She trod warily over the ground stubble and as she parted a clump of bushes all hell was let loose! Sister Margaret had walked straight into an attack!

The boys had joined up with another gang and were playing 'wars', and, thinking she was the enemy, had pelted her with missiles forcing her to duck and dive to avoid them.

"Boys, boys!" she shouted at them. "Listen to me! Listen, will you?"

The attack stopped as suddenly as it had started and faces stared at her from the trees where they had climbed. Clambering down, Joe apologized now to Sister. "We thought it was the enemy coming after us," he explained. "We didn't know it was you Sister."

She adjusted her habit while extending a conciliatory hand out to Joe. "It's alright Joe," she told him as the others climbed from the trees and joined him. Sister Margaret studied them. They were five brothers so completely different in looks and character as ever brothers could be.

Joe, the eldest, stood reverently before Sister now with his blond hair and square face. John beside him was dark and swarthy looking. Arthur was blond with fine chiseled features and expressive blue eyes. Charlie was dark like John and then, lastly, Jimmy the youngest, squinting up at Sister, having left his glasses at home.

"Boys..." she started again, "why have you left Liz all alone in the park? Isn't that rather unkind?" She inclined her head to one side in a questioning manner as she looked at them. The boys stood in silence.

"We were just 'aving a game of war, Sister. Liz can't play 'cos she's a girl," Joe reasoned with her in a polite manner. He had a lot of respect for Sister Margaret. Wasn't it she who came each week to the house with sweets and comics for the family when he was so ill and confined to bed? The comics were like gold dust to the boys, each reading them in turn from cover to cover and sucking the sweets to the very last drop. They weren't used to such luxuries and were quite sorry when Joe eventually recovered and the treats stopped.

"Now, Joe," Sister persisted, "you can't leave Liz all on her own. It's not safe."

"Sorry, Sister," they said, one after the other.

They all loved Sister Margaret. It was she who comforted their mother during her 'down spells', when life as a single parent became too much for her. She made life bearable for them at these troubled times by taking some of the seemingly insurmountable burdens that weighed the family down.

"Let's talk about it, Janey," she would say in a sympathetic manner to my mother when she was once more going through one of her tearful episodes. Sister would sit me on her lap and enfold her arms around me, while at the same time drinking the inevitable tea as she listened…

Joe took my hand now. "Come on Liz, it's almost time ter go 'ome anyway."

He hauled me into the cart and we started the journey back. As we trudged through the churchyard, Jimmy whined to go in the cart. He wasn't much older than me. It had been a long day and he was tired, and, like the rest of us, hungry. We had eaten all of the sandwiches as soon as we had got to the park.

"No point in waiting," Joe had said as he had eaten more than his fair share.

Joe now pulled me deftly on his back while Jimmy was plonked in the cart. Charlie and Arthur took a handle each to pull him along and John brought up the rear. As we passed the church, the boys turned in unison to the large clock on the front of its edifice. Yes, bang on time!

Although my mother couldn't get rid of us quickly enough in the morning, she worried and made a fuss if we were late getting home in the afternoon. The clock was the family's lifeline as we never had one that functioned properly in the house and we certainly couldn't afford a new one.

"Quick, nip out and see what the time is," my mother would say on any given day to whichever boy was playing nearest the front door. A loud groan would go up as the unfortunate victim would have to get up and tumble into the street. He would run hell-for-leather to look at the church clock and then hell-for-leather back to continue what he had been intent on doing before he was so rudely interrupted.

Catastrophe wasn't far off, when one day the clock unbelievably stopped working.

"Not working? What do yer mean?" My mother looked hard at John as he dashed back home with the devastating news. "It must be working! 'Ow can we manage without it?" she insisted, a worried look on her face.

"It's not working mum," John said in an exasperated tone. "Go and see for yerself if yer don't believe me!"

"I will too!" My mother put her hat on and opened the door. "I'll 'ave to speak to Father Joseph about this. 'Ow will I know when to send yer all off to school."

She walked up the street in an indignant manner, determined to have this out with Father Joseph, as though he owed it to the family to keep this essential piece of equipment functioning always.

Within a few days of my mother's visit, a collection was being made by the church on behalf of the clock. Everybody in the street was called upon and expected to contribute. We obviously weren't the only ones to rely on it. My mother dropped a sixpence into the box, after holding on to it for as long as she could, a hurt expression on her face. For some reason she thought she should be exempted from contributing, even though we probably used this facility more than anyone else.

"I 'ope that as I'm making this sacrifice, we won't 'ave ter wait too long for the clock to be working again," she said frostily to the collector.

"It's being worked on now," came the reply.

My mother breathed a sigh of relief. How could we possibly manage without a clock. It was almost like losing your right arm. We did have Auntie Queenie living in one of the rooms upstairs and she had a functioning clock, but we bothered her as little as possible. My mother relied on her small rental of the room to survive. But Father Joseph, true to his word, had the clock restored within a few days and life was able to get back to normal.

⁓

…Five scruffy, weary and famished boys, now, with one sniveling little girl perched very uncomfortably on Joe's back, traipsed home. A little way from the house he plonked me on to the pavement.

"Come on, Liz, yer can walk the last few yards," he said, panting slightly.

I skipped a little in front, feeling more rested for the piggy-back ride. However as I reached the house, the sound of a growl suddenly stopped me in my tracks. The vicious, snarling little dog from next door was quickly upon me. He had been hiding behind the end of the garden fence and took me completely by surprise.

As I screamed, Joe, like a flash of lightning, stepped quickly in front of me just as the dog did its usual trick of whipping around in retreat. He had achieved his aim of frightening the life out of me and now he would back off, but he wasn't quite quick enough as Joe shot his foot under the assailant and booted him clean off the ground. The dog sailed through the air before coming back down to earth spread-eagled on all four paws.

His yelping, as he scampered back to home ground, quickly brought our equally aggressive neighbour like a bolt from the blue through her front door.

"Yer cruel vicious brute!" she hollered at Joe, picking the dog up and fussing it. "I saw what yer did to my little Bobby and I shall be round to yer mother later, just see if I won't."

Joe just shrugged his shoulders and pushed me into the house. "Silly old bag," he muttered to himself, as we all traipsed along the passage after him.

Later that evening, we were all seated around the big family table in the kitchen ravenously consuming the inevitable stew, (our staple diet), which was more vegetables than meat. My mother magically succeeded in making it so delicious with its thick gravy poured over a big plate of potatoes and dumplings. We never tired of it and even today it's still one of my favourite meals.

Mrs Rumble, as good as her word, stood rapping at the back door now. She had made her way round and seen us through the kitchen window. My mother hurried to let her in and she came straight to the point, while looking enviously at our appetizing stew.

"Your Joe," she said, an indignant look on her face, but still eyeing our plates, "your Joe…" but before any more was said, she turned to my mother and modulated her voice, "now Janey, yer know I'm not one to complain don't yer?"

Mother, not sure whether to nod or shake her head, just looked uncertainly at her, knowing full well that Mrs Rumble always had something to gripe about. She chose to ignore the snigger that had come from the boys.

"I'm not one to complain, as yer know," the whining voice persisted, and my mother gave the boys a warning look, "but your Joe almost killed my little Bobby just cos 'e went up to greet Liz when they came 'ome," she lied. "'E kicked 'im clean up in the air! It almost gave me a heart attack, I can tell yer!" She clutched at her chest as the boys spluttered into their stew with mirth. My mother looked aghast.

"Is that right, Joe?" she demanded, knowing how much the dog meant to her neighbour.

"No it aint right," replied Joe, unabashed as he continued to consume his stew. He had a nonchalant expression on his face that so typified him. " 'E went fer Liz, so I kicked him up the arse!"

A stunned silence ensued, broken only by John's explosive guffaw into his stew, splaying it in all directions.

"Eeeeee!" exclaimed Mrs Rumble, shocked to the core. "Eeeeee! What do you think to that then? What sort of language is that to be using?"

My mother, to save face, leaned across the table and clipped Joe smartly across the ear. His plate shot to one side, went up in the air, and came down plop into his lap.

"You old cow!" he shouted in a rage to Mrs Rumble. But he was more upset at losing his stew than anything else and he looked in sadness at the mess accumulating on the floor.

As we all looked on, somber now, Joe rushed through the door and tore upstairs to Auntie Queenie. My mother looked at Mrs Rumble in an apologetic manner. "You see 'ow difficult it is fer me," she implored of her, "with no man to discipline 'im?"

But Mrs Rumble wasn't that bothered anymore and left now with a smug expression on her face. She had achieved what she had set out to do. Joe had been clouted, and that made her feel a lot better.

"We'll let it go this time, Janey," she said, sliding out the back door, "just as long as it doesn't 'appen again." And with a sharp sniff of the nostrils she sailed away.

In the meantime Auntie Queenie had replenished Joe upstairs. "A growing boy needs his food," she informed my mother when she came down later with him. "I'll skin that woman alive if she comes around causing any more trouble. Don't you fuss now Joe," she consoled him. "I'd believe you any time over her. Grumble, that's what her name should be, not Rumble."

We all laughed at this, but my mother was too busy cleaning up the stew on the floor to see the funny side of the quip. "You should be doing this Joe," she told him, but Joe was laughing with the rest of us. He had forgotten the confrontation with Mrs Rumble, or should I say, Mrs Grumble, as she was in future referred to by us.

Joe suspected that his mother was afraid of our formidable neighbour but he certainly wasn't. He was afraid of nothing and no one.

"If that dog goes for Liz again," he told us younger ones later, "'e'll get another kick up the arse!"

We all fell about laughing at this remark. However, after this upsetting episode, Joe developed a very negative stance towards dogs in general. He wouldn't necessarily harm them, but he wouldn't give them the time of day either.

"Clear off!" he would shout if any were brave enough to approach him. This attitude persisted until an incident occurred later in his life when he had matured somewhat and had entered into matrimony with Jessie.

SCRUFF

Joe had met and married Jessie who lived next door to the flat in which we, as a family, eventually moved to; it being more modern and more spacious than the house in Kent Street which we had completely outgrown.

Jessie lived with her parents Lill and Fred and when she and Joe became one, Joe moved in with them. He had become a drinker but Lill and Fred had looked upon their future son-in-law with great pleasure as he courted Jessie. They were drinkers themselves so they recognised in Joe a fellow being and welcomed him with open arms. He only had to transfer his belongings from one door and through another, just a few steps away along the balcony on the fifth floor of the modern block of flats.

Their complete social life revolved around the local pub, as was the custom of most Eastenders, just as people in the suburbs would be intertwined with their local church. Joe's habitual drinking meant that each evening he would be with Jessie and her parents in their local pub talking and imbibing with the other regulars. Nobody was ever lost for words and the longer the drink flowed the louder the talking became.

On one particular evening, Lill and Fred decided to leave earlier than usual. They left Jessie and Joe still bantering and chatting with the usual crowd, and to those left in the pub the time just flew by. It was with some surprise then when the cry went up "Time Gentlemen Please!" The landlord, having rather indulged himself, suddenly realised to his horror that it was way past closing time, a quite serious offence in those days. He went around now taking half consumed drinks away from his customers.

"Time Gentlemen Please!" he hollered again. "Now come on Joe, do you want me to lose my licence?" He pushed him and Jessie gently towards the door. As they staggered rather unsteadily out into the street they were not to know that within a very short space of time, life for the family was to take on a completely new dimension.

To say that Jessie and Joe had had rather more than they should have would be some understatement. It was more by accident than design that they found their way home at all that night, but as they now lumbered past the doors of the pub Joe suddenly stopped in his tracks and looked back.

"Whash that?" He had noticed a slight movement to one side of the pub door, but it was quite dark now and he couldn't easily make out what it was. He moved towards the object as Jessie clung to his arm in alarm. "Oh Joe, what is it?" she exclaimed in a frightened voice "is it a bomb?" The war, you see being well into its fruition. "Don't be bloody silly, Jesh!" Joe told her enunciating each word carefully, as he was having considerable difficulty with some of his speech, having drunk more that he should. "Well I never, itsh a little dog" he said, almost tumbling over it as he went nearer.

They both stood contemplating the shivering animal huddled close to the door. It appeared to be sleeping but opened its eyes at their approach and feebly wagged its tail at them.

"What can we do, Jesh?" Joe looked anxiously at the dog. "We can't jush leave it 'ere, the poor little bugger must be frozen!" He gingerly scooped the dog into his arms and surveyed it. "What you doing 'ere then?" he asked the dog unnecessarily, while holding the bedraggled creature aloft, and wondering at the same time on the best course of action.

"We'll take 'im 'ome he decided then, his mind made up, we can't jush leave 'im to freeze to death 'ere, can we?" Joe tucked the dog under one arm and Jessie took the other. She wasn't at all sure that this was the right thing to do, but if this is what Joe had decided, that's how it had to be, but as they negotiated their journey Jessie started to limp badly. "Oh Gawd, Joe; my poor feet!" Don't go so fast she implored him now. Jessie, being a mere 5 feet nothing, tried to compensate for her lack of height by wearing shoes with a six inch heel, and always complained when she had to walk any distance, but Joe wanted none of it, he was more concerned for the shivering creature tucked under his arm at that moment and he gave his wife short-shrift.

"I've told you before, Jesh", Joe admonished her, wear more sensible shoes, I don't want to keep 'earing about your poor bloody feet!" They continued haphazardly towards home with not another word from Jess.

Surprisingly they came in sight of the block of flats without any mishap and Joe steered his wife, who was hobbling quite badly now, towards the elevator, but she hung back scared. "Joe, you know I can't go in lifts, you know I'm claustrophobic!" Joe clicked his teeth in annoyance. In the first flush of courtship and marriage he would think nothing of carrying her, light-hearted and laughing, up the five flights of stairs to the balcony where they lived with Lill and Fred, but not this time.

"Jesh, you either come in the lift or you stay down 'ere. Please yerself, I can't carry both you and the dog." She had no option then but to quickly follow on. The dog had already started to take over their lives.

In the flat they found Lill and Fred sprawled on the settee in front of a warming fire, and as Joe plonked the dog down on to the rug in front of it, Lill shot up in alarm.

Oh! my Gawd, what's that?" she exclaimed as she gawped at this shivering apparition crouching in front of the fire.

"Itsh a dog, Lill," he told her.

"I can see that, Joe, but what's it doing 'ere?"

"Someone's slung it out, Lill, what could we do, we couldn't just leave it, could we?" he threw the dog a compassionate look. "We 'ad to bring 'im 'ome".

Lill attempted to pull herself together at this. "Ow! poor little bugger," she said, "now 'ees shivering." She advanced forward and picked the dog up. "Bloody 'ell Joe," he stinks like a sewer she exclaimed, quickly passing the dog over. Joe in his inebriated state hadn't at first noticed this until Lill pointed it out to him. "You'd probably smell like a sewer, Lill, if you'd been slung out!" he said, in defence of the dog. "We'll just 'ave to bath 'im that's all."

"What at this time of night?" If Lill hadn't been so fond of her son-in-law, she'd never have put up with this.

She looked at Fred who sat, mildly amused at this altercation going on between them. He was an amiable man, as fond of Lill as Joe was of

Jessie. He just sat smoking his pipe now and his only contribution to the difficult situation had been to agree with: "Yea, poor little bugger" when Lill had uttered this comment.

He looked with interest at the dog though, noticing how thin he was. "'Ee looks bloody 'ungry to me," he ventured, "a good meal is what 'ee needs". Having said this, Fred returned to his pipe, happy with his contribution on the matter.

"'Ee'll need a bed to sleep on," Jessie ventured, getting quite excited now at the thought of keeping the dog. "Yea, and a dirt-box as we ain't got a garden, 'oo knows the last time he cocked is leg?" Having made this further piece of advice Fred wriggled down further in the settee, but Lill admonished him with "Come on then get your bloody arse off that settee," she told him authoritatively now; "you and Joe can bath 'im in the kitchen sink, while I get 'im something to eat."

Fred, anxious to avoid this, queried Lill with: "Bath him with what? We ain't go any dog shampoo". The thoughts of this late night activity didn't appeal to him at all. "That's awright," Lill retorted, "we'll just use some of yours." She wasn't going to let Fred get out of it.

Fred was quite affronted now. "We can't use that; you bought me that for Christmas". "I'll buy you some more for next Christmas," Lill told him. "Now come on and get to it." Fred arose sulkily from the settee, pipe still in his mouth. No good arguing with Lill, she always got her way. He threw a baleful look at Jessie and Joe now. "Come on then let's get on with it" he commanded them, as though it had been his idea in the first place.

While Joe and Fred set about preparing hot water, shampoo and towel for the dog, who was now comfortably ensconced on the hearth-rug and didn't really appreciate being disturbed, Lill busied about in the kitchen trying to decide what to prepare for him to eat.

"We ain't got any tins of dog meat; ee'll just 'ave to 'ave some of the weekend joint," she decided.

"No! 'ee can't 'ave any of that," said Fred and Joe in unison. "We'll need all of that for ourselves." To sacrifice some of their weekend joint to feed a dog didn't credit thinking about.

"Well, that's all we've got to offer 'im," replied Lill, as she hauled an enormous joint of beef onto the end of the draining board. "You lot will just 'ave to eat a bit less, it won't do you no arm; and 'ee can 'ave one of them cream cakes for afters."

Never having had a dog before, Lill didn't realise that dogs didn't have 'afters'.

As the dog ravenously ate the meat and cream cake that was put down for him before he had his bath, he shivered and darted wary glances around him. It was quite obvious that had anyone attempted to remove the sumptuous meal from him they chanced losing their hand, so hungry was he. He just woofed it all down, cream cake and all just vanished without a trace.

The very necessary bathing of the dog then was something of a comedy act. Joe and Fred were in convulsions of laughter as the poor confused creature shook himself repeatedly, completely drenching the two of them with soap-suds and water.

"Give over!" Fred hollered at him. "It's you what needs the bloody bath, not us; you'll put my bloody pipe out in a minute!" Fred had held on rigidly to this throughout.

"Ow, look at my floor!" cried Lill. "Now there's more bloody water down there than in the sink!" Fred and Joe plodded on; eventually wrapping the dog in one of their bath towels and giving him a good rub and then a good brush with a hair brush that Jessie had found in her parents' bedroom. She had also concocted, while this was all going on, a bed of sorts for this now sweet smelling creature: a cardboard box with a rumpled jumper reposing in it.

"Ere; ain't that one of mine?" Fred protested, and going to rescue it.

"Leave it, Dad, begged Jessie, "you don't wear it much; looks better on 'im!"

"Why one of my jumpers? Why not one of Joe's? 'ee brought the bloody thing 'ome." But Joe pretended not hear and fussed the dog who, realising he was on to a good thing, now gazed up at his benefactors with large limpid eyes.

"Ow ! Just look at 'im," enthused Lill. "Don't 'ee look lovely, just like a bug n a rug," she laughed.

"Bloody well ought to an all," spat out Fred, "'ees ad my shampoo, my airbrush and now my bloody jumper!" He gave an uncharacteristic scowl on saying this.

"'Ow can anyone be cruel like that; slinging 'im out on is ear?" commiserated Lill, giving the dog an affectionate look. She was very soon to find out!

"What we going to call 'im then?" said Jessie now. "We can't keep calling 'im 'the dog.'"

Fred, puffing away at his pipe as he gave some thought to this matter, announced, "Scruff! That's what we'll call 'im." And so Scruff it was.

Having got the dog settled, the family now realised how exhausted they all were. "Look at the bloody time!" exclaimed Joe, looking at the clock on the mantelpiece, "it's 'arf past bloody two; good job I've got no work termorer."

They all trooped off to bed; closing the kitchen door quietly behind them so as not to disturb Scruff, who appeared now to be in a deep sleep, little snores emitting from him.

…Some undetermined time later Lill suddenly sat bolt upright in bed. "What's that!" She shook Fred awake. "Quick, go into the kitchen," she told him, "there's something wrong with Scruff."

Fred looked sleepily at the bedside clock. "Bloody 'ell. Lill, it's only 'arf past four…"

"I know" said Lill, "but there's something up, you'll 'ave to go."

A howling came from the kitchen. "Fred get up," Lill pleaded.

But Fred was having none of it. "Let Joe get up and see to 'im, 'ee brought the bloody thing 'ome." Lill clambered out of bed herself. "You know 'ow Joe likes is rest at weekends on account of 'ow 'ard 'ee works all week," she told him, resentfully.

As Lill passed Joe and Jessie's bedroom door on her way to the kitchen however, she noted that it stayed firmly shut. "It's strange 'ow some people 'ave a problem with their 'earing at times," she announced to whoever chose to listen.

Coming back to the bedroom with Scruff in her arms, she informed Fred, "'ee was lonely that's all; 'ee better stay in 'ere with us."

19

She dumped Scruff on the bottom of the bed, making quite sure it was on Fred's side.

"'Ee's done a poo on the kitchen floor an all, Fred, you'll 'ave to see to that when you get up".

"Why me?" queried Fred. "Why should I 'ave to do it?"

"Well, you're the 'ead of the oushold, Fred. You must see to these things."

Fred cocked his head to one side. "Funny 'ow I suddenly become 'ead of the 'ousehold when something bloody unsavoury needs doing." He snuggled down further in the bed; at least things were quiet now, he consoled himself.

Lill didn't bother to answer but just got into bed beside him. Everybody could go back to sleep now. "Just make sure you stay put," she told Scruff, in what she hoped was a very firm voice. The dog gave her a grave look as everybody finally settled down but he obviously had no intention of 'staying put' as Lill had commanded him, because when Fred awoke in the not too distant morning he found himself looking, not at Lill's face, but into the intense gaze of Scruff.

"Bloody 'ell, Lill!" he exclaimed, as he shot out of bed.

⁓

At breakfast, Fred sat looking sombre. He'd been up and out with Scruff to a spare piece of ground behind the flats after first clearing up the poo. He didn't feel he'd had a proper night's sleep.

"Now we know why you was bloody slung out," he told Scruff, as the dog looked innocently up at him from his lap.

"Ow, leave 'im alone Fred, you'll upset 'im," Lill implored.

"Oh well, we mustn't upset 'im must we," came Fred's retort.

"Eel settle once we get organised," Lill assured him.

"It's worse than 'aving a baby in the 'ouse" complained Fred. "At least you can stick a bloody dummy in its mouth to shut it up!"

Through all this discussion at breakfast, Jessie and Joe's bedroom door remained firmly closed. Nothing but nothing must disturb Joe's weekend lie in. "'Ee works really 'ard all week," Lill would vehemently maintain!

⁓

Within a few days Scruff did indeed get all the family organised. Fred was to get up first, and after the early morning cuppa he and Scruff visited the spare ground at the back of the flats, which was once a beauty spot when the flats were first built, but now it was neglected, and overgrown with grass and weeds. Fred would stand puffing on his pipe while Scruff meandered around; he had scorned the dirt box, it was beneath him to use that.

"Now come on, Scruff, do your duty for King and Country," Fred hurriedly told him while he drew harder on his pipe, and at the same time pulled his coat collar further around his ears. "For Gawd's sake 'urry," he urged the dog, "so we can get back out of this freezing cold. HURRY UP WILL YER!"

On returning from their early morning sojourn, Scruff would immediately look for his breakfast of cornflakes with Gold Top milk and woe betide anyone who left him short of this luxury. "Ow, 'oos used all of Scruff's Gold Top milk?" Lill would berate all and sundry, "you know ee don't like the ordinary milk!"

"You've got a fine little dog here," the vet had said when Lill and Fred took Scruff for a check-up. He obviously realised how lucky this nondescript little animal was to be taken in by such a nice family, having just listened to Lill's dramatic account of 'stray dog found abandoned, 'alf starved and near death's door'.

She bristled with pride now at the vet's words. "Nothing but the best 'ee 'as," she told this nice man. "But 'ee's intolerant to tinned dogs meat; just won't touch it," she stated with some authority.

Fred clicked his teeth in annoyance at this. "No, cause 'ee won't touch it, 'cos 'ee's too bloody fond of what comes out of the oven, and 'ee won't even eat 'is cornflakes in the morning unless it's got Gold Top milk on 'em, 'ee's no bloody fool!" Having had his gripe, Fred now got back to his

21

pipe but the vet gasped at this worrying piece of information of all this fatty milk the dog was consuming, but he laughed now as he turned to Lill.

"Well, well, well," he told her, "he should live to a ripe old age, with all the pampering he gets; that's if…" he laughed again, "…that's if the Gold Top milk doesn't get to him first!" They all had a good laugh at this.

"You're bloody right an all," Fred told the vet as they left, with Scruff tucked under his arm, his pipe still clenched between his teeth, and he gave him a hearty slap on the back, causing the vet to cough and splutter.

Back at the flat, a little gate had been erected at the front door to stop Scruff from wandering out. So when a welfare visitor noticed it as she passed on her way to assess a new baby a few doors along the balcony, she eyed it with suspicion. She wasn't aware of a baby at No. 65, it wasn't on her list. It was important that every infant be registered with the local Health Authority, and so, on her way back, she knocked with some trepidation at the flat.

Scruff was laying very comfortably in his favourite chair and ignored the knock, but Lill went immediately, thinking it was the postman. "Hello!" said the welfare visitor with forced cheerfulness, as Lill came on the scene. "I don't remember seeing No. 65 on my books; I *am* sorry, I would have visited you to see how things are." She gave Lill a quizzical look. A bit old for a new Mother she thought, perhaps this is Grandma. "I hope you don't mind me knocking," she finished lamely, after seeing the astonished look on Lill's face.

A peal of laughter came from Lill now as she caught on. This of course was a Post-natal nurse, who had thought, on seeing the gate, that there was a baby in the house. "Ow, I don't mind at all," she told this lady. "You wait ere and I'll bring my baby out." She dashed into the lounge and scooped Scruff up into her arms. "'Ere 'ee is," she told the astonished welfare visitor. "'Ere's my baby; ain't 'ee lovely? We put the gate up at the door to stop 'im getting out; not that 'ee's ever bothered, 'ee's too comfortable indoors," she chortled" The welfare nurse laughed with Lill, but departed more than a bit embarrassed.

Scruff thrived on his lavish upbringing and became quite a

presentable looking dog. His regular brushing produced a lovely sheen on his coat, his eyes were bright, and all in all he was very acceptable and spoiled rotten.

"Here you are, your majesty. 'Ee who will not eat tinned meat," Lill would tell him when she put the delicious smelling food down for him. He would initially draw back, a hurt look on his face. It wasn't his fault he couldn't eat tinned meat. Lill would laugh and ruffle his head. "I'm only joking," she would say. Only then would be condescend to eat his meal.

In spite of his small size Scruff was quite a good house dog. "I wouldn't fancy anyone's chances if they broke in 'ere," Lill would tell all and sundry. "'Ee might be little but 'ee's got a good guarding instinct. 'Ee would 'ave a go at anybody that broke in," she assured them, but nobody was ever quite sure what actually happened to Scruff's guarding instinct the night that they actually were burgled.

They had got home quite late from the pub. It had been Alf's birthday; one of the regulars, and everybody made a real night of it. "Roll out the barrel; Down at the old Bull and Bush"; all the old favourites had been sung while everyone celebrated this birthday, and the beer flowed freely.

Staggering out of the pub, way past closing time, Lill, Fred, Joe and Jessie made their way home. "By, that was a good night." Fred was on a real high as he chose not to think about the following morning, and he did a little dance along the street.

"Pull yerself together," Lill told him laughingly, "you won't feel like dancing when you wake up termorrer."

"Ow Gawd, Joe, my poor feet." Jessie was making her usual complaint, having stood at the bar for four hours, and now the long walk home. Joe looked up to heaven. "I've told you before and I'll tell you again, Jesh." Joe was having difficulty pronouncing Jessie's name again. "Get yerself some sensible shoes. I don't want to keep 'earing about yer poor bloody feet."

On eventually reaching home, Fred fumbled around in his pocket for the front door key. "Jush a minute." Fred was also having trouble with his pronunciations. "Jush a minute, I've got it 'ere somewhere… 'Ere! Whash thish?" He glared at the door. It was OPEN. "Whash thish?" he said again as he poked at the door. "OW MY GAWD! Someone's been 'ere; someone's been 'ere; QUICK!" he said, as he and Joe tried to get through the door together.

"OW MY GAWD!" They surveyed the disorder inside; someone had made a good job of turning the place over, but, "Wait a minute, where's Scruff?" a terrified Lill asked, as she looked farther afield now for their precious dog.

"In the bedroom, quick!" responded Fred, having noticed both doors wide open.

A thorough search began as the carnage in the lounge was momentarily forgotten. "Scruff come on, where are you? It's awright, we're 'ere now." They called and searched to no avail, and Lill and Jess broke down in tears.

"Why did they 'ave to take Scruff?" sobbed Lill as she collapsed now on the settee.

"I expect 'ee went for them and they 'ad to shut 'im up," Fred offered unhelpfully, while Joe just stood looking distressed.

"I don't care what they took from 'ere, but to take our little Scruff!" Lill broke down again.

"Right!" announced Joe now, taking the lead, and he strode to the phone on the sideboard, at least the burglars had left them that; the sooner they got the law here, the better. The police assured him that they would be right there, and in the meantime Joe paced back and forth in the lounge, uttering threats of what he intended to do to the offenders when they were caught.

"OH, SHUT UP, Jess; for crying out loud!" he hollered at this wife, as she made her distress known to everybody in no uncertain terms. "I know you're upset, we all are," he said now, less aggressively to her. They were all rapidly becoming very sober.

The constable, when he arrived, looked around him with a practised eye while drinking the cup of tea that Fred had made for him. "Yes," he surmised, "I would say that more than one person was involved in this.

Don't disturb anything and tomorrow I'll send someone to check for fingerprints."

"It's our little Scruff we're worried about," Lill told him, still crying bitterly, as she envisaged all the horrible things that could be happening to him. Jess made *less* noise now after Joe's shouting at her.

"Well, at least they left you the piano," observed the constable as he eyed it, "but of course they'd have had a job moving tha… Ere! Old on; old on a minute," and he advanced towards the piano, and bent down to take a closer look. "What's this then?" A little black nose peeked out now from under the piano. Scruff had finally decided that it was safe to make his presence known.

Lill and Jess jumped up to rescue their little treasure, and Lill cried even more as she hugged him and whispered in his ear, "It's awright darling, you're safe now. You're safe with us now".

A heavy burden had been lifted from the family and they were able to laugh as they saw the constable out after his having had another cup of tea to celebrate.

When Scruff finally stopped shaking, he jumped down from Lill's lap and found his way to the hearthrug to warm himself in front of the blazing fire. He had been cold and uncomfortable squashed under the piano for all that time and now he stretched himself out and luxuriated to the full before finally, with a big sigh, he rested his head on his front paws while cocking an eye up at Joe.

Joe cocked an eye back at him and with a cynicism that only Joe could muster, he admonished the poor dog with:- "Bloody fine guard dog you turned out to be. 'Ooo let them burglars in then? 'Ooo did that? And people 'ere crying their eyes out cause they thought you'd been murdered." The dog was deeply offended at this, and shot back under the piano.

"Ow, Joe," Lill chastised him, "look what you've done, you've really upset that dog. Come on darling, come out." But for all Lill's coaxing, Scruff refused. He knew just what Joe had meant and was deeply ashamed, so he stayed just where he was.

… Scruff, of course, was a much loved dog, but there was an occasion when, because of him, the family almost lost the flat.

On a day when it was raining 'cats and dogs' outside, Lill opened the front door to an official from the Council. He had a grave look on his face as he walked in. "I understand you are harbouring a dog here," he announced, while being ushered to a chair. "Now you must know that this isn't allowed," he told Lill and Fred, while peering over his spectacles at them.

"I'm not going to try and deny it," admitted Fred, which would have been very difficult to do, with Scruff being very much in evidence.

"'Ee don't cause no trouble to anyone," pleaded Lill. "Ee don't bark or anyfing. Our daughter and son-in-law found 'im in the street, 'alf starved and at death's door. What would you 'ave done Sir?" she asked as she ingratiated herself to the official.

The man gave an embarrassed cough as he weighed up the situation and studied the inevitable cup of tea in his hand. "Well now," he looked at Lill and Fred, a sympathetic look emanating from his face. "Well now," he started again, having been rather put off by the intense anxious looks displayed by both of them. "I know how it is," he told them. "I happen to be a dog lover myself; I know how they can pull at the heart-strings."

All this time Scruff had been clutched in Lill's arms with Fred sitting next to her and fondling the dog's ears.

"But you know," continued the official, "you know," and here he gave another little cough, "you must know we can't allow this situation to continue with the strict rules in place regarding keeping a dog or cat in the flats, and you being on the fifth floor and everything," he finished lamely.

It was very difficult for him. He realised that these people would live in a tent rather than part with that little dog. "Okay then," he brightened considerably now, and Lill and Fred looked at him expectantly. "Here's what we'll do." His manner was quite jubilant as he said, "I'll put you on the waiting list for a house; you'd have a small garden then for your little Scruff to play in." Fred's eyes brightened considerably at this. No more turning out on freezing cold mornings for Scruff to do his duty for King and Country, but Lill wasn't so keen.

"Ow, well now," she said, "we're very 'appy 'ere, sir," she pleaded, but the official ignored this. "Yes, that's what we'll do," he insisted, "we'll put you down for a nice house." He took a book from under his arm and scribbled away, detailing this transfer from flat to house.

Lill and Fred sat very quiet after the official's departure, as they contemplated doing something they hated the thought of. They had lived in the flat for ten years, loved it here, but because of little Scruff they would have to move. Why, what harm had they done to anybody? No harm at all. Scruff would hate it as much as they.

Fred sat puffing his pipe staring into space and Lill sat with Scruff on her lap, feeling empty. Even the dog knew something was up. "Come on, let's have a cup of tea," said Fred. "Ev'rything'll be awright, you'll see." A cup of tea sorted everything out in their lives.

What eventually happened was anyone's guess, for as the months went by they never heard a thing from the council. Did that very nice man forget to put the wheels in motion? Could he not bring himself to do it?

⤚

Lill and Fred never did move from the flat, and they never had another dog either. Years later when Scruff passed away there was a big void in their life, but at least they knew now that they were safe. There would be no move to a strange territory after all. They could stay where they were with the precious memories of their darling little dog.

"I swear that sometimes I can still see him sitting in his chair there," Fred would often tell people. "One in a million 'ee was," he reminisced, looking blankly ahead. "One in a million that's what 'ee was, and don't you deny it, Joe." He pointed his pipe at his son-in-law-in-law on hearing a sardonic chuckle coming from him, but Joe good naturedly agreed with Fred now.

"Yes, Fred, 'ee was one in a million, and I wouldn't dream of denying it." He got up and gave Fred a gentle slap on the back, "and I think you're one in a million for 'ow you coped with the little rascal." They all laughed at this.

27

"True, how true," Lill chipped in now. She threw her husband an affectionate look "you '*ave* been one in a million, Fred, you really 'ave." What she, and only she and Fred knew, was that their darling Scruff was not far from them, oh no!

One very early morning, after he had died, she and Fred had tearfully carried his lifeless body, wrapped in yet another one of Fred's jumpers, to is favourite spot at the back of the flats where he liked to meander while Fred had stood and almost frozen to death. They had tenderly buried him there, safe in the knowledge that he was still near to them and they, in return, were near to him. The comfort that they gained from this was paramount to them, and they planted a little cross and filled this once-neglected spot with an abundance of flowers, so that it was neglected no longer. Scruff would be happy there, they told each other with feeling, because he would somehow know that they were not far away from him. So, it was never a case of 'Goodbye, Darling' but more, "Now, Scruff, you make sure you stay put!" as Lill would so aptly tell their little rascal, before she then took Fred's arm as they crept away.

DISGRACE

My brothers were to a certain extent quite unruly. I'm not saying that they were disrespectful in any way to my Mother, who ruled them with a rod of iron, so that they were quite frightened of her at times, but with no Father around, this iron discipline was essential for the wellbeing of the family.

"Janey, don't!" Auntie Queenie from upstairs would intervene when Mother was laying into one of the boys for some misdemeanour, but she would pay little heed to her sister.

"Don't tell me 'ow to bring my family up," she would retaliate; and that was that.

Outside of the family though the boys tended to run riot, and egged one another on. One such occasion took place within the church and brought a lot of shame to the family when they really overstepped the mark at one of the regular film shows, put on by the church for the young children living in that area. These film shows were hilarious and noisy occasions, much looked forward to by the tribe of scruffy, snotty nosed kids, who all came from desperately poverty stricken homes in and around the vicinity of the church. This era of the nineteen thirties, tottering between the two world wars, was rife with mass unemployment, causing families to exist on a pittance.

My own family were poor; not because of this circumstance, as my father, being a very skilled man was in regular employment, but most of his wages went on drink with very little left over for his family, so we were not much better off than the rest of this motley crowd. As these children shambled in, this impoverished state showed in the shabbiness of their clothing; their shoes in a worn down state, the innards packed with cardboard as protection against the cold and wet seeping through the soles. Their faces were pale and pin pinched through malnutrition, their noses were snotty, and some of the younger ones had hacking coughs, heard continuously throughout the film show.

The government at this time, I remember, had set up soup-kitchens and many of these young families could be seen queuing each day for their bowls of soup and bread. Nobody was too proud to partake of this service, it was what helped them to survive, and my Mother was happy for the boys to go along to fill their hollow legs, but she herself wouldn't be seen dead there…

At the back of the hall now a series of long trestle tables had been erected and standing behind these tables stood the ladies of the church, smiling benignly at the children as they passed. These kind ladies had spent the day cake-making, and their efforts were displayed now on the tables, the cakes interspersed with large jugs of lemonade.

The children eyed the bounty longingly as they filed past, but they would have to wait until the end of the film-show and, Mrs Bates, the lady in charge was alert to some of the boys who surreptitiously attempted to rifle a cake as they passed the end of the tables. She would bring a small ruler down on their thieving fingers. "WAIT!" she would shout at them, and at the same time would command, "And wipe your nose!" She was a good kind soul really, with the welfare of these poor unfortunate children in mind, but she wouldn't be taken advantage of, oh no.

Mr Longbottom, the organiser, stood at the front of the hall, gently reprimanding some of the boys as they squabbled with one another to attain the best seats. He chided them with, "Now, boys, steady now," as he sorted them out, but he did this with a laughing, acceptable manner, and nobody minded his gentle reprimands; he loved these ragamuffins as though they were his own, and so he welcomed them with great pleasure to these 'not to be missed' evenings. In return the children had a great respect for him.

"Sorry, Mr Longbottom," some could be heard to say, as they conformed.

While this was all going on, my brothers made their entrance with me in tow, and I noted as we appeared how Mr Longbottom had inclined his head and cast a wary eye in their direction. The Bone boys were notorious for trouble making at these film shows and had been warned several times about their 'frenetic' behaviour. Father Joseph had sent Sister Margaret around to the house to speak to my Mother, just last week, regarding their unruliness.

"You know, Janey," Sister had said in a forbearing manner to her, "the church goes to a lot of trouble to put these film shows on for the children, and it's not very nice when the boys misbehave." And so they had been given a stern warning from my Mother, with no ifs or buts: "Be'ave or suffer the consequences!" she had said.

Mr Longbottom relaxed his glare now as the boys walked in quite orderly, with Joe propelling me by the shoulder and shoving me unceremoniously onto the end seat. Obviously his warning to them at the previous film show regarding their behaviour had had an effect; but I'm sure that this nice man was fully aware of the mickey-taking by the boys regarding his unfortunate surname.

"When 'ee sits down," Joe used to quip to us, "'ee's way above everybody else because of his long bottom," and of course we would all fall about laughing, but I don't suppose there was much that the poor man could do about this situation, as long as it didn't get out of hand.

As we sat orderly on our seats, Joe's manner, I noted, was completely nonchalant. At twelve years of age he considered himself above this churchy entertainment, but he was assigned by my Mother for the purpose of keeping the rest of us in order, especially in view of the recent complaints, and so he sat quietly now, but with his feet propped up on the chair in front of him.

Everybody sorted out now; the lights dimmed and the show started. The children fidgeted with expectation as they riveted their eyes on the screen. The promise of another fantastic evening presented itself and for now, their hunger and deprivations could be forgotten for a while.

There was something very appealing emanating from these youngsters who bore their hardships with fortitude, and their excitement spilled over now into uncontrolled shouting as the Lone Ranger made an appearance on screen with his famous horse 'Silver'.

"HI, HO, SILVER!" he would exclaim, waving his hat in the air, as 'Silver' pranced up, his two legs clawing into space; and when the Indians arrived on the scene in pursuit, the noise was absolutely deafening... 'Tonto' though, his part Indian ally was always there to save the day.

That finished; the children quite hoarse by now, settled expectantly for the antics of Charlie Chaplin and Laurel and Hardy. The laughter rang out, not only from the children, but from Mr Longbottom and the ladies at the back. Everyone was having a fantastic time; everyone, that is, apart from Joe, who sat throughout, a bored, long-suffering look adorning his face. This kids' stuff was all 'old hat' to him but he nevertheless contained himself throughout.

At the end of the show, as the lights came back on, Mr Longbottom stood up, still laughing. "Wasn't that fantastic?" he called out to the kids; some of whom were already perched on the edge of their chairs, ready now to dash to the ladies at the back to be first in the queue for their lemonade and cakes, but Mr Longbottom held them back as he repeated his question. "I said 'Wasn't that fantastic?' children!"

"YES...." they all shouted in unison.

"Well!" continued Mr Longbottom. "I think we should give a loud 'Three Cheers' to Father Joseph, who goes to all this trouble to arrange these shows for us; what do you think, then?"

"YES..." everyone shouted back again, with certain boys actually falling off their seats, so eager were they for their refreshments, but Mr Longbottom was having none of it, and continued to hold them, while actually picking one or two of them up off the floor where they had toppled.

All this time I had noted that look of nonchalance on Joe's face; this really was too much for him, he would just be glad to be shot of it. It was probably only the promise of the refreshments at the end that held him. He was very clever, in his underhand way, of managing to consume twice the amount of anyone else. He clicked his teeth in annoyance now. "Just get on with it," I heard him mumble.

"Alright, then," Mr Longbottom continued. "Come on then children. 'THREE CHEERS' for Father Joseph. HIP HIP..." his hands flew up in the air for effect and to conduct the loud 'HOORAY' from the kids, but a very different response came from Joe at the back.

"DOGS' SHIT!" he had retorted, a cynical smirk hovering around his lips.

I held my breath, while I looked nervously at Mr Longbottom. The laugh on his face was replaced for a split second by momentary concern, while his hands remained suspended in the air. Did he hear aright? He was clearly thinking, but he obviously pushed the unthinkable to one side as once again he brought forth a huge grin.

"I didn't quite hear that" he laughed, so let's really hear you this time," and he cupped one of his ears as he called out once again: "HIP HIP!"

This was surely torment for the children, as in their famished state the refreshments were now paramount in their minds, but patience took over with them as there was an intaking of breath while they determined to do right by Father Joseph, and they endeavoured to make the supreme effort.

"That's right," encouraged Mr Longbottom. "Come on then, 'HIP HIP!'"

"DOGS' SHIT!" came from the back. My brothers had taken their cue from Joe, and had shouted the obscenity all together in unison, completely overriding any concerted effort from the children.

I squirmed in my seat, while the boys fell about laughing. They'd certainly made a good impact, judging by the silence that ensued. I fearfully stole a look at Mr Longbottom as an expression of amazement on his face, quickly turned to thunder. This time there was no mistaking what had been shouted out, and as the eager HOORAY! died on the children's lips, they turned around and gawped at the perpetrators of this obscenity.

The ladies at the back also stood dumbfounded and, like the children, their mouths were agape.

Suddenly, like a mad bull, Mr Longbottom, beside himself with rage, proceeded to crash his way through the seats to get at the boys. Children and chairs were scattered in all directions as he blundered through. This nice, kind man had been pushed to the limit. There was only so much that even he could take, and as he manoeuvred his way toward the boys like an angry drunkard, they then realised the enormity of their behaviour and a frightened look registered on their faces. This time they had definitely gone too far, and a silence came over them as they watched Mr Longbottom's approach, and I sat on my hands as though this might give me some sort of security, flicking my tongue around my dry lips.

As he reached the boys, Mr Longbottom literally fell upon Joe, and clutched at his ear, yanking him to his feet. "GET OUT!" he shouted. "ALL OF YOU; GET OUT!"

The boys timidly stood up and followed Mr Longbottom as he, still clutching Joe's ear, shoved them all outside and, to add insult to injury, I heard Joe say to him in a somewhat contrite manner, "What about our refreshments, then?" Had he sat and suffered for nothing? But that was the very last time the boys ever entered that hall. It was just as well Joe had no knowledge then of what was to come as a result of his terrible indiscretion. He had gone beyond the bounds of decency; there was no going back, as far as the church was concerned.

As I sat now, mortified by what had happened, Mr Longbottom came back into the hall and approached me. "Come on, Liz," he said, kindly, as he took my hand, "come and have some refreshments. I feel quite sorry for you, being saddled with that lot." And I joined the other quite frightened children, as they made their way slowly towards the ladies at the back. All the fun had gone out of the evening, and I felt the tears well up in my eyes now as I watched Mr Longbottom making a supreme effort to conciliate himself again with the children as he tried to brush the incident to one side.

"Come on kids" he laughingly addressed them. "We're alright aren't we? We enjoyed the film show, didn't we?"

I felt a rage build up inside me now, as the tears continued to course down my, by now, grubby little face. HOW DARE they? I thought. HOW DARE they upset Mr Longbottom like that! I was suddenly very fed up with my brothers, and as I walked from the hall, a pious look adorning my face, I informed the boys, who were sloughing around waiting for me, "Mr Lonbottom doesn't want you to any more of his film shows, so there!" But this made no impact on them at all. "And Father Joseph will be coming round to the house," I added. This last remark of mine did have some effect, and stopped them momentarily in their tracks, but then, my brothers just grabbed me. "Come on, Liz," they said, "blow that lot in there, let's go and ge' our chips."

I should explain that it was the practice for us on these Friday nights to stop off at the local fish and chip shop. Auntie Queenie would have given us our weekly penny on this day and we would spend it on a penn'orth of chips on our way home from the film show to finish off the evening.

A queue awaited us at the shop and the boys joined it impatiently, pushing and shoving as they were, as usual, hungry and couldn't wait to get their chips.

"AWRIGHT, AWRIGHT! Stop yer shoving!" the man behind the counter bawled at them. "Just wait yer turn like everyone else."

As Joe and John eventually took their chips, they sidled along the counter towards a large jar of pickled onions at the end. "AND YER CAN LEAVE THEM ALONE!" the shop manager was on to them immediately. The pickled onions were for people who bought the fish *and* chips, not for those who could only afford a penn'orth of chips. My brothers made a face; this time they didn't get away with it. They took the vinegar instead, and sprinkled it liberally over their chips until they were sodden.

By the time I got my helping of chips, Joe and John had finished theirs, and as I joined them outside, they immediately fell on me like a couple of vultures.

"You've got too many there, Liz, you'll never eat all those; and look, that one's got a black spot on it!" The boys knew how finicky their sister was, and in spite of my cries of, "Leave me, leave me alone!" as I squabbled with them to save my chips, they quickly consumed the lot, then they had the task of dragging me home, bawling my head off.

My Mother was waiting for us at the front door, her having heard my plaintive cries as we neared the house. "And I suppose you've scoffed all 'er chips again!" she admonished them as we entered the house. She gave both the boys a good cuff around their ears. Apart from flinching, the boys said not a word. When she got to know what else they'd been up to, that's when they would start to worry. As it happened, they didn't have long to wait.

THE THRASHING

The very next evening after the disgraceful incident in the church, as we sat in the kitchen eating the inevitable almost meatless stew, a loud knocking became even louder, as though somebody couldn't wait to get in!

"Alright!" my Mother exclaimed in alarm, as she hastily made her way to the door. "Hold on," she continued, as she made her way quickly along the narrow passageway to the offending racket.

The boys exchanged furtive glances. They knew full well who was at the door; I had told them that Father Joseph would be coming round, and a scared look showed now on their faces... Trouble!

Suddenly, a body flung its way into the kitchen, quickly followed by my Mother, a surprised, questioning expression on her face. "What's all this?" she asked, of no one in particular. "What's this?" But what the boys had been dreading, was now happening.

As Father Joseph stormed in, he pointed an accusing finger at Joe, and I noticed that his hat stayed firmly on his head as he made this gesture. Most unusual really as I knew that Father always removed his hat when entering the house, but now he pointed at Joe as he spat out, "You're the instigator! You're the one!" I wasn't at all sure what that word meant, but I knew what Father was here for.

"You DISGUST me!" He made a move as though he was going to strike Joe, but he controlled himself, and turned to a by now very frightened Mother. Father looked her squarely in the face. "Have they not told you?" he enquired of her.

"Told me what?" she replied, looking even more alarmed.

"Come outside, Janey, I don't want to repeat here in front of Liz what went on in the church hall last evening. Come out here," and he propelled her through the door into the passageway.

The boys stopped eating their stew; suddenly they weren't very hungry.

"He must be taken in hand, Janey," we heard through the door.

"You shouldn't have done it, Joe," Charlie now said to him, and the boys nodded in agreement.

"You all shouted it as well," Joe accused them hotly. They just sat in silence. Their bravado of the previous evening in shouting out that obscenity, didn't seem such a good idea now.

We heard the front door close now, as Father Joseph left the house. My Mother came back into the kitchen, and she was crying. "How could you?" she shouted at the boys. "How COULD you! Oh! I'll have to get your father," and she dashed upstairs to summon her sister.

Auntie Queenie, after listening to my Mother's tearful explanation of the shocking event perpetrated by the boys, Joe being the instigator, came hurrying down the stairs, moved quickly through the kitchen, while throwing Joe a look of mortification, then exited through the back door into the garden to fetch her bike. She was a church-goer herself and was disgusted at Joe at this particular moment. She knew where to find my father. He would be in the usual pub, just a ten minutes' bike ride away.

My Mother stood wringing her hands as she stood in front of the boys now, guarding the back door to prevent Joe bolting through it to escape what he knew was to come. "Just sit right where you are," she told them all "just don't move, any of you," which was quite unnecessary, as the boys sat as if in a frozen state. Not one of them moved a muscle, until… CRASH! went the front door, for the second time that evening.

SMASH! went the kitchen door now, as my father threw himself in, crashing the door against the wall.

We all shot up, terrified; we knew how my Father was when he was in one of his rages. We scattered to one corner of the kitchen, cowering against one another; all but Joe, who stood with a determined, challenging look towards my Father who, without a word, was undoing his leather trouser belt from around his middle. As he advanced towards Joe, he twisted the end of it around his hand and held it aloft. There was a menacing look stamped on his face as he made for his son, but Joe was ready for him and, as my Father got close, Joe reached out and grabbed him. If there was one thing that Joe was not, it was a coward. In for a penny, in for a pound! This was something he could not get out of, so he met it with a challenge!

As the two of them grabbed at one another, they almost immediately fell to the floor, where they rolled over and over as if they were in a wrestling match.

Up on their feet now, they reeled around the room like two drunkards, Joe with his teeth clenched, my Father brandishing his belt. He didn't care where he hit Joe, just as long as he got the whips in; and all the time, we others were jumping about in our attempts to dodge the melee, while my Mother was crying out: "That's enough now, that's enough!" but my Father was consumed with rage, and would not stop until his rage abated, and Joe got the thrashing of his life.

When my Mother finally succeeded in pulling my Father away, he stepped back, breathing heavily. He himself hadn't got off scot-free, as Joe, being a solid thick-set twelve year old, had managed one or two wallops of his own.

The offending belt was slowly and meticulously replaced back around the waist of my Father's trousers, while he endeavoured to control his breathing. He uttered not a word. His rage had been brought on, not so much because of what Joe had done, but more because he had been dragged from the pub, where he spent most of his evenings with his drinking cronies. That would take some living down. Precious time and pints had been missed, apart from the humiliation Auntie Queenie had caused as she rained words down on his head regarding his responsibilities instead of wasting his time and money in the pub every night.

Without further ado, my Father now blundered through the door into the passage, where Auntie Queenie had stood as a silent witness, a bland look on her face. Why did she bother, the look clearly conveyed; she knew what he was 'useless'.

As my Father quickly passed by her, he looked her squarely in the eye. "Don't you EVER speak to me again," he told her, with emphasis.

She looked back at him with an equally aggressive stance. "Don't worry," she retorted, "I wouldn't want to *ever* speak to you again," and she never did.

Amazingly, Joe never held this beating against my Father, which took him some days to recover from. In fact, it was he alone who was with him at the end when my Father died. They had associated together in the ensuing years when in adulthood Joe himself became a habitual drinker. He chose to forget the hardship caused to my Mother through my Father's drinking; but John, on the other hand, was of a different calibre. He never was able to forget or to forgive.

Unlike Joe, who had thrown off his sultriness as he matured, having developed an amiable, easygoing nature, John, as he matured, became much more serious. He had, for a start, inherited my Father's vicious temper, and he didn't suffer fools easily. This mentality was coupled with an intense sensitiveness, and as he had observed over the years my Mother's struggle to raise the family single-handedly he had harboured a hate towards my Father; so much so that he refused to have any contact with him.

When Joe later disclosed to the rest of us how my Father, at the end, had asked for John, we decided to keep 'mum', and did not disclose this to him because we knew that it would cause him great distress. He hated his Father, yes! But he was still his son and had he known of my Father's asking for him, his extremely sensitive nature would have taken over, and caused him great sadness, and so we said nothing. Let sleeping dogs lie, seemed the best option.

My Mother had been legally separated from my Father, but a condition of this separation was a monthly visit from him to the family, in the home; and during these visits, in my Father's more lucid moments, when he was free from drink, he would make a genuine effort to communicate with John. "I 'ear you've been picked for the school football

41

team John; you'll need some decent boots then?" He looked at John as he said this; silently appealing for his acceptance, but John looked away; he wanted nothing from him.

"I'll leave some money for them, eh?" proffered my Father; "yes," he answered himself, "I'll leave some money when I go." By now, he was getting a bit fed up with trying to converse with us children, who sat stony faced around him, and not uttering a word. His efforts to make amends were falling on stony ground and when, amazingly, the new football boots materialised, John refused to wear them, preferring instead to wear the second-hand ones found for him at the school.

How could you forgive a man, even if he was your Father, who could stand by while his wife struggled with the unremitting task of raising alone, five boisterous demanding boys, and all that goes with it? Boys, who at times, much as they loved their Mother, had that firm need for a Father figure.

My Mother, at these visits, would make herself scarce. Nothing that she could ever say to this inadequate man would ever make any difference. She also wanted nothing from him any longer. She had regretted calling him to deal with Joe. Life with him had been one big regret, so she had just walked out of the room, leaving him with us attempting his false promises of recompense.

At this particular visit her energy levels were at their lowest. Charlie had been very ill with rheumatic fever. He had very unwisely stood in the pouring rain a few weeks earlier while queuing with a fried outside the local cinema. Then he had sat throughout the film in his soaking wet clothes. When he got home much later had shivered violently, and the next day he was delirious with fever.

Joe and John did what they could to help my Mother with the nursing of Charlie; helping her to lift him and sponging him with cold water to bring his temperature down, and at the same time, I was in the other bedroom, very ill with one of my regular chest infections. The doctor was in and out, quickly going from one to the other of us, and my Mother had been run off her feet.

My Father had scooped me up when he came, and now as I

languished on his lap, listening to the stilted talk between Father and sons, I realised, even in my wan condition, that it would have been better had he not been there at all. The hate in John's eyes and the silence of the rest of us, coupled with the purposeful absence of my Mother, dug deeply into my sensitive nature and made me really miserable.

"Bye then, Janey," my Father would call, as he left the house. "Let me know if you need anything."

My Mother never even bothered to reply to his empty words. "Good riddance!" she remarked as she re-entered the room on his departure. She picked me up in my weakened state. "Come on, Liz, back to bed now he's gone; and he even forgot to go in to see how Charlie was," she stated indignantly.

I lay back weakly against the pillows. Sister Margaret would be coming round. She would be bringing sweets and comics with her, and she would stop and have a cup of tea with my Mother. We always looked forward to Sister Margaret's visit. She was like a beacon of light in our turbulent lives and made our fraught existence in these punishing times a bit more bearable. Oh yes, we all looked forward to this special person coming! Young as she was, she had a definite stabilising effect on the family and we would certainly have been lost without her. I hope she stays for a long time today, I told myself, as I fought the overwhelming tiredness which was forcing my heavy eyelids to droop. "Mustn't miss her... mustn't miss her," I was saying. But, of course, in the end I did miss her, as the little packets of sweets left on my pillow told me, when I eventually came out of my exhausted sleep.

"Never mind," my mother was saying to me now, as she noted my distress. "Don't cry," she said, "because she's coming back temorrer. Don't cry now." But I did continue to cry because tomorrow seemed to me to be a very long time before I would see Sister Margaret again, and so the tears continued to flow as I once again gave in to the fevered sleep that had been responsible for my missing this dear person. But I clutched at the sweets that she had left for me, as I would continue to clutch them until she came again – 'temorrer'.

TUPPENNY RUSH

As the church silently refused to accept the boys to any more of their film shows, it was decided by my Mother to allow them instead to go to the Saturday morning 'Tuppenny Rush' at the local cinema, after persistent cajolery from Joe.

There would be no getting in free at this cinema though. It would cost tuppence, and there would be no nice refreshments at the end of the film show, but that didn't bother Joe too much, in fact it suited him fine. He could shout and swear as much as he wanted, and no one coming round to the house to report him.

It was a long walk to this Saturday morning jaunt however; not just around the corner, as it had been to the church film shows. There was no money to take the bus; just a lengthy trek there, and a lengthy trek back.

As we at last reached our goal on that first Saturday, with me riding on Joe's back; a shock awaited us. A long queue went to the end of the street and continued right around the corner from the cinema.

Joe plonked me down on the pavement, and sized the situation up. He would have to do something about this, he was clearly thinking, as my brothers looked at him in dismay. They were already tired after their long walk, without having to stand at the end of this long line and Charlie, still weak from his illness, had just sat down on a small wall, silently whimpering with distress.

Suddenly Joe's face lit up as his searching gaze alighted on a boy, standing patiently at the front of the queue.

"Oi! Look who's 'ere," he called out to us. "Old Spindle-legs from school. Watch yer Spindle-legs, what yer doing ere then?" he called out, in a taunting manner, as we and everyone else standing around, turned to gawp at his victim.

The poor, unfortunate lad, just standing and minding his own business, coloured up and squirmed as he manoeuvred his stance to hide his stick thin legs behind the boy who stood in front of him. His under-developed shins had always been a continual 'butt' at the school, for unkind quips from insensitive bullies like Joe…boys never wore long trousers in those days, until they were at least fourteen, or were starting out to work. This poor boy had a while yet before he could hide this continual embarrassment of his thin legs, but he was getting a bit tired of taking this recurrent abuse, and he turned to Joe now. "Awright, Boney," he spat out, "and what about your Pansy BLOND HAIR? Just like a soppy girl. What about that then?"

It was Joe's turn to colour up now. He objected to being called a 'Pansy'. That was a definite assault on his masculinity. Spindle-legs had touched a very raw nerve when he called Joe that. He had always hated his startlingly blond hair; associating it with being a bit effeminate – why couldn't he have had the swarthy dark looks of John? It would have been much more in keeping with his volatile nature, and our surname of Bone didn't help either: it was always 'Boney' to the more brave.

Joe raised his fists and lunged at Spindle-legs now. "Come on, then!" he shouted at him. "I'll show you what a 'Pansy' I am," and he walloped the poor boy straight into the crowd of youngsters who were standing patiently in the long queue.

'Spindle-legs' went sprawling backwards with arms stretched out in an effort to break his fall. He struggled to regain his footing now and then; quickly, he lowered his head and came at Joe full pelt; making violent contact with his lower chest.

Joe staggered back, a surprised look on his face. He'd taken on a bit more than he'd bargained for. The wind was momentarily knocked out of him, and he struggled to regain his breath before he came forward for retaliation, but at that point, as the boys grappled with one another, the commissionaire, who had been standing at the front of the queue, hurried onto the scene.

"'Ere! 'ere!" he admonished the boys. "Stop that! Did you 'ear me?" he shouted. "Stop IT!" But these bold words from the poor little man resplendent in his smart uniform fell on deaf ears.

The moment he opened his mouth, his hat was knocked clean off from behind: on one hand then he tried to retrieve this, and on the other he attempted to break up the fight: fists flying, and 'Spindle-legs' snivelling and crying all through the melee, but this gallant boy wouldn't give up; he was giving as much as he got. He had had enough of being made fun of on account of his legs. They may have been weak, but you couldn't say that of his spirit.

Suddenly! Joe stopped fighting; he looked around at all the confusion; the shouting and cheering going on. This was better than any film. The poor little commissionaire was frantically running after his hat, further up the queue where someone had kicked it, as he had attempted to intervene in the fight. Jo realised then that the column of wild youngsters was moving. The doors of the cinema had been opened, and the fight was forgotten as everyone surged forward.

I was grabbed by Joe and hauled after him as he surreptitiously wormed his way to the front, leaving the others in his wake. His attempt to cause a distraction for this very purpose had worked brilliantly, and we sailed into the cinema well ahead of the others who had been patiently waiting in line, and no time was lost in selecting the best seats.

For the duration of the film-show then, all bedlam was let loose, with caps flying in the air as fights broke out among this frenetic, undisciplined throng of youngsters, jousting one another for supremacy, and the poor little usherette walking hurriedly up and down the steps with her torch flashing along the rows of seats, as she endeavoured to pin-point the trouble makers, but they just ridiculed her efforts to bring some order, and she was forced in the end to call the manager onto the scene. He lost no time then in grabbing the offenders by their ears and throwing them out, but Joe escaped this by quickly dodging under his seat so that when the torch flashed in our direction, it just revealed a frightened little girl (me) sitting in innocence, and clinging onto her seat, for dear life, terrified at all the savagery that had been going on; while the film continued to boom out, with cowboys and Indians all chasing one another and arrows flying in all directions through the air. I had seen very little of all of this, as I had sat ducking and diving throughout, endeavouring to avoid the wallops being meted out to Joe; he being the instigator of most of the trouble.

As the performance finally came to an end, we trailed out, with me once again being dragged along by Joe. I snivelled as I endeavoured to keep up with him. I hadn't enjoyed myself one bit: not like I used to at the church film shows, and there would be no nice Mr Longbottom here now, to take me by the hand and lead me to the ladies at the back of the hall to partake of their lovely cakes and lemonade. No penn'oth of chips on the way home with the penny that Auntie Queenie used to give us. Things couldn't be much worse.

Joe scanned the teeming crowd of youngsters, making their way to the cinema's exit now, his sense of responsibility suddenly coming back to him: he was accountable to my Mother for our welfare. Where was Charlie then? He wasn't with the rest of my brothers. Unbeknown to us, Charlie had never come into the cinema, but had remained in his exhausted state sitting on the wall outside! Panic overtook Joe as he hastened to go and find him, there was no way he would dare to venture home without one of his brothers, my Mother would wallop him hard, but as we made our hurried way to the exit sign, our movement was barred by the Manager who stood with his feet astride, a stern look on his face – the poor little beleaguered commissionaire who had suffered so much as he had tried to control the crowd outside before the film-show, was pointing to Joe as he told his employer "That's him, that's the one who caused all the trouble." I noticed that he had retrieved his hat, however, which now sat squarely on his head. He had obviously reported all, to his superior, and here they were, waiting for us.

Joe put on one of his practised innocent looks, but I knew that this time, his luck had run out. "What! He said "What 'ave I done?" but the Manager wasn't so easily fooled, he'd come across a lot like Joe. He looked him squarely in the face now. "Don't let me see you or your tribe in this cinema again. DO YOU HEAR." He enounced his words very precisely; leaving Joe in no doubt that he meant exactly what he said.

"Now GET OUT!" he spat at Joe, and we all walked meekly through the exit door under the baleful glare of the Manager and the now triumphant commissionaire, so that was the end of our Saturday mornings 'TUPPENNY RUSH' and as we undertook the journey home, me on John's back, and Charlie on Joe's, an air of despondency prevailed. Joe's wild behaviour had ended yet another of our treats. No film-show at the church with lovely refreshments after and now, no more 'Tuppenny Rush'. Nobody said a word apart from Jimmy, who squinted up at Joe now.

"It's all your fault Joe," he said, but Joe didn't care too much, and as we at last reached home he made his way to the front room and surveyed himself in the mirror that hung a bit haphazardly on the wall above the fireplace. He hooted with laughter then as he saw his reflection.

"Well, would you look at tha'" he told us "Spindle-legs has given me a black-eye. I wondered why it was 'urting so much." He laughed again, "The Cheeky Bugger, you wait till I see 'im," but this was said in admiration of what Spindle-legs had done to Joe, rather than in a threatening manner. This brave boy had stood up to him, even if he had cried and snivelled all through their fight and when Joe next encountered him at school, he decided to befriend him. "Hi yer, mate!" he hailed him.

Nobody, after this dared to taunt this boy any longer, because he was a friend of Joe's and woe betide anyone who said a word out of place to 'Spindle-legs' Joe would have them down on the ground like greased lightning. The two became bosom pals and would walk around the playground, sometimes in deep conversation with their arm around each other's shoulders. Their friendship lasted throughout their schooldays and a few years later, when they happened to bump into one another at a social occasion; this now tall handsome chap grabbed at Joe's hand and shook it firmly. He stood well above Joe, he being much taller, and he presented a very distinguished appearance in an immaculately tailored suit.

"Look Joe" he quipped, "I don't have any problems with my legs now that I can keep them covered: long trousers can cover a multitude of sins, can't they?"

Certainly this nice man left Joe in the shade with his polished presence and self assurance. Joe, who was short and thick-set in stature, in opposition to his friend's regal appearance, also lacked the social graces that his former school chum possessed and an unusual reservation took hold of him as he in awe conversed to the best of his ability.

Time, they say, is a great healer, and I might add; time has the potential also of change. Certainly in the case of Joe and Spindle-legs it excelled itself as it transformed and turned around the circumstances of these two beings.

LOST

Saturday morning; no school; all day to themselves, and they needed all day to make one more.

The boys dodged about the pavement outside of the house; bumping into one another, with their planks of wood going from one to the other, while I reposed on the front step, with my chin resting on my hands, and I watched the whole complicated procedure.

They planned to go on a long all day ride the next day, but they were short of a scooter for Jimmy. They now however had all the necessary bits and pieces spread round about them on the pavement, and they stood silently surveying all the clobber with thoughtful expressions on their faces.

Two planks of the wood, contributed by my father, stood propped up by the door – two small ball-bearing wheels of equal size, found on the dump adjacent to the park – a bolt for attaching the planks of wood together, and a smaller carved out piece for the handle –bar, also contributed by my father. All of this strewn about them. Now they just had to assemble everything together, and for the next few hours it was, hammer, hammer, hammer, saw, saw, saw, and squabble, squabble, squabble with:-
"NO! Arfur, THAT'S not straight, 'old it more firmly" and "'old it tighter John, 'ow can I ge' the bolt in if yer keep lettin' it slip?" Joe's voice was getting louder and more exasperated by the minute. "CHARLIE" he bawled out now. "Where's those bloody ball-bearings? GET EM OUT A YER POCKET; they're no bloody good ter me in there!"

"Joe, watch yer language!" my mother's warning voice sailed from inside the house.

Bobby from next door peeped around the bit of fence which separated the two front gardens.

Since he had felt the weight of Joe's boot, all aggression seemed to have left him and he eyed the boys now in a mild interested manner. After a while he cautiously inched forward on his belly; wanting to get in on the act.

"Stay clear, Bobby" Joe told him in a firm voice. He didn't hold it against the dog for the trouble he had caused, but at the same time he didn't want him getting in the way. Bobby's ears went back and he retreated to a safe distance, but he continued to watch with intensity now every move the boys made.

This endeavour of my brothers went on for most of the day, with just a hurried break for chip butties and a pot of tea, made with the grouts left over from breakfast, which were still in the teapot. Nothing was ever disposed of in the kitchen until its use had well and truly gone beyond redemption.

After several hours the finished article was proudly wheeled through the back gate into the back yard.

John sported a bloodied nose; the result of a heated argument with Joe, and in the affray that followed, Joe's fist had accidentally come into contact with this very sensitive feature of his, but John made no fuss, he was; like the rest of his brothers cock-o-hoop over the finished article; even so his eyes still watered from the blow, and on my mother's instruction he hurriedly swilled his face under the kitchen tap to abate some of the bruising resulting from the 'accidental' contact with Joe's fist, but now it was all forgotten as they surveyed the almost perfect finished article.

Tomorrow couldn't come soon enough for the boys; a whole day for the five of them to go as far as they wanted, and without having to drag me along with them.

They had spent some of the last evening nailing a metal Oxo tin to the lower strut of Jimmy's new scooter, just like they had on theirs, this made an excellent container for the sandwiches it would hold, and then a large bracket was fixed to the front strut of the scooter, and into this would be strapped the bottle of lemonade, so essential for the journey when they would stop on Joe's command to "have a quick swill"

The ball-bearing wheels on each scooter were meticulously oiled; that was very important, and the bolts checked that they were securely slotted into the fixture that kept the two planks of wood adjoined together. They wanted no repetition of what happened to Arthur on their last ride, when, as they took a sharp turn at the end of the road, his scooter; because the bolt hadn't been fixed securely enough, decided to part company. The front strut went one way and the lower strut went the other, and Arthur sailed straight over the top, landing on his head.

The boys laughed and laughed as they stood and surveyed the scene of the disintegrated scooter and Arthur sitting rubbing his cut and bruised skull. That must not happen again, for all the mirth it had brought about, when this unforeseen accident had happened.

As we sat, that Saturday evening at the large table in the kitchen, we became aware of the wheedling voice of our infamous neighbour.

"Look, Janey, come and 'ave a look out the front wiv me" she whined, as she poked her head round the back door.

"Now, you know I'm not one to complain" (the understatement of the year) "but just come and 'ave a look at the mess your boys 'ave made." She guided my mother through the back gate and around to the front to make her aware of the shambles that the boys had left behind, and Joe and John were dispensed forthwith to clear up and placate "Moaning Minny" as they called our complaining neighbour.

…Good fortune reigned on the boys as they arose early next morning to a bright and shiny day. Great excitement abounded as they milled around the kitchen, bumping into one another. After their hurried breakfast, they cut huge chunks of bread, spread hastily with margarine, and then layered with lumps of cheese. All, then, was wrapped up and shoved hastily into the large metal Oxo tins on their scooters. These tins had been supplied to the boys by the spinster sisters who ran the small general shop further along the road.

Bottles were filled with powdered lemonade that the boys had made the night before, and then slipped into the bracket on the front strut of their scooters. No time must be lost, and they cursed one another as they blundered about.

"Gerrart of the way!" and "now look what yer've done" as Jimmy, the youngest, who couldn't get a word in edgeways, cried that he couldn't manage the bread-knife, until my mother came to his rescue and sorted him out...

As everyone eventually stood in the street with their scooters; Joe already flamboyantly drinking from his bottle, as he eyed his brothers; my mother hurried out with Jimmy, "Now yer be quite sure yer take good care of 'im Joe" she said, as she looked him squarely in the eye, commanding his attention. "See 'ee don't lose 'is glasses." She had fixed these securely to Jimmy's head with elastic.

The wearing of these glasses by her youngest son was absolutely essential, owing to his having a lazy eye, and if the glasses were not worn, the eye would creep into the corner of the socket; giving him a cross eyed look.

"BOSS-EYED BONEY!" the kids at school would call him (our surname being Bone) if he was careless enough to forget to wear them. This used to upset Jimmy very much, and so it was imperative that the glasses were not lost; but Joe was, by now, well versed in the art of taking care of his younger sibling, and just gave my mother a wise forbearing nod. "Get near the front, Jimmy," Joe commanded him, "where I can watch yer; and make sure 'ee stays there," he told the others.

As the boys clattered off along the street, over the uneven paving, Bobby charged after them, while barking his head off. "No!" Joe shouted at him. "Go back Bobby, yer can't come." The dog stopped in his tracks, and slowly turned away, his tail between his legs. For the rest of the day the poor unhappy creature just lay, waiting for the boys to come back, and wouldn't bother with anybody, even when his owner found a biscuit for him, he just wasn't interested, he had just wanted to be with the boys.

... Nine o'clock! And there was great concern within the household. Where were the boys? Darkness had crept in through the evening. The usual big pot of stew sat waiting on the hob. They would be ravenous, but where were they?

"They'll get nuffink if they're much longer" my mother mumbled, in an attempt to cloak her concern, but as evening wore on, she became very fearful. Auntie Queenie was summoned from upstairs and after a quick discussion with my mother she retrieved her bike from the back yard and departed post haste for the police station.

"Quick, Liz!" my mother instructed me, now in a hoarse voice, "go and get Mrs Gold from next door ter come in. Quick!" Her voice broke a bit at this!

I literally fell through the front door in my haste. "Quick, get Mrs Gold," I repeated to myself as tears blinded my exit.

Bang! Bang! and Bang again; I smashed the knocker on her front door. I was beside myself, imagining the boys lying and dying somewhere, isolated, never to be found again!

A startled Mrs Gold hurriedly opened the door, an incredulous look on her face.

"Why Liz!" she exclaimed. "What's all this? Yer frightened the life out'er me. What is is, Ducky?"

The sight of Mrs Gold, already in her long flannelette nightie, topped by big metal curlers in her hair, all kept in place by a brown hairnet; and with night cream plastered all over her face, should have had me laughing, so funny did she look, but the situation was too serious for that and as she noticed my tear filled eyes, she pulled me inside.

"'Ow! My ducky, tell me wha' it is?" she asked as she dabbed at my face with a corner of her nightie, while I spluttered an explanation out to her.

"Let me ge' a coat on." In those days we didn't have such things as bath robes or dressing gowns, and once away from the living room fire the rest of the house was freezing. Coats were donned for a measure of warmth. She hurried to the line of hangers in the passageway which had been put up a bit haphazardly by Mr Gold who always confessed to being useless as a 'andy man; "but 'ee 'as other attributes" his wife would defend him to other people. Nobody, however ever discovered what these other

attributes of Mr Gold's were and one was just left to guess, but Mrs Gold loved him for how he was, and in her eyes, "tha' was all tha' mattered."

The message I had conveyed to Mrs Gold in my tearful manner, left her in no doubt but that she was needed urgently and she guided me through the front door. "Come on, my duck, dry yer tears now, they'll be found, yer'll see," she comforted me as we went hand in hand back home, but we found my mother beside herself, and she threw her arms around our neighbour's neck as we entered the house. "Doris!" she cried, "they're lost. Wha' can I do? Wha' can I do?" she repeated. A look of surprise momentarily crossed the face of our neighbour; it was most unusual for my mother to be showing such emotion. It wasn't really in her nature to be like that. She wasn't exactly unfeeling towards her brood of children, but more like a Sergeant Major for most of the time, but then, who wouldn't be, with five boisterous, and sometimes very unruly boys to contend with.

Mrs Gold looked around the room. Sister Margaret and Mrs Rumble, who for once sat saying nothing, had already been summoned, and both just stared into space, an anxious look on their faces.

"Now come on, Ducky,'" said our gentle neighbour as she surprisingly took command of the situation. "Your Joe won't let nuffinc 'appen to the boys, yer know tha'!" she conveyed to my mother; all the while nodding her head in a wise manner. "They're lost, that's all, they went too far bu' the police 'll find 'em, you'll see. So let's all 'ave a cup a tea" and she bustled in a confident manner to the kitchen with Sister Margaret in her wake.

As we sat drinking this comforting beverage, Mrs Gold pulled me onto her lap. I was exhausted with emotion. My eyes became heavy and I was losing the battle to keep them open as the discussion and assurance regarding the boys welfare rumbled on. "Yes, Ducky," and "No, Ducky," from Mrs Gold faded into the distance. "Three bags full ducky." I was telling myself sleepily, but a measure of comfort enfolded me as I lazily listened to these words, brought more to enforcement as time ticked on; then suddenly, WHAM!! Everybody was jumping to their feet as a thunderous knocking from the front door penetrated the mournful atmosphere…

Bobby, who had been snoozing on Mrs Rumble's lap, fell to the floor as his owner jumped up in alarm. He went into a serious spate of growling and barking, so alarmed was he at this sudden intrusion.

My mother literally flew along the passage to let these noisy intruders in; she knew instinctively who they were, "Thank Gawd, thank Gawd," she mumbled as she went.

A hefty foot then kicked open the inner door where we all were, and a huge policeman stalked in, with Jimmy, dead to the world, in his arms.

"We've go' the others," he informed us, as everybody rushed out to the street.

There before us was the police car, with Joe, John and Arthur sitting in the back; their scooters standing upright on their laps.

Charlie was squashed in front of the vehicle, his scooter having been stowed away in the boot of the car, along with Jimmy's. As this forlorn foursome trooped into the house, my mother, overcome with emotion, just stood crying. "Thank gawd, thank gawd," she said again, all her wrath forgotten in her intense relief at seeing the boys safe, but not a word was uttered from her brood as they staggered upstairs to their beds.

"Wait!" called my mother to them. "Yer stew," she implored to them, "yer must be starvin'." but her concern fell on deaf ears: bed was the only thing the boys were interested in. No one, nor nothing was going to keep them from falling flat on their faces across these as they gave into complete and utter exhaustion; their clothes and shoes still on their bodies.

"There we go, Ducky, wha' did I tell yer? I said they would be awright, di'n't I?" Mrs Gold took my sobbing mother in her arms.

"And Joe's even made sure that Jimmy's glasses 'ave stayed on 'is 'ead," I contributed with some relief. It was important to me that Jimmy still had these. I didn't like him being called 'Boss-eyed Boney" by the unkind lot at school...

It was a sorry tribe that emerged from their beds the next morning; still very tired, but feeling considerably better after polishing off the re-heated stew for breakfast. Jimmy remained in bed though, still with his glasses on his head. He hadn't moved all night. He stayed unmoving in his state of exhaustion; so much so that he slept the sleep of the dead and it would be some time yet before he became alive. "Leave 'im." My mother had instructed the others, but when she saw them to the door, for school, she put her hand to her mouth as she watched them limping along the street. "Oh my gawd!" she exclaimed as she took note of the fact that each boy was practically minus the right shoe which had peddled them all those miles the previous day. The left shoe was okay; that had merely rested on the scooter, but the soles of the other had almost ceased to exist, and what was left was just flap, flap, flapping on the ground as the boys walked along.

Joe and John had made a hurried attempt before they left home to tie sole and shoe together with string, which gave them some leverage, but Charlie and Arthur just hobbled along as best they could on their almost non-existent sole flapping between foot and ground.

As it happened; only a few weeks had elapsed since Father Joseph had come to the house regarding the boys' absence from church on Sundays. "Where are they?" he had asked.

"Well Father," my mother replied, "they 'aven't any decent shoes a' the moment ter wear fer church; it wou'n't be righ' to send 'em in the scruffy shoes tha' they 'ave, would it?"

Father stood thinking about this. "Bring them along some time during the week, Janey, and we will see what we can sort out," he finally told her, " we can't have the boys missing church on account of this."

And so my mother had dutifully taken the boys along to be fitted with new shoes and here now, they were already in tatters. What could she do? The scooters had been confiscated; relegated to the back yard, where they stood forlornly in a neat row, and not to be touched. It was quite sad really to see the boys' only method of transport just standing redundant like this, rejected and abandoned. Joe and John looked at them contemplatively through the back window on the day in question and turned to my mother.

"Mum, if we promise not to go too far could we…"

"Don' you dare ask" she cut them off in mid sentence. It was bad enough that Father Joseph's new shoes were already worn out and now, here was the inevitable letter from the school's headmaster. Dear Mrs

Bone! It started... I stood protectively behind my mother and looked over her shoulder as she mumbled the contents. She ran a hand then over her furrowed brow as she lay the letter to one side. "Mr. Stevens wan's a see me, Liz," she told me wearily, "about the boys' shoes"..."I would appreciate," the letter had finished, "that you come to see me at your earliest convenience, so that we might discuss the matter!"

My mother was in deep thought as she slowly arose from her chair, and I watched her as she stood and agonised over the letter. What could she do?... In the end, after much soul-searching, she decided to take the bull by the horns and make a clean breast of things on a visit to Mr Stevens. She dragged me along for moral support.

"Their scooters 'ave been confiscated" she told this sober man as he peered at her over his glasses, while at the same time he drummed his fingers lightly on the desk before him.

"That is a great pity, of course," he conveyed with condolence to my surprised mother. "I'm sure that they get a lot of pleasure from riding them, but I think that their use, in future must be limited, because we can't of course have the boys coming to school all the time with one of their shoes practically falling of their foot, can we?"

My mother eagerly clutched at this 'olive branch' being held out to her, and shook her head vehemently.

"Ow gawd, no, Mr Stevens; we can't 'ave tha' can we? Tha's just wot I told the boys. Yer can't keep goin' to school wiv one of yer shoes fallin' off yer foot: tha's just wot I tol' em."

A forbearing look flicked across the Head's face as he contemplated the next step. "Look," he said. "Maybe on this occasion we could perhaps involve the school welfare to fit the boys with appropriate shoes... although they probably won't be new," he warned my mother with emphasis. "They would more than likely come from a pool of almost new shoes, would that be acceptable to you" he said, as he pointed his glasses at her, awaiting her reply.

"Ow well, Mr. Stevens, tha' is very good of yer: thank yer very much," my mother grovelled to him, in her immense relief. This relief was probably brought on by the fact of her realising that she would not now have to go cap-in-hand to Father Joseph to explain the demise of the boys' new shoes. They could continue to turn up for church on Sunday without him knowing anything about what had happened to the spanking new footwear that he had provided. "Thank gawd for tha'," she was probably telling herself. "Thank gawd for tha'."

She shook the forbearing Head's hand as we took our leave. "Now don' yer worry, Mr. Stevens" she told him as we slipped away. "I'll make sure tha' the boys take good care a their shoes now, ufferwise they'll 'ave me to answer te. You jus' see, you jus' see," she finished, at the same time giving him a knowing wink.

I wouldn't mind betting that Mr Stevens had a good laugh to himself after we very soberly left him in spite of all the long-suffering looks thrown across his desk to my mother, and the frequent raising of his eyebrows to her – yes, I bet he had a really good laugh. I know I would have done, had I found myself as he had done in the ludicrous situation that had just taken place within his office. Mrs Bone, with her brood of boys and their continuous, practically non-existent right shoe. What a laugh!

A BUCKET FULL
OF DUNG

There was never any spare money in the family. In fact there wasn't even enough to live decently; my Mother having to manage on a weekly allowance, by 'court order' from my father, which was barely enough to feed us, let alone anything else; yet my father would moan about parting with this pittance. He chose to forget that he himself could afford to visit the pub every evening, socialising with his cronies, and so, of course, none of us children ever got, what's taken for granted today: a thing called 'pocket money', apart from our weekly tuppence on a Friday from Auntie Queenie. So the boys were always looking for ways to earn a little, be it doing jobs for the neighbours, like chopping wood or running errands, cleaning windows, or helping out after school in the various shops round about by weighing-up biscuits or other products, or even sweeping and cleaning up.

Joe was old enough now to do a paper round. He was supplied with a rickety old bike by the newsagent and got quite expert at shoving the papers through the doors without even getting off this monstrosity, which creaked and cranked at every turn of the pedal. The chain hung loosely almost to the ground and –was forever coming off, making the job twice as long.

"And just make sure you git it right!" the newsagent would bawl, as Joe Left the shop while studying his long list. There were plenty of others who would like the job if he didn't get it right. He knew this and so he would wobble around on this decrepit bike with a determination that only he could muster, until all the papers were delivered, in the right order.

John had also found a way of making some money. He would watch out each day for the tradesmen with their horse-drawn vehicles coming along the road, and when he spied them, as they turned into the street, he would rush into the kitchen to retrieve one of the buckets from under the sink while calling out to me, "Quick, Liz, get the shovel!"

On this particular day, it happened to be the Rag and Bone man, and we heard his plaintive cry long before we actually saw him. He was singing loudly as he appeared, in a resonant voice so that everyone could hear him. "Bring out your Rags, Bottle and Bo…hones. Bring out your Ra-hags, Bottle and Bo…hones." He kept up a continuous wailing of this, until little kids would suddenly come darting from their homes with one or two bottles, or some rags, which entitled them to just one go on an amazing little roundabout that he had somehow constructed on the back of his cart. This was by far my favourite tradesman, as I, sometimes, ran out with the other kids, while clutching perhaps a couple of jam-jars or some rags saved purposefully for this occasion, and I would sit on his rickety contraption, grinning from ear to ear as we swirled around…

John and I shot out now and followed the tradesman until the horse delivered a nice dollop of steaming manure. Our luck was in on this particular day, as the horse, seeming to know what we were after, excelled himself as he deposited a huge pile of this evil-smelling stuff right in front of us onto the road. The stench was overpowering, but John, quick as lightning, ignored this, and with great enthusiasm started to shovel the manure into his bucket, while I stood to one side holding my nose.

Suddenly, from nowhere, it seemed, a boy rushed up and blocked John's way, so that he couldn't get to the rest of the manure. "'Ere! Gerrof!" shouted John at him. "I was 'ere first. Gerrof!" But there was no way that the boy was going to give up on this lovely manure. "'alf and 'alf" he said to John, as he determinedly stood there poised with his bucket and shovel. "No, gerrof" John shouted again. "I was 'ere first!" and he shoved the boy to one side. A squabble quickly ensued and the boy became exasperated on realizing that he wasn't going to get any of the manure. And so, without more ado, he picked John's half filled bucket up and tipped the contents all over his head! "Awright, 'ave it!" he said in a rage.

I looked on in horror then, and watched, as this foul-smelling and very liquid stuff ran in soggy lumps all down John's face. The culprit, very pleased with himself, made to run off, but John was too quick for him. He grabbed at the boy's jumper and at the same time hooked his foot around one of his legs, and he brought him down. The two of them rolled round and around on the ground, cursing and throwing punches at one another. They were both in a frenzied rage, and were quite oblivious of all that unmentionable stuff splattered on the ground accumulating on their clothes.

The perpetrator of this brawl eventually managed to break away and, giving John one final wallop, he ran off. But he didn't go scot-free, he had almost as much manure on himself as his victim had. In his haste, he had also forgotten his bucket which stood empty on the road, the shovel standing within it.

John go to his feet and watched now as his attacker beat a hasty retreat, but there was no victorious look from him, instead, he stood stinking and dejected. Bang went his bucket of manure, the stuff that now plastered him from top to bottom.

It was this, you see, that John traded to some of the houses round about. The streets might look shabby and non-descript, but some of the gardens were lovely. Mr Chambers, for instance, spent hours during his retirement tending his gardens, both back and front, with attractive shrubs and flowers for all to see at the front, and an assortment of vegetables and fruit at the back, some of which he would graciously give to my mother. "Surplus to requirements," he would tell her, with a grin, and she in turn would repay him in kind, by doing a little ironing or mending for him, he being a widower.

There were one or two others like Mr Chambers. They would gladly part with a sixpence now and then for a full bucket of manure from John. "As long as you promise that it's quite fresh," they would tease him as they surveyed the potent stuff, steaming away in his bucket.

"Just collected it," John would tell them, not realising their gentle taunting of him. "Ain't that right Liz?" He would turn to me, and I would vehemently nod my head in agreement. I knew how much John needed that sixpence, and sometimes he would give me a penny of it for carrying the shovel for him.

"Come on, Liz, let's get home," he said heavily to me now. The day was utterly and completely ruined, and all expectations of that treasured sixpence had been blown sky-high. He picked up the bucket in one hand and the shovel in the other, and we trudged along in sombre mood; he'd lost all interest in the manure now. We must have presented a bizarre sight as we walked disconsolately along, but as we neared the house I suddenly felt a tingling of excitement surging through me, and I ran quickly ahead. I couldn't wait to tell all at home of this extraordinary happening that had just taken place, and as I reached the house I literally fell through the back door shouting, "Quick, Mum! QUICK! Some boy's thrown SHIT all over John. QUICK!"

Unfortunately, at that moment, my Mother was sitting having a cup of tea in the kitchen with Sister Margaret, and as she picked me up off the floor where I had tumbled, she admonished me, while at the same time giving me a warning look regarding my using that word in front of Sister. But so anxious was I to impart this incredible news, that I couldn't stop myself from repeating it. "A boy's thrown SHIT all over John!" I said, in case people hadn't heard me the first time. My mother dragged me to her. "Where is 'ee?" she said, looking me straight in the eye. Had I not heard what she'd said?

"'ee's coming" I said. "'ee's coming along the street." My mother dashed to the front door with me in her wake. I wasn't going to miss this for all the tea in China!

As she opened the door, John met her on the step, and I heard her gasp. "What the!" she said, as she watched him dripping manure all over the step. "WHAT! GET ROUND THE BACK!" she bellowed at him now. "Don't stand there dripping; ge' round!" she repeated.

"I told you, Mum," I called after her as she hurriedly made her way to the back of the house to meet John. I was thrilled at the reaction to this drama which was unfolding. "I told you," I persisted, as I followed her closely. "I said that boy 'ad thrown 'shit' all over John. I didn't make it up, did I?" My mother stopped momentarily in her tracks and turned me to face her, eyeball to eyeball and said, "Liz, if I 'ear you saying that word again…" She gave Sister an apologetic look, then, "She get's i' from the boys," she told her, and this was true. My mother never made a habit of swearing. To her, this would seem very unladylike, the same as a woman smoking or drinking; the boys, however, swore like troopers, just as their father did.

"If I 'ear you say tha' word again," she continued, looking hard at me, "I'll give you such a thump, yer see if I won't".

She rummaged under the sink for a bucket.

"STAY WHERE YOU ARE!" she hollered at John through the opened back door as she filled the bucket with water from the tap.

"JUST STAY THERE and DON'T MOVE!" she commanded him.

She stepped into the backyard then and threw the contents of the bucket all over John, and then hurried back to refill before going back again.

After standing somewhat uncertainly while all this was going on, Sister Margaret suddenly came into action. She quickly filled the large washing-up bowl standing on the draining board with water, and went out to do likewise to John.

Back and forth, back and forth they went.

I stood transfixed by all the goings on, and then I laughed and laughed; I couldn't help myself.

The proceedings were suddenly interrupted however by the entry through the back gate of Mrs Rumble, our troublesome neighbour.

"Eh, Janie", she said to my mother, "trouble again?" She gave a meaningful look to Sister. "They'll 'ave to be taken in 'and. And you know, Janie, they **will** you know."

My mother momentarily stopped what she was doing, and glared now at this interfering busy-body. Emboldened by the presence of Sister Margaret and suddenly very fed up with this woman, she took a step towards her. "Why don't you just MIND yer own BUSINESS for once?" she spat at Mrs Rumble!

A look of complete surprise came upon our neighbour's face; she couldn't believe the venom in my mother's voice, and for once she was lost for words. Then… "E-e-e-e-e," she uttered – her favourite expression. "E-e-e-e-e!" she exclaimed once again, as she beat a hasty retreat back through the gate. "Wha' an insult!" we heard her saying to herself as she bustled off.

The dousing of John continued until it would seem that every trace of the manure had been sluiced away.

Sister Margaret went into the kitchen. "I think we had better have another cup of tea" she said.

My mother took a chair into the backyard for John to sit on. "STAY THERE!" she commanded him, as though she were talking to a dog. "STAY THERE and dry off!" she boomed "and I'll bring yer a cup a tea." She mellowed a bit now, though, as she realized that it wasn't something that he'd done on purpose; he was, after all, just trying to earn a few pennies.

My mother and I, and Sister, sat solemnly drinking our beverage now, as we surveyed John through the window. He drank the hot sweet liquid with a resentful look on his face. "What a good job it's a blazing hot day for drying him off," said Sister, but John looked a picture of dejection. He was mortified by what had happened, and he'd lost a sixpence into the bargain.

He wasn't to know then, that our kind retired neighbour of a few doors down had seen what had happened through his front window earlier on, and would come along to hand John the treasured coin. "You put up a good fight there, John" he told him. "Good on yer!" And as he handed him the sixpence, he added, "That's an advance on the next bucket of manure yer bring me." But John had known nothing of this as he sat patiently drying off, that this kind neighbour had seen all, and he brightened considerably then as he clutched the treasured sixpence.

The hot sweet tea, being drunk by us onlookers in the kitchen soon had a relaxing effect, and I became conscious then of a shaking of Sister's shoulders. She was laughing, and a spluttering came from her as she made a determined effort to stop herself; but the tea sprayed from her cup as she guffawed into it. She could control herself no longer, and a peal of laughter rang out from her.

"Oh, Janie!" she said then, "the look on your neighbour's face, when you told her, in no uncertain terms to MIND HER OWN BUSINESS," and she exploded with laughter again.

My mother, on giving this some thought, began to see the funny side, and she started to laugh heartily herself. "I certainly told 'er, didn't I, Sister?" she said, as she continued to laugh. "I'll probably pay for it later, though: Mrs Rumble's no' likely to le' it go. I'm bound ter suffer fer me moment of madness soon," and another high-pitched burst of laughter, almost bordering on hysteria came from her as she continued. "An' I be' when tha' day comes, yer won' even be around ter protect me!" The two of them could hardly converse coherently now, so much were they laughing, and I laughed along with them. I knew how frightened my mother really was of Mrs Rumble, but for the moment she chose to forget this. How lovely it was, though, to see the friendship between these two. I always felt so happy when Sister was with us, but now it was time for her to leave. I didn't want her to go and clung onto her hand.

"Goodbye, John," she called out to him as she went out of the gate. "Call around with Liz later," she told him, "and I'll see if I can find some sweets for you. Goodbye."

In one way then, it had turned out to be John's lucky day after all. What with the treasured sixpence from our kind neighbour and now the promise of sweets from Sister Margaret, it hadn't turned out so bad, had it?

HOSPITALISED

I tossed and turned and whimpered as once again my mother sponged me down with cold water from a bowl. She had been up and down all night coping with my coughing and the high fever that accompanied it.

"Quick, Joe!" she called now, from the bedroom. "Go to the surgery and get Dr James fer Liz; tell 'im it's urgent!"

Joe came to the bedroom, already pulling on his trousers. He took one look at me before he disappeared hastily through the front door. My delicacy had always been a cause for concern within the family. The boys had always been robust, but in comparison my thin frame, topped by an elfin face with dark circled eyes, gave the appearance of what my mother described as a 'alf-starved sparrow; clearly revealing my frailty.

At mealtimes, as the boys squabbled over who should have what was left on my plate, my barely having touched it, my mother would come down heavily with her elbow in the middle of the table. She would stretch herself out and cuff the boys around their ears. "That's right!" she would shout at them. "Fight over 'er food, don't worry tha' she's not eating it. All you greedy lot can think of is yer own stomachs!" The boys would pull back guiltily.

Sometimes though, when I was well, she would take me to the nice pharmacist in the chemist situated at one end of Hoxton Market. This was a favourite day out for my mother, who once a week would walk with me to the bus-stop just around the corner from where we lived, and we would take the bus to the market. She loved the atmosphere there; the friendly stall-holders with their usual greetings of 'ow are yer terday then, Darlin'? What's it ter be then?" My mother would give a brief nod, but would continue to walk toward a more urgent matter in the chemist, further along the market.

As we approached this double-fronted building, standing with doors wide open, it being a very hot day, my mother sailed through them in search of our benefactor, the pharmacist.

"Well then," he would say as he spied us coming toward him, and at the same time he would be sizing me up, to see if I had been responding to the various tonics that he had been recommending for me over a period of time.

"How is she then?" he would ask my mother, while nodding in my direction. "Is she eating any better?"

My mother would shake her head. "No' really," she would respond. "Look at 'er: a puff of wind would blow 'er over; she don't eat enough ter keep a sparrow alive."

The chemist would rub his chin and look contemplatively at me. "Well, there's only one thing for it now, he decided. "Parishes food, that's what it will have to be," and he stretched behind him to take a bottle off the long shelf. He held it aloft. "See that?" he asked of my mother. "One of the finest tonics around." If that doesn't work, nothing will. Yes, we'll get her onto that." And he tipped and turned the bottle of deep red liquid while displaying it. "Full of iron that," he assured my mother as he slipped the bottle into a paper bag, while taking the money. Full of hope, we made our way now to the assortment of stalls along the market, making a beeline for the one selling second-hand clothes. We got the usual greeting once again, while my mother was having a good sort through, of "Nice day ain't it, Luv?"

My mother gave a perfunctory reply in an abstract manner as she concentrated on her search, then, "Ere we are Liz," she said as she held a garment aloft, while eyeing it up and down. It was a small gabardine mac hanging neatly on a hanger. "Look at tha'" my mother said, "Just what yer'll need fer starting school."

"'ow much?" my mother enquired of the stall-holder. The woman ran a glance over us, obviously sizing up what we could afford, and she mentioned a very reasonable price.

"Slip it on, Liz; see if it fits," and my mother helped me to try the garment for size.

I stood proudly as we noted that it did indeed fit well, but then I became aware that the belt was missing. "I can't wear it without a belt, Mum," I said with disappointment. My mother looked enquiringly at the stall-holder.

"Well, well, now don't yer fuss, Darling," the woman tried to console me. "It's sure ter be in me stockroom at 'ome. I'll find it, Luv. Just yer 'ave it, and come an' see me next week; I'll find it fer yer, yer'll see." She popped the mac quickly into a bag before my mother could change her mind, and each week we would enquire after the belt.

"I'm still lookin', Darlin'" the stall-holder would tell my mother. "Now don't yer worry, I'll find it fer yer." But of course, she never did, and starting school in a mac minus its belt made me feel quite sad. I would stand in the playground at play-time, my fingers in the empty loops, hoping that nobody was noticing the absence of the belt, because without it, the garment just hung on me… I had wanted to be able to strap myself into it, which would have made me feel very smart and proud. I was bitterly disappointed and got no pleasure from the wearing of this garment at all, and my mother would have to force it on me, in spite of any protests I made each morning.

A treat for my mother while in Hoxton was a visit to the jellied-eel and pie shop. "Come on, Liz," she'd say. "Let's get somefing ter eat; I'm 'ungry." She'd quicken her pace towards her goal.

I'd trail reluctantly behind her. This was a place I hated going to.

In front of the 'Pie and Eel' shop window were displayed large flat trays of squirming eels, and the woman standing behind these would be brandishing a huge knife and she would cut the eels in half as they were squirming around, getting them ready to be cooked and made into jellied eels. "A very nourishing food," my mother never stopped telling me.

This ugly woman, who brandished the knife, would beam at me as I walked in with my mother. Whatever her feelings for the unfortunate eels, she was obviously fond of children, and she would go to hug me as I passed her, but I would quickly extricate myself from her clutches and make for the furthest table, away from all the slaughter being carried out at the front.

My mother would laugh at my squeamishness. "I don't wan' nuffin' ter eat," I would tell her, feeling quite faint as we sat down.

"No need to ask 'er what she don' want," she called to the man who was serving; just bring 'er some pie an' mash and 'opefully she'll eat some of i'." She'd take her plate of jellied eels then and would eat them with relish.

"This is what yer should be eating," she would say, while pointing her fork at the mass of jelly on her plate. "This would soon make yer strong." But I didn't want to know; I continued to feel faint just thinking about it.

As we eventually made our way out of the shop and into the bustling market once more, with me taking the longest route around the back of all the chairs, my sole intention being to avoid at all cost the trays of squirming eels and their over-affectionate slaughterer, we almost collided with a man standing to just one side of the doors. My mother put a restraining hand on my shoulder and gave the man a questioning look which clearly said, "Did he have to stand quite so close to the exit?" But as I looked at him, I experienced a wave of sadness. The man was carrying a tray, low on his chest which was supported by a strap around his neck. On the tray were matches which he was trying to sell. He looked haggard with his dark-rimmed eyes and hollow cheeks, and I felt desperately sorry for him.

When we had got a little way past him, I tugged at my mother's sleeve. "Mum, mum," I whispered in her ear as she bent down to me. "Mum, buy some matches off that man, quick! Buy some matches," I said urgently.

My mother, rather surprised at my request, glanced back and gave the man a cursory look, before turning once more to me.

"But, Liz, I don't need no matches," she said, dragging me away.

It was quite obvious then, that my acute sensitivity had not been inherited from her! I walked tearfully along beside her; she could have bought some matches; why didn't she? But my mother's conscience wasn't bothering her; she was only interested in exploring the rest of the market.

We continued past one of the several pubs in that area of Hoxton. The smell of beer wafting through its open doors made me feel nauseated, and I held my nose.

"Wha' are you doing, Liz?" my mother was saying to me with a trace of annoyance, when suddenly, something came flying through the pub's open doors, and landed on the back of her neck.

Quick as lightning, a man dashed from the pub to rescue the lighted cigarette butt which he had carelessly thrown through the open door, and which was now trapped by the collar of my mother's jumper. He literally flew to my mother's rescue, closely followed by the landlord, who had seen what had happened from his position behind the counter.

He bawled at the offender now, "How many times have I told you about that? Can you see now how dangerous your throwing lighted cigarette ends through the door is?" Fortunately the quick action of this careless man in retrieving the cigarette from my mother's neck, saved her from too much harm and she was coerced, unwillingly, by him to enter the pub for a conciliatory drink to make amends.

I had a lemonade put into my hand, as I stood at the door and, as I leaned against it, I took note of the men inside, just propping up the bar with large pints of beer in their hands, as they talked nonsensical, meaningless chatter with each other. I wondered how with all the poverty, they could afford to do this. I thought of the poor haggard match-seller, outside the pie and eel shop, who obviously couldn't even afford a decent meal. I thought of my father. He also could afford to prop up the bar each night with his cronies. I couldn't reason the comparison of these differing people; of course, I was too young to understand then, but my thinking sowed the seeds of a hatred of pubs, an abomination that would follow me through life. I was to come across the curse of drink again and again, but this was my initial introduction to this aversion, and as my mother and I later made our way home, I informed her, "I'm never going ter drink when I grow up, Mum; never!"

My mother threw a hard look at me, my having said this with such intensity, but she said nothing. Maybe she was thinking of the happening some weeks back when, having got off the bus at the market, we had first made our way, as was usual, to the court offices where she would collect the small monetary maintenance allowance paid in by my father through Court Order but on this occasion, there was nothing. My father had failed to 'cough-up' that week, and my mother, on being told this, stood dumbfounded. Bang! went the only pleasurable event in her weekly toil – no sorting through the market on that day; no visit to the pie and eel shop she so much enjoyed; nothing: and so we had trailed miserably back to the bus-stop and home. This was the one day in the week that my mother looked forward to and it was one more nail in my father's coffin as far as she was concerned; but no matter, my father did not get off scot-free. He was soon visited by the police, who had the full measure of him. Pay up or be banged up in prison! It wasn't the first time that he had had this warning, and at least he had the sense to realise that prison would mean no job; no job would mean no money; no money would mean no drink! So once again he was forced to pay up. This was the lesser of two evils as far as he was concerned, but it didn't quell my mother's tears that day on the bus, as we made our way home.

I stole a concerned look at her then: "Mum, don't cry," I had said quietly. "Don't cry, 'cos we can come again next week, can't we?" She just patted my hand, but continued to look vacantly through the bus window. "Yes," I told myself, "we can come again next week."

The kind pharmacist's magic tonic of that day made little difference, I'm afraid, to my dire and delicate constitution, as I was soon very ill again. The doctor had wasted no time when he saw me and just went straight back to the surgery to call an ambulance.

In my delirium, as I lay prone with fever, things seemed to be happening from afar. I was mildly surprised therefore to realise that my mother was crying. "She will be awlright, wont she?" she asked of the doctor, as he went back through the bedroom door. He paused for a moment, his hand still on the knob, before answering. "Well, like most things, it's in the 'lap of the gods,'" he replied, after glancing once more at my frail frame on the bed.

This didn't console my mother at all and she continued to cry bitterly. She realized how very ill I was. I lay there for most for the day in my serene state, before the ambulance arrived to take me to hospital.

I found that, by laying quite still, the pain in my chest wasn't so severe. The fever that ravaged my body that morning had the effect of tranquilizing me, and so I felt quite calm. I was aware of the boys coming in and out of the bedroom. They realized that I was very ill and they would hold my hand. "Yer'll be awright, Liz," they told me in a whisper. "Yer'll soon get' better in 'ospital: yer'll see."

A little while before the ambulance arrived, Arthur came in to me. "Look, Liz," he whispered as he leaned over me, "Mr Evans 'as sent these for yer," and he placed a small packet of biscuits into my hand. "They're yer favourites, ain't they?" he said, as he closed my fingers around them. "Yer always like ter eat them, don't yer?"

I gave a weak smile as I gripped hold of the biscuits but I said nothing, and then we heard the clanging of the ambulance, as it turned into the street and pulled up outside the house.

I was conscious then of being wrapped tenderly in a blanket, with as little movement as possible on account of the pain in my chest, which was like a knife being plunged and twisted into it. I remember being carefully carried along the narrow passage and through the front door to the waiting vehicle, its engine still running.

The ambulance man then trod carefully up the steps and he passed me to the attending nurse, the two negotiating the laying of me methodically on the bed.

The whole street, it seemed, had turned out to watch the spectacle of me being taken away. As I looked from the high bed, through the window of the ambulance, I saw Mrs Rumble, our quarrelsome neighbour, as she stood clutching Bobby in her arms. Since Joe had given the dog a good kick some weeks earlier, Bobby had quietened down considerably. He had certainly taken Joe's message on board. His owner stroked and whispered to him now, as she watched with worried eyes my impending departure.

As I continued looking through the window in a strange sort of detached abstract way, I took note of Jimmy, half hiding behind my mother, a scared worried look on his face. Joe stood to one side of her, his usual blank expression on his face. He wasn't much given to showing emotion, even if he felt it within himself. John also stood with her.

Other neighbours of ours stood around, talking to one another, as they cast furtive glances in my direction, but as the ambulance moved off, their talking ceased, and they just followed us with their eyes as we sped away, the bells clanging loudly again.

Further up the street, and just before we turned onto the main road heading for the hospital, the ambulance slowed a little and there, standing quietly outside his bakery, was kind Mr Evans, a sad, grave expression showing on his face. Standing beside him were the two spinster sisters who owned the little general shop, and between them stood Terry, a boy of about eight or nine years of age.

The sisters had more or less adopted this attractive small boy from when he was very young. He came from the usual large, poverty stricken family, so prominent in those days. They lived just across the road to the spinster sisters, so Terry wasn't far from his natural parents, but he was living permanently now with his benefactors. They had more or less adopted this irresistible youngster, after looking after him for a prolonged period when his mother had been very ill. They had grown to love him in fact, having no children of their own. In an unspoken pact, Terry had become theirs, and they treasured him like no other child had ever been treasured. To all intents and purposes, he belonged solely to them and they had no intention of letting him go!

Sometimes, if we had visited the spinster sisters' shop, Terry would be behind the counter with them, feeding his face and laughing.

"Oh, yer rascal Terry!" the sisters would chide him. "Yer'll never eat yer tea, stuffing yerself like that." They would chuckle at us waiting to be served. "But we still love 'im," they would remark, while giving their mischievous treasure hugs and kisses. How can yer 'elp but love 'im? As it happened, my brothers couldn't stand the sight of him, spoilt and greedy as he was, while they themselves were always hungry, going into the shop merely for paltry portions of this, that and the other for my mother. I suppose it was rather insensitive of the sisters to flaunt Terry's wellbeing in front of us in this manner, knowing how poor we were; luxuries like sweets and chocolates were a rarity for us but for Terry, the abundance of these was taken very much for granted, and so enthralled were the sisters with their prodigy, they could deny him nothing.

"Silly SOD!" exploded Joe, his face looking like thunder. "What a twerp," he added, as we walked from the shop. The expletive uttered first from him was loud enough for the sisters to hear, and they followed us out with their eyes shock registering on their faces; but they stood now, with Terry between them as the ambulance passed, and their expressions were very different. Compassion emanated from their kind faces, the concern they felt for me being very evident and they both clutched at Terry, as though it might have been him in the ambulance.

The vehicle picked up speed as we turned onto the main road, leaving everybody behind. Only then did the tears come to my eyes…

"Choc-a-block!" the charge nurse announced, as on entering the hospital the ambulance crew methodically started to make their way with me to the children's ward; but there was "No space in there," he informed us. "Women's medical," I would have to go there, he announced in a harassed authoritative tone; and so, that's where I was taken.

As I was transferred from the ambulance man's arms to a cot and made comfortable, the ward sister lost no time in placing a thermometer gently under my arm, and gave a little gasp as she withdrew it. "Don't worry, Darling, I'll give you something to bring that down," she told me kindly, as she at the same time tried to relieve me of the, by then, rather soggy biscuits still clutched in my hand, but I held on tightly to them. Arthur had bought these for me to eat when I felt better, and I resolutely refused to part with my precious token.

"Alright, my darling, you just keep them," sister spoke softly as she attended to my needs.

The next few days for me were a blur of nurses coming and going.

They fed me liquid from a feeding cup when my temperature reached a dangerous level. Day faded into night; night eventually gave way to day; how many? I don't know and, in my fevered state, I didn't care. And then, suddenly early one morning, the fever was gone. I lay quietly in my cot and took stock. I remembered that at some stage during my days of oblivion I had vaguely been aware of a commotion taking place at the entrance to the ward. I had turned my head weakly then towards it, and saw my mother remonstrating with a nurse who barred her from coming into the ward. "Just let me have five minutes with 'er," I had heard my mother say, but the young nurse resolutely refused. "I'm sorry. I can't let you in – visiting time is over; you'll have to come back tomorrow," she said.

It appears that my mother, having missed the bus, had turned up just as the visitors were leaving. She was not going to be let in because, unlike today, visiting times then had to be strictly adhered-to for the smooth running of the ward. My mother had ultimately conceded and reluctantly walked away, after first looking in my direction.

I had whimpered and put my fevered hand through the bars of the cot to her, but she was gone and the nurse came to comfort me. "She'll come back tomorrow, Liz," she whispered to me, but I wanted her **terday** not termorrer. I had cried and drifted back to my fevered sleep, but now, as I opened my eyes this early morning, I noted the sun that was streaming through the windows into my cot; the fever and pain had gone. I weakly raised myself up on my elbows. Although my prolonged high temperature had at last decided to leave me, it had ravaged my small body, and drained me of most of my physical strength. I turned my head now towards the locker at the side of the cot having become aware that Arthur's biscuits were no longer in my hand, and there they were, in the little cubby-hole, still in their small wrapper, and although I didn't want to eat them then, I knew that I would. Maybe I will soon go home now, I thought.

I looked around the ward then to observe the goings on. There was another cot, I noticed, directly opposite to me where a young baby bounced vigorously up and down, up and down, while holding onto the end of it, and I vaguely remembered now its crying during the night. The women in the ward were complaining bitterly. "NURSE!" they were calling out. "Carn't yer do soemthin'? 'Ow are we supposed ter sleep wiv all this racket goin' on?"

The nurse went into the small kitchen at the end of the ward and returned with a bottle for the baby. "It's not my fault the baby's in this ward" she told the women, but things did quieten down as she fed and changed the little one and the women settled once again to sleep for what was left of the night, but they had to have a final grumble. "Only another two hours, and yer'll be waking us all up again," they told the poor harassed nurse and, indeed, it wasn't much more than two hours before the breakfast made an appearance, with its huge teapot rattling away on the decrepit trolley being manoeuvred with some difficulty along the ward. "Sugar? Milk?" was being called out by some little careworn woman, who looked as though she hadn't had much of a night herself.

That finished, and now a silence pervaded the hurriedly-tidied ward. Matron would soon be doing her daily round, and as she made her dignified appearance that day, she was accompanied by a young doctor of foreign origin. I should have been afraid as they stopped at my cot. The doctor's face, I noticed, was completely disfigured by scarring, as though perhaps he had at some time been caught in a fire, and yet, as he bent over me, I was only conscious of his amazingly kind eyes, and the slightly lop-sided schoolboyish smile that he bestowed upon me. He touched me gently. "You're back with us now, then, Liz," he said. "You've had us all very worried. Has the pain in your chest gone?" I nodded shyly, as he ruffled my hair, and I remembered then how at sometime during the dead of night, that first night, he had been summoned to me in my delirium as I lay in my befuddled state, just moaning. His eyes had been worried as he slid his stethoscope over my inflamed and congested lungs, and he conversed in a quiet voice with the ward sister who stood at his side; but he turned to matron now with a huge grin, as this formidable woman, who obviously adored, him returned his look with admiration, ready to cater to his every command.

"Just make sure she has plenty of fluids, Matron," he instructed her, and she dutifully made a note of this on the board that was suspended at the end of the cots. He took the board from her then, with a smile playing around the edges of his mouth while he added a postscript before moving along the ward to the other patients, who were quietly sitting bolt upright in their beds like a row of tin soldiers.

Before these very important morning visits, there had been the usual mad scramble by the two poor overworked nurses to get everything into apple-pie order. Everybody was strapped securely in their beds with not a cover out of place. "DON'T move a muscle, any of yer until matron's been, or else!" the poor harassed nurses had told their patients with mock authority, and as doctor walked with matron along the hushed ward, not a sound was heard, nobody even dared cough, so afraid were they of matron. The reverent tones of "Yes, doctor" or "No, doctor" could only just be heard from his patients, as they cast a wary glance at matron. Even if some might have been in pain, I don't think they would have been brave enough to mention it, so afraid were they of this dragon, but they all had that look of adoration in their eyes as they conversed with doctor, nodding or shaking their heads in compliance with whatever was being said by him. Just seeing and speaking with him each morning was almost like a cure in itself, but as soon as he and matron passed from the ward, all bedlam broke loose, as bedcovers were slung off and the patients tumbled with alacrity onto the floor, mingling with one another and talking in loud raucous voices.

"Where's our elevenses then, nurse; don't we ge' none terday then?" All reverence went out of the window once Matron had gone, and even the baby, who had sat wide eyed and quiet throughout the visit, now seemed to sense the freedom prevailing, and proceeded to yell his head off.

I was soon to come into contact again with Dr Arzapardi, after I had left the hospital, in much more congenial circumstances, my having made a slow recovery, but in my mind's eye today, after all the intervening years, I still recall his face quite clearly and I remember how I wasn't afraid.

What was it about this doctor that made him so admired? His badly-scarred face hadn't stopped those looks of adoration from the female fraternity. Fortunately, the scarring stayed clear of his magnetic eyes, as though, in whatever terrible circumstances his disfigurement occurred, he had somehow managed to protect them. His mouth also had escaped whatever trauma he had endured, and so that attractive smile of his had not been obliterated. These facets of the doctor's features served, I think, to detract a person's gaze from the obvious scarring of the rest of his face.

His nationality remains a mystery to me. I was too young at the time to query this. The name Arzapardi should give a clue, I suppose, and I do wonder sometimes when did he obtain the terrible facial scarring? Was it here, or in the country of his birth? But does it matter anyway? It certainly didn't detract at all from his popularity in any sense or form; he just seemed to have that rare presence, possessed by very few, and those fortunate enough to come into his administrations were just very privileged.

Later on, on the day of his visit to the ward with Matron, she herself came bustling back and made a beeline for my cot. This was most irregular for Matron, who was a stickler for protocol. Her visit had been done for the day, so what was she doing here now?

The looks on the ward patients' faces, who had been revelling in their disarray quickly showed amazement at her Majesty's entrance. This was very strange for Matron to turn up unexpectedly like this. They stood gawping at her now in silence while the two little nurses, a shocked look on their faces, made a fervent attempt to tidy up. But Matron, at this precise moment, wasn't much interested in what was going on in the ward, but more concerned in the post-script that Dr Arzapardi had added to my board during their morning visit, before he had quietly replaced it at the foot of my bed.

As she studied this now, that look of adoration slowly came back on to her face.

"Oh! That lovely man," she told all and sundry. "That lovely man," she said again as everyone stood, a stupefied expression adorning their faces. This was most unlike Matron to be so confiding, her frosty exterior having been put to one side for the moment. "Just listen to what he's put onto Liz's board here, just listen," she purred; and she read out again in a clear voice now as she turned this way and that so that everyone should hear:

"All Liz needs now," she enunciated in clear tones, "is plenty of TLC. Oh! What a lovely man: isn't that just like him?" She replaced the board thoughtfully, still with that dreamy look, but then she suddenly stiffened and drew herself up to her full regal stature, realizing that she had allowed her authoritarian manner to slip. She looked sharply around the ward now at the disorder. She took note of the unbelieving expressions still on the women's faces and she drew herself up briskly.

"Nurse!" she called in her normal icy tone. "Look at the state of this ward. Get it cleared up immediately – and some of you women walking around half naked. Get your dressing gowns on!" she admonished them.

"Yes, Matron," the guilty parties immediately chorused, while at the same time making rude signs at her departing back, as she flounced from the ward with her usual aplomb…

Later on that day of Matron's visit, I was surprised to see, walking towards me in an energetic manner, her long head-veil billowing out behind her, none other than Sister Margaret. She was accompanied by the ward Sister, and they stopped beside my cot.

"Well, Liz!" she exclaimed, while giving me one of her lovely smiles, "you look so much better." She turned to Sister standing beside her, and who had obviously given special permission for this late-morning visit. "Doesn't she look well, Sister?" she asked of her. "It's obviously to do with all the loving care that Liz has received while she's been here," she enthused, "she's so much better."

This pleased the ward Sister, who fairly bristled with pride and agreed that, yes, I had had to have a lot of care.

"Well, Liz," said Sister Margaret, turning once again to me. "I have some exciting news for you. What do you think? We are sending you to the seaside for two whole weeks to get you really well again."

My face dropped, and I felt tears rushing to my eyes with the shock of this sudden announcement. I didn't want to go to the seaside, I wanted to go home. I had missed my brothers. I had missed Auntie Queenie upstairs in her cluttered room where I often sort refuge from the bedlam going on downstairs, with the boys fighting and squabbling, and my Mother's empty words of "STOP IT, or I'll get your father!"

I would sit at Auntie Queenie's feet, dreamily lapping-up the warmth from the small fire in her room. She would knit, knit, knit, the numerous socks and gloves which seemed everlasting for our large family who, though lacking in general clothing, at least had their hands and feet kept warm by Auntie's industriousness.

My mother struggled all the time to keep the boys clothed, but they actually only possessed just one pair of pants each, and Wednesday was 'inside out' day when the boys religiously turned this garment to the clean side, the younger ones being reminded by my mother in the morning, "Have you?"

"Yes, Mum," they would say before she could finish; "we know it's inside out day today."

On a Saturday evening, the pants would be washed and draped over the fireguard in front of the fire to dry. Five pairs of steaming underwear, fresh and clean and being made decent for church the next day...

No! I didn't want to go to the seaside. I missed so many things at home; even Bobby the dog next door, who no longer went for me since his contact with Joe's boot. Now he would sidle up to me, and I would pet him, and speak lovingly in his ear.

I stiffened then, as an anxious thought occurred to me. What about John and his manure? He needed me to carry the shovel for him.

"Quick, Liz, get the shovel!" I heard him call in my mind's eye. Oh no! I could not go to the seaside, there was much too much at stake here. "I want to go home," I cried now, much to Sister Margaret's disappointment. "I don't want to go to the seaside. I want ter go home," I protested, with a sullen pout... but all to no avail.

CONVALESCENT

I walked along the platform, holding onto Sister Margaret's hand. Her other hand was being held by another thin, pasty-faced little girl, rather like myself. We had stopped off at the station tea-bar for some milk and a bun, but now we trundled along to the waiting train.

"Isn't this exciting?" Sister exclaimed as we settled ourselves down in the carriage. She tried to jolly us up, but her efforts fell on deaf ears, as the other little girl and myself just looked miserably at one another across the carriage.

"We'll soon be there" Sister persisted, as the train sped on its way. "It's not a very long journey," she told us, "and just think, tomorrow you might go to the beach, and you can make sand castles".

The little girl and I nodded politely at Sister with sad eyes, and when she realised that she was flogging two dead horses, she just shut up.

I felt myself dropping off. I was very tired after having a disastrous last night in hospital, and it was all over a bed-pan.

"Nurse!" I had called out in the silent darkness of the night, where the only light in the ward had come from a dim lamp on the desk where the night-nurse was sitting.

The desk had been positioned in the middle of the ward, so that the nurse could survey all the patients and, as she sat there, the eerie glow of the lamp silhouetted her head in a ghostly circle, while she bent over some charts upon which she was recording the patients' temperatures and summaries regarding their welfare.

When I realized that she hadn't heard me, I called louder, "NURSE!"

At this, she shot off her chair. "Hush. Liz" she said hastily as she hurried to me. "You'll wake everyone up, shouting like that," she told me rather unfairly. "Anyway, what do you want?"

"I need a bed-pan," I told her.

She bustled off to the sluice area, and returned with the required item. She slipped it under me with the instruction to call her 'quietly' when I had used it.

I watched her walk away then to the kitchen annex. "I might as well have a cup of tea," she was telling herself, and I heard her greet another nurse from the adjoining ward. They chatted away to one another and after a while it was quite obvious that nurse had completely forgotten about leaving me on the bed-pan.

I called quietly to her several times. I hadn't dared shout but my calls went unheeded. I cried noiselessly to myself as I tried to remove this monstrosity from beneath me, but in the endeavour, all the urine flowed up the hollow handle of the bed-pan, and soaked into the cot.

I lay miserably in this sodden state, before I eventually relapsed into a restless sleep, conscious of the fact that not only was I soaked, but that I smelled to high heaven as well...

"Liz! Why didn't you call me when you had finished with the bed-pan?" nurse chided me early the next morning, as she eyed the empty item that I had toppled onto the floor during the night. "Come to the bathroom" she said, her voice full of pique. She proceeded to strip everything off me, while filling the bath, where she scrupulously scrubbed me clean.

"No point in getting back to bed" she said in annoyance, as I sat watching her strip all the smelly bedding, and dumping it moodily into the soiled linen container by her side. At least I smelled more sweetly now, but I couldn't stop myself nodding off as I sat there, so tired was I after my traumatic night-time experience. And here I was now, dead to the world, the train wheels going clackety-clack, clackety-clack in my subconscious, Sister having long ago given up trying to converse with me or the other little girl.

The train stopped with a jolt now, the sudden movement arousing me from my slumber. Someone lifted me up and carried me out of the station to a waiting car. A man's voice spoke to Sister: "It's not too far to the convent," this voice said, as he sat me down in the back of the vehicle, and I struggled to keep my heavy eyes open as I looked around.

Sister sat between me and my little companion as we sped on our way. She chatted to the driver who she called Roy, and they discussed the weather.

"Yes, it'll be nice enough for the beach tomorrow," he told her, and I felt a small tinge of excitement, as he said this; my apprehension wavering a little, as I began to accept the inevitable. I had never been on a beach before, but then I had never been away from home either; but it was as well that sister Margaret was with us, otherwise I might have cried. I wasn't to know then that she was to leave soon after we reached our destination. She was merely escorting us to the convalescent home but then she had to go back.

"Cheer up, Liz," she said to me later, as she noted my silent distress at her departure. "You're going to have a lovely time here," she assured me, "and before you know it, you'll be back home again."

She walked with Roy back to the car, and smiled as she waved goodbye to us.

I felt very alone as I looked in silent protest at the departing car, but once I had resigned myself to the inescapable situation, I did indeed enjoy my stay at the convent. The nuns were kindness itself and I remember trips in the jaunty bus to the beach, with us all sitting and clutching our buckets and spades.

On some days we would go for long walks in the countryside, through some woods, whose terrain sprouted clusters of wild flowers, a few of which we were allowed to pick to take home with us.

On the way back to the convent, we'd find high grassy banks to roll down, then we'd find another, and run up it with glee, and down we'd roll again, the Sisters standing to one side, holding our flowers and laughing. It was no wonder, then, that with all of this fresh air, my once depleted appetite grew to all proportions, and my once wasted frame filled out, giving my appearance the more appropriate stance of a healthy five-year old. It left the kind pharmacist in Hoxton Market and his well-intentioned tonics rather in the shade, I'm afraid. Obviously, plenty of fresh air was what I had really needed to cure me of my state of weary inertia.

One bone of contention, however, at the convent was their rigid obsession regarding bowel performances of the children. If you didn't open your 'bowels' after breakfast, you didn't go out, but just sat instead in a long row, on various sized chamber pots, in a huge bathroom, with one of the Sisters industriously knitting at the head of the row, and waiting for eager voices, informing her that "Sister, I have been!". If you performed, you might just be in time to join the others on their exciting excursions, but if you didn't, you just sat there until you did.

I had been caught out once like this, but I didn't intend for it to happen again and so, ever after, when sweet Sister Elaine came along in the mornings with her little note-book to enquire "Liz, have you been?" I would look at her unflinchingly and lie to my back teeth as I assured her that "Yes Sister, I 'ave been!" I probably wouldn't go to heaven now, I told myself at this time, because sinners didn't, did they? But I took the risk anyway and carried on with my morning resolve, as I reasoned daily that nothing could be worse, no, not even going to 'Hell', than being stuck on a big pot each morning and missing all the delights of beaches and grassy banks.

Anyhow, in the meantime, nothing terrible happened to me after going a whole two weeks with rarely being able to say in all honesty to dear Sister Elaine "Yes Sister, I 'ave been." My system didn't seize up; I ate well; no, I had no need for the big pot, and no one was any the wiser, so as far as I was concerned. "All's well that ends well" seemed an apt summing up to my young but reasoning mind, as my convalescence neared its end.

THE HOMECOMING

What a welcome!

As we approached the house, its exterior festooned with balloons, and all the neighbours congregated together outside the front door, it really was a lovely sight. They laughed and waved and they hugged me as I alighted with Sister Margaret from the car.

Mrs Rumble stood, with Bobby in her arms, and I swear that dog was smiling at me, his mouth spread wide open, revealing all his teeth.

Mrs 'Ducky' stood, still as usual with her hair curlers in, and she took me in her arms. "Ow! My duck," she said, as she plastered me with kisses. "Ow, my duck," she repeated. "You 'ad us all so worried bu' look at yer now! Ducky' just look at yer, now. Yer look a new li'le gel wiv all tha' colour in yer cheeks, an' I swear yer've grown all of two inches, I swear yer 'ave."

And so, here I was, and a few tears of happiness pricked my eyes as I then went into my mother's arms. She had been standing, flanked each side of her by Joe and John, just as they had been standing on the day that I had been taken away to hospital, so very ill. Joe stood now with that characteristic sullen look on his face, John just looking non-committal. Neither of them were prone to revealing their innermost feelings; the turmoil that they were both probably experiencing at that moment.

As I was ushered indoors, I felt I would burst, so happy was I.

"Liz," Arthur spoke to me now. "Liz, Mr Evans wants yer to go in termorrer fer yer broken biscuits.

I looked at him in surprise. "I can't go in termorrer, Arfer," I told him, "cos it's only Tuesday an' I don't ge' me penny off Auntie Queenie til Friday."

It was the practise for me to visit Mr Evans in his baker's shop on Fridays, after collecting my weekly penny from Auntie upstairs. I would purchase with this a small bag of broken biscuits, and sometimes, just sometimes, you might find lurking among these broken biscuits, a lovely shiny sixpence: a popular ploy of dear Mr Evans to entice the children to buy the broken biscuits on occasions when he found himself inundated with them.

"It's awright," Arthur told me now. "Mr Evans said yer can take the penny in on Friday." So, after my enforced rest the next day, on the advice of the hospital, I paid that visit to Mr Evans, who had a smile lingering around his lips as he handed me the biscuits.

"Ere yer are, Liz; 'oo knows, yer might be lucky fer tha' shiny sixpence terday eh?" he told me in a low, confiding voice.

I laughed, and took the bag off him, but before I rushed home with them to the ever-hungry boys, I stood outside the shop and rummaged through the biscuits and, lo and behold, there it was: a lovely shiny sixpence!

My feet grew wings as I flew home to my mother, shouting the good news as I raced through the back door. "Mum, quick look!" I called to her as I sought her out. "Quick, look!" I squealed, as the boys fell on the biscuits. "I've go' one of Mr Evans's lovely shiny sixpences fer yer." I couldn't have been more excited had it been a hundred pounds. Sixpence in those days was a useful little coin to have: you could buy all sorts of nice things with a sixpence.

And so, my homecoming was a joyous occasion in all sorts of ways. I loved being back with the boys, with Auntie Queenie, with Mrs Ducky next door; yes, even with Bobby, who would creep up to me now whenever I made an appearance outside, and I would ruffle his head and tell him "Wha' a good boy 'ee was". Oh yes, it was lovely being home, and me being so much stronger. And then, of course, there was Sister Margaret's visits once again; how could we do without those? Oh yes, my homecoming was certainly a joyous occasion!

THE ACCIDENT

Throughout my childhood with the boys, I can never ever remember boredom entering into their lives. There was no television or suchlike then as there is now; no computer with its endless games and entertainment; but no matter, the boys were never idle for things to do.

Firstly they had their collection of marbles: big ones and small ones all intricately swirled with wonderful colours. They would hold them aloft in the light from the window and, looking through one eye, would twist them this way and that to highlight their beauty.

They would then sit on the floor and tip the marbles from the drawstring cloth bag made for them by Auntie Queenie, and they would then spend time bargaining with one another, swapping the marbles while putting the special ones to one side. They would then go out into the street and challenge one another as they rolled the marbles in the gutter, smashing into their opponent's prize possession to claim it for themselves.

Charlie was champion at this, his aim being very precise, and he always ended up with most of the other marbles, although the special intricately-coloured ones were always kept securely in the boys' pockets, not to be played with as they were too precious.

Jimmy usually finished up in tears, having lost most of his marbles, his eyesight not being as good as his brothers. Then they would placate him with, "'Ere, 'ave these," and they would ply him with some leftover marbles to shut him up.

Then there were the boys' flick cards, obtained from the Brooke Bond tea packets, with all sorts of interesting pictures and information on the front of them. The boys would keep these in an elastic band and sit around in a circle swapping them with one another before going just outside the front door to line the cards up against the wall, and then flick at them from the remainder in their hands. Any card they managed to flick down was theirs, to be added with the others inside the elastic band, and then, back indoors they would go to study the pictures and read all the interesting facts regarding them. It might be the Houses of Parliament or London Bridge in question, a famous art gallery or concert hall. A whole realm of information would be assimilated by the boys, their faces set in concentration, as they studied everything on these amazing little cards. It was surprising the amount of knowledge they drew from their collection with the hours they spent digesting all of these facts and data.

The most popular pastime for all the kids in the road of an evening, however, was swinging on the street lamps dotted along the road outside. Strong rope was needed for this, the clothes-line in the back garden being ideal for this very purpose.

It would take the boys ages to undo and unravel the rope from the two posts at each end of the overgrown garden. They would then sneak it through the house and out of the front door while my mother was otherwise occupied. Once in the street they lost no time in putting into operation the difficult task of slinging the rope, with all their might, time and time again in their endeavour to hook it over the metal struts protruding from the top of the lamppost. "Ooos" and "Ahhs" were uttered as John and Joe slung the rope repeatedly without success.

"Hurry up, hurry up!" the others clamoured in exasperation, with Jimmy jumping from foot to foot as he noticed the boys at the other end of the street already swinging wildly and with glee around their post and having a high old time.

Joe had indeed noticed this, and it grieved him enough without all this shouting. He let go of the rope for a minute while he went to Jimmy and boxed his ears. "Right, take tha," he told him, before returning purposely to the job in hand.

At last the rope twirled itself around the metal strut, and a cheer went up from the others. Now the rope was aligned and equaled out, and a good strong knot was tied at the bottom, joining the rope to form the seat for sitting on, and before anybody else had a chance, John slipped quickly into it, pressing down heavily to test its strength before Joe sent him sky high around the post.

"Weeee!" John chortled loudly as he flew into the air while we all stood and stared wide-eyed and clamoured for our turn, but John wasn't ready to relinquish his swinging act yet. "Higher!" he shouted to Joe as he came back to near ground level. "Higher!" he commanded. Joe stepped forward and clutched him as he came within reach. He held John aloft, then, with one almighty intake of breath, he swung him with all his strength high into the air.

We stood open-mouthed and alarmed then as we watched John swing completely out of control as the rope suddenly twisted and unbalanced him. It smashed him forcefully against the metal post. There was a sickening 'thud' as he slammed against it, his face taking the full force of the collision, and he fell from the swing to the ground. He lay very still now, with blood pouring from his mouth.

The swing was forgotten then as everyone crowded around John. He lay almost unconscious and he groaned softly, his eyes closed.

Joe ran quickly to a neighbour, his face as white as a sheet, and this kind man came and gently scooped John into his arms before carrying him home.

My mother was beside herself and made no attempt to stem her tears as her son languished on the shabby old settee in the front room, his face already swelling with a mass of bruises. She dodged about making cold compresses from an old towel, and she enclosed his entire face within them. "Aw, John," was all she could say.

For several days John lay prone on the settee as he slowly recovered from his injuries and shock. It wasn't until several days later, as the swelling started to subside, that it was discovered that a double molar had been knocked clean out from one side of his mouth, undoubtedly lying somewhere in the gutter outside.

Children, then, didn't receive the dental treatment as they do now, and for a long time, John had a noticeable gap in his lower jaw where the large tooth should have been. However, nature took over as this gap slowly began to close when his remaining molars spread to close this unsightly space. The offending aperture in his jaw miraculously disappeared, bringing his stunning good looks back again.

Some years later, when John reached the age of seventeen, great amusement was caused within the family when one day he recounted to us what had happened during an important medical he had undergone earlier in the day to join the Royal Marines. What's more, he had recklessly signed up to a twelve-year contract with His Majesty's Service.

The medical had been very rigorous but he, being a very fit and suitable candidate, had, without any difficulty, been accepted. The part of his recounting of this medical that had us laughing was the half-hour that he had spent with the dental surgeon. This poor, bewildered man had stood and counted John's lower molars several times while rubbing his chin. Then he counted yet again. "How strange," he said to John, who knew full well what he was alluding to. The surgeon was obviously hoping for an explanation of why he was a molar short but with no gap to show for it. John kept 'mum' however. He knew why, but he wasn't letting on. He never was one for unnecessary words anyway, and so the surgeon just had to accept the situation without further comment.

Maybe the thought of that extremely traumatic accident was too painful for John to remark upon; who knows? Things like that are probably best forgotten. The incident certainly made no difference to his suitability for enlistment. My mother had been devastated at his clandestine enrolment in the services, but she had had to accept that it was what he wanted to do and no amount of persuasion would make any difference, and so, on that day, when John told us of the incident with the dental surgeon, she laughed along with the rest of us. 'If yer can't beat 'em, join 'em,' was probably her philosophy at that time.

THE PARTY

An event that has stayed in my mind through all these years, and was my first inkling of how unscrupulous some people can be, was to do indirectly with my dramatic stay in hospital when I was so very ill.

An invitation had been sent to me from the hospital after my recovery, inviting me to their annual children's Christmas party. There it was that day, lying on the front door mat; a large white envelope with a funny face drawn in one corner, and it was addressed to me.

My mother picked it up, full of curiosity, and then her eyes widened as she showed it to me.

"Look at this, Liz," she said. "An invitation from the 'ospital for you to go to their Christmas party. Well I never!" she exclaimed. "'aint that kind of 'em!"

I scanned the invitation proffered to me with mixed feelings, as I still associated the hospital with my being so ill, and yet, the thought of a party beguiled me. I'd never been to a party.

My mother took note of the uncertain look on my face.

"What is it, Liz?" she asked me. "Wouldn't yer love to go? It'll only be fer 'alf a day, you wouldn't 'ave ter stay overnight." She seemed to sense my anxiety and was anxious to defer my fears.

"But, Mum." I said, gradually warming to the idea, but still not quite sure. "Mum, I 'aven't got a party dress," I reminded her.

She thought for a moment and then: "We'll go and see the nice lady on the stall in 'oxton Market," she enthused. "She sells all sorts of things, and she's very reasonable; I'm sure we can find the money some 'ow."

I had my doubts about this woman who had fitted me out a while back with a smart school mackintosh but had never got around to supplying the promised missing belt for it, which had taken all the pleasure from me as I wore it for school with embarrassment, but I kept quiet about this now. I didn't want to upset my mother. "And just think," my mother continued to enthuse, "that nice Dr Arzapardi might be there." This finally convinced me, and I knew that I must go. The thought of seeing my favourite doctor filled me with pleasure...

⤚

Here we stood then on the appointed day, at the entrance to the big children's ward, with me fervently clutching my mother's hand, but still a little uncertain.

The stall-holder in Hoxton Market had done me proud this time and had decked me out in a very elaborate party dress full of frills and bows, so that I quite resembled a fairy, even down to the silver sandles on my feet; the only thing missing being the wand, of course. By today's standards, I would be a laughing stock by the sophisticated young set, with their modern cropped trousers and state-of-the-art tops but, no matter, I thought then that I was the 'bees'-knees' – wonderful, in fact.

I stood wide-eyed now as I surveyed all before me. The ward had been industriously decorated with balloons and paper-chains. A long table, I noticed, stretched the length of its middle, all decked out with Christmas crackers, and a vast array of highly coloured jellies and trifles mingled with plates of ornate little sandwiches.

I was somewhat surprised to note some little, animated toddlers occupying cots placed strategically to one side of the ward. These little ones were obviously well enough to attend the party. Those who were more ill had been transferred elsewhere.

Sister and the nurses all wore party hats and were blowing up balloons for their patients. My eyes finally alighted then on a wonderful sight. Right

95

at the end of the ward, there it stood, in all its glory: the biggest Christmas tree I had ever seen, with its twinkling lights and miniature Santas festooned all around it. And then my excitement grew even more, as I spied none other than dear Dr Arzapardi himself. He was helping to seat the children and generally joining in the fun. I ran to him and clutched his hand. His poor scarred face was wreathed in big smiles and no one gave a second thought or a second glance to his disfigurement. To all and sundry he was just something very special and all the children loved him, as I did. He was everything to me at that moment, and my mother had just crept away quietly. I didn't even wave her off.

Towards the end of this lovely party, none other than Father Christmas made an appearance and he positioned himself in front of the Christmas tree. He carried a large sack over his shoulder, which he plonked down in front of him.

"Well, have you all had a good time?" he called to us.

"Y-e-es!" we hollered back.

"Okay," he laughed. "Well then, let's get around to giving out the presents." He delved his hand into the sack and proceeded to distribute his booty.

When my name was called, I shyly stepped forward. Two brightly coloured parcels were lovingly given to me and, as I eagerly turned back with them, I noticed, with disappointment, that Dr Arzapardi was no longer with us. He had apparently been called away, and a woman who was helping out at the party, took charge of me. She seemed nice enough and helped me to unwrap the first present. As the glittery paper fell away, I gasped. There, sitting on my lap now, was the biggest box of chocolates I had ever set eyes on! It had a beautiful picture of a country garden on its lid, and a big red ribbon was tied around it, finishing in a flouncy bow on top! I put my hand to my mouth; this was truly wonderful. I wanted to go home there and then to show the boys and Auntie Queenie. I wanted them to have the chocolates. I wanted to see the delight on their faces as they sampled each one. This was a luxury unknown to the family; a once in a lifetime happening; and I wanted to go straight home, but the woman was now unwrapping the second present.

"Come on," she urged me, "what do we 'ave 'ere?" I turned my attention to her as she once again unravelled the paper. A teddy bear emerged and I immediately fell in love with it. I had a teddy at home, and I would still love it, even though it was now very shabby. At one point in its life, it had lost one of its eyes, and my mother had gone to a lot of trouble to replace it, but as she had handed it back to me, I had looked at it and burst into tears.

"For gawd's sake, Liz" she had said to me in annoyance. "What's wrong now?"

"Mum," I'd said, wiping my tears with the back of my hand and making an effort to stop crying. "Look!" I pointed to teddy's eyes. "'e's got two different size eyes now, so they're all wonky." I didn't like to mention, also, that the one she had sewn on was a slightly different colour.

"Trust you ter notice; yer don't miss a fing do yer?" my mother said in exasperation, as she yanked the eye off, but it made no difference as to how I felt about teddy. I'd rather he had only one eye, than look boss-eyed with two, just as Jimmy did, when he forgot to wear his glasses. But here now was this wonderful new teddy with its two shiny black eyes, and I clutched him to me. I would love the both of them, I told myself.

Father Christmas continued calling name after name, as he delved into his sack, and I started to get a bit fidgety.

"I want a wee," I told the lady.

"There's the lavatories," she said, looking around. "Leave yer presents with me; I'll look after 'em." I handed her my lovely presents and hurried away.

"Don't rush," the woman called out to me. "Take yer time." But I didn't want to take my time; I wanted to get back to her as fast as I could and, as I bolted back, I remember I was still pulling up my knickers! But then I stopped: the woman was nowhere to be seen. She had done a complete disappearing act, together with my lovely box of chocolates and teddy.

I felt the tears spring to my eyes as I frantically looked around and I started to blame myself. Why did I have to go to the lavatory? I should have held on. Why did I part with my lovely presents? I should have held on to them. I was overcome with grief. I wanted to tell Dr Arzapardi but he still wasn't there.

I became aware then of my mother calling to me as she stood at the doors of the ward, my coat in her hands and she beckoned to me. I made my way to her. "Come on, Liz. 'ome we go." She looked then at my crest-fallen face. "Cheer up," she said. "'aven't you 'ad a lovely time?" She slipped me into my coat and I just nodded that I had, but it wasn't until we were on the bus home that I suddenly threw myself onto her.

"Ow, Mum," I wailed as I clutched her around her neck. "She took me presents and I couldn't find 'er." I sobbed all through the telling to her about what had happened.

"My lovely teddy and the chocolates; she took 'em," I told her.

My mother was horrified. "Why didn't yer say at the 'ospital?" she asked me. "We could 'ave told Sister; she would know the woman." She took me onto her lap. "Ow, Liz," she commiserated, "'ow can anyone be so mean? I just 'ope it comes back on 'er, I really do."

The episode remained in my memory always, and sometimes as I sat cuddling my shabby one-eyed teddy at home, I would ponder on what had happened to that brand new teddy with the lovely shiny black eyes, and my mother's words would register in my head: "I 'ope it comes back on 'er, I really do."

Although I wasn't sure of the implication of these words, I hoped, like my mother that yes, it would come back on 'er, and that she might eventually realise the grief that she had brought to a certain little girl.

MOVING ON

After the formative early years with my brothers, a creeping certainty had come looming on the horizon. The dreaded war that had been threatening the nation over a period of time had suddenly burst upon us and its inevitable arrival brought with it a hasty, contrived evacuation scheme which caused devastating fracturing of close-knit London families, and in doing this, nothing for these kinsfolk could ever be the same again.

My own family seemed to be split right down the middle and were never to be whole again. I myself was to be plucked from my mother and brothers at the tender age of seven and sent post-haste to the country before the incessant bombing of London began.

Jimmy also was hastily dispatched to the country, but the four older boys stayed and took their chance with my mother. Miraculously, they all came through the bombing unscathed, but not my mother, who died when the hospital she was in at the time was bombed.

There was to be a sad parting of the ways then and I was to lose almost all contact with my brothers during this fraught, dangerous and uncertain period of our lives. But my intention was not to forget my siblings, not to forsake them. No, they had been a major presence and influence in my early years but if my constant tagging along with them was a necessary forbearance on their part, there is no doubt, I'm sure, that they were quite happy, eventually, to shed this encumbrance. However, to me, the parting from the boys, the transition from the uncertain days of life while in their precarious care to the even more sustained and unexpected precariousnesss that awaited me, was a painful process. I missed and pined for them at first, but during our lengthy separation they were rapidly maturing under their own steam so to speak, and getting on with their vastly contrasting lives in the ensuing years.

Their differing characters led them into a diversity of avenues thereby forcing them into different directions which entailed long periods of separation from one another until they became almost like strangers.

Ultimately, we would come back together, changed people and in much sadder circumstances, having lost our mother. This event seems a shadow to me now, dimly remembered, with me still being very young and away from her at the time of her death.

My eventual reunion with my brothers found me a serious and disillusioned young teenager, the result of my unhappy years away from them. I was, however, later able to be reintegrated into their lives, to pick up the threads of our former shattered existence and to follow our destinies.

JOE

Joe emerged from a volatile youngster into a good-humoured, quick-witted, amiable man. He was lacking, to a certain extent, the sensitivity of one or two of his siblings and sailed through life with brashness and a desire to just live for the enjoyment of the moment.

He scorned the idea of joining any of the armed services of the war, although he was very fit. He chose instead to go into munitions, having no other choice. This, as Joe put it, was 'bloody continuous hard work and long hours'. The reward, however, was in the money he earned, which was very important to him.

He married Jessie, his teenaged sweetheart, who lived with her parents Lill and Fred in the block of flats, to where we, as a family, had eventually moved, having completely outgrown our small, shabby house in Kent Street.

As we were just a few doors away from Jessie and her parents, it took Joe no time at all to transfer his belongings through one door and into another. He and Jessie were young, yes, but they had never had eyes for anyone else, only for each other; complete soul mates, in fact.

Right from the beginning of Joe's move, he was doted on by Lill and Fred. They were blown away by his forceful character, tempered by an infectious sense of humour. You couldn't be downhearted with Joe around – well, not for long anyway!

He, Jessie, and her parents were all drinkers, and their lives revolved around their local pub.

There was no ambition for the niceties of life with them, no urge for betterment in any way, material or professional wise. No thought for tomorrow – "just live for terday and enjoy it, coz you're a long time dead," Joe used to quip.

Money flowed in the pub with carelessness and as freely as the nonsensical talk and witticisms that revolved among the punters as they downed their pints around the bar. Every weekend was a party and the more drunk the drinkers got, the more the money flowed.

There came the day then when Joe's luminous life was complete. Joe junior came into the world – his pride and joy in every sense of the word. Never was a son more favoured than little 'Joe boy' as he was called by everyone; the term 'boy' being a typical East End idiom.

With his placid, happy nature, 'Joe boy' was the light of his parents' and grandparents' eyes, but there was to be no siblings for this happy little chap, because in all the nine months that Jessie carried him, she was unable to go anywhere near a pub because of the debilitating nausea she experienced after even a whiff of beer. She was unable even to pass one, but would have to cross over the road to the other side.

Of course, this had been a complete disruption to the families' social lives. It was like Jessie being in total isolation. To go a whole nine months, cut off, as it were from civilisation, as Jessie would put it, was just unbearable.

Joe junior then was left in no doubt on growing up, as to why there could be no siblings for him. "I couldn't go through that again," Jessie would say as she, on regaining normality, stood once again at her husband's side round the bar, her favourite tipple clasped in her hand.

Unlike his father, who had always been a tough nut, 'Joe boy', in contrast, was an attractive gentle being, with a smile for everyone; there probably wasn't a mean bone in his body. He was loved by all.

Although Joe, as he matured, had become more amiable, there obviously still lurked within him that volatile streak that had so beset him in his youth, and one particular evening this hidden vice came suddenly and unexpectedly to the fore.

There was a strict rule in those days, as I believe there still is, with regard to children not being allowed in pubs, so I'm not really sure why 'Joe boy' happened to be there on this occasion with his parents.

Into the pub then walked one of the regulars and as he spotted 'Joe boy' he chucked him under the chin. "And what might you be doing here?" he asked of him. "Don't you know the rules?" he quipped. "Come on then," he said, taking 'Joe boy' by the hand, "let's go and buy an ice-cream."

Unconcernedly, Joe carried on his conversation with another of the regulars, with Jessie hanging onto his every word.

Time went by, however, and Jessie became very worried at the non re-appearance of the man and 'Joe boy'. Her subsequent agitation finally got through to Joe who then stopped his chatter in mid-sentence.

"Where's Joe boy?" he asked Jessie now.

Tears welled up in Jessie's eyes as she answered him.

"I've been trying to get through to you Joe; it's well over an hour and they haven't come back. Oh, Joe, do yer think 'ee's alright?"

Joe took immediate action.

"Tom!" he called to the landlord of the pub, "where does the fellow that took Joe boy live?"

"I'm not sure," replied the landlord, "somewhere around 'ere, that's all I can tell yer Joe."

Everything went quiet as Joe made for the door.

"I'll find 'im," he said menacingly over his shoulder. As he entered the street, he saw the man with Joe boy walking hurriedly back to the pub. He had a hold of one of Joe boy's hands, and in the other hand Joe boy held an ice-cream.

Rage overtook Joe as he collared the man and dragged him into the pub.

"Where 'ave you been?" he demanded, noting that the ice-cream cornet that his young son held was untouched; it was as though it had just been swiftly put into Joe boy's hand.

"'as 'ee touched yer, Joe boy?" Joe asked of him, but Joe-boy silently looked away with an uncharacteristic serious look on his face.

Joe turned to the man; he looked hard at him, and noted the shifty, guilty look in his eyes, as he tried to defend himself. He said in a whining conciliatory tone,

"Now 'old on, Joe, would I? Now would I touch your ..." but he got no further as Joe, in one fell swoop, knocked him to the ground, for what he might have, and most likely had done, to Joe-boy.

The man went down like a lump of lead. A silence took over in the pub as he struggled to his feet, his nose streaming with blood, but he might as well have not bothered because Joe immediately knocked him down again and this time the man made no attempt to get up but just lay there.

Tom, the landlord, who up to that point had turned a blind eye, now came onto the scene.

"Alright, Joe; that's enough. Leave 'im now," he ordered, as he surveyed the culprit lying prone on the floor, and he tipped the jug of water that he held in his hand straight over him.

"NOW, GET UP and GET OUT!" he shouted.

"GET OUT and STAY OUT!" he told this scum as everyone then watched the battered and bruised man making the supreme effort as he crawled on all fours towards the doors, and Joe gave him a final kick up the rear to help him on his way.

There was no soft soap treatment in those days for paedophiles: the man never came near the pub again. Good riddance to bad rubbish was the general consensus among the punters and they patted Joe on the back.

"Good on yer, mate," they chorused, as they got back to supping their pints, but 'Joe boy' was never quite the trusting, gentle boy again, and he always refused to talk about his long absence.

Joe tried to trace this obnoxious predator, this piece of scum, but was told by the police that he had probably gone 'underground'.

"Good," said Joe, "because that's where 'ee belongs, and what's more, ee'd better stay there!"

It was quite obvious that the matter still rankled with Joe.

There was, in those days, a silent resolve amongst the East End fraternity to extrude a zero tolerance towards the misfits in our society, be they poofs, paedophiles, or whatever, but if these misfits didn't impinge their presence on them in any threatening way, then they were quite safe and left alone.

Take Jeffrey, for instance, a regular at the pub. He would make an appearance most nights, in his tight trousers, and flamboyant hat to talk and joke with the other punters. He was theatrical, ostentatious, and very popular with everyone.

"What yer Jeffrey! 'ow are yer, darling," the others would call to him as they supped their pints; and "If yer wear them trousers much tighter, yer'll do yerself an injury," they'd tease him, but Jeffrey took it all in good part. He knew what he was, so what? It didn't stop him from being accepted by the others. He would just laugh at these taunts.

"Don't be naughty," he'd just tell them. Oh no, there was no harm in Jeffrey: he just wanted to be one of the crowd, with all the back-slapping and ribald comments flying around. Unlike the predator of 'Joe boy' he was welcomed and perfectly safe with all the customers at the pub…

Soon after their son's birth, Jessie and Joe were required by the council to move out of the flat that they had so happily shared with Jessie's parents, Lill and Fred.

Overcrowding, was the reason given, but it was with great reluctance that this parting of the ways came about, even though a perfectly nice small house with a garden was offered to them, just a short distance from their previous abode.

"It ain't right though, Joe, is it?" Jessie grumbled. She missed the close alliance with her parents but Joe, for once, stayed 'mum'.

"It's the rules, Jess," he simply told her, and that was the end of the subject.

Jess realised then that she would have to get used to their changed circumstances, but she sorely missed the hustle and bustle of life at the flat, the intimate intertwining of family. The overcrowding, as the Council had put it, hadn't bothered her at all. In the spaciousness of the house now, she felt lonely, isolated, 'out on a limb' so to speak, but over time, these acute feelings mellowed a little. After all, they weren't that far from Lill and Fred, Joe would remind her, and Jessie would keep reminding herself of this fact, as she and Joe gradually accepted the situation…

A quiet knock on the front door one Sunday afternoon took both of them a bit by surprise. Who could possibly be calling today? Any other day, yes, but not a Sunday; that was one day they liked to be left alone, in peace. But Joe made his way amiably to the door now, full of curiosity. Who could it be on a Sunday? His surprise,e then, was complete as he opened the door and came face to face with no other than a Minister!

Joe looked intently at him as they stood surveying one another before anything was said between the two of them… The face of this man standing on the doorstep was vaguely familiar to Joe. Who was it? he was asking himself. This person, standing meekly before him, was somebody quite well known, he knew that, and he racked his brain quickly for a split second as he endeavoured to come up with the answer. And then he knew. DAVID SHEPPARD, that's who it was, the famous cricketer, standing here before him in a cleric's collar, and the momentary look of intense concentration on Joe's face turned now to incredulity. What on earth was this famous man doing standing here before him in a dog-collar?

"I'm sorry to disturb you," the Minister was saying now, as Joe stood with his mouth agape. "I'm making a few calls on my parishioners each week to ask them if they would be interested in joining my church."

Joe was momentarily stumped for a reply straight off. His being referred to as a parishioner was very off-putting to him. Church was for weddings and funerals surely… the pub was their church; they hadn't got time for anything else.

"No, I don't think so," Joe said, hesitantly. He didn't want to offend this renowned cricketer, now turned Minister as he endeavoured to come up with the answer.

"We're very busy people you see; we wouldn't 'ave time for church, would we, Jess?" He turned to his wife now, as she joined him at the door. "Anyway, don't you play cricket now?" Joe asked this extremely nice man, hoping to turn the conversation around to something more amenable to him as he suddenly felt a bit guilty now about the long hours he and Jess spent in the pub.

The Minister just brushed this enquiry of Joe's regarding his cricket prowess to one side. There were more important issues at stake here. "No," he simply said. "I'm a Minister now," and the atmosphere between him and Joe became a bit tense and slightly embarrassing. The Minister knew that a lot of drinking went on in this East End community, and his campaigning for converts was not easy.

"Have you any children?" he said brightly now to Jessie and Joe, "because we have a wonderful Sunday afternoon school for them, and the children love coming."

This was music to Joe's ears. "Yes," he answered quickly, "and as a matter of fact, our 'Joe boy' is there now. Jess takes him every Sunday, don't yer, Jess? 'ee loves it don't 'ee?" Jess nodded rapidly in the affirmative, and Joe's manner relaxed now, as he put a hand lightly on the Minister's shoulder. The fact that 'Joe boy' actually attended this man's Sunday school made him feel a lot better, but this momentary lapse into cordiality with the Minister had the unfortunate effect of loosening his tongue somewhat. "We like 'im to go because it gives us the chance of 'aving an hour all to ourselves on the bed! Do yer know what I mean?!" he said while giving this young representative of the church a nudge nudge – wink wink. It never occurred to Joe that the Minister might think that what he had just said was in rather bad taste, especially on the Sabbath, which should be about spiritual things and not earthly pleasures, but Joe would never see this of course, being blind to such matters. Religion meant nothing to him and Jess.

As Joe related this happening to the family some weeks later, there was a mixed reaction. Amazement from them that this famous cricketer had relinquished his fame to become a humble Minister, and admiration that he had been so brave as to venture among the impassioned ungodly of that pagan area of the East End. They just laughed at the thoughts of it – the Minister attempting to draw Jessie and Joe into his flock! What a hope! And although I laughed with them, uppermost in my mind was the feeling that here indeed was a brave, dedicated man, who cast aside fame to commit himself to something more important. Although far less financially-rewarding, his calling to the church and all it entailed, and the saving of souls, was by far the more urgent feature in his life. No! Joe would never understand that. He and Jess were obviously never going to be among the chosen ones. Their priorities were of more earthly things. Spiritual matters never entered their heads, ever. As Joe had often said, "Life is short, so yer might as well enjoy it!" and that was that, as far as he was concerned, but you could never blame the Minister for trying, even if his endeavours of conversions did mostly fall on stony ground. There were a lot like Jessie and Joe around, he probably realized all too clearly, but he would undoubtedly keep trying.

A short while after Jessie and Joe's enforced move into their small house, Joe had the offer of a big promotion from the very successful engineering firm that employed him. The promotion would mean a much fatter wage packet, and very exciting challenges but, with great reluctance, he turned the offer down.

The transition would involve a move to France to set up a subsidiary company. The offer to him however was an absolutely unthinkable option, with Jessie in tears at the very thought of it. Her family and 'Joe boy' and their very set lifestyle were being threatened. Not in any way could this promotion be considered.

Joe refused the compelling project put to him, then, with profound misgivings, and another employee quickly claimed it, leaving Joe agonising over his controversial decision for some time.

The refusal however was never regretted by Jessie and himself, and I personally think that they made the right choice. They were too embedded in their family and lifestyle ever to be able to adapt to foreign changes, surely, and Joe would never have considered leaving Jessie to go it alone in France; so, all said and done, yes! they did the right thing…

Jessie fussed around Joe one morning who, unbelievably had got up feeling very unwell. He sat quietly then in his favourite armchair.

"Now, Joe, are yer going to be alright if I take Mum out shopping this morning?" she asked anxiously of him. Joe was never unwell.

"Jess! Don't make a fuss," Joe answered her. "Of course I'll be alright; just get going or yer'll be late." Jess, with some hesitation went off, but got back as quickly as she was able. It was so unlike Joe to be ill.

"Joe, I'm back," she called out as she entered the house once again but there was no reply. Joe, while she was gone, had quietly and unobtrusively died. Her best friend and partner for all of those years had gone. No fuss, no chance to say goodbye. He had just silently passed away.

JOHN

John, unlike Joe with his carefree, impetuous manner, had matured into a serious, reserved, discerning adult. He was very handsome with his dark swarthy looks. He didn't suffer fools gladly and took life with a seriousness and profoundness that Joe had scorned.

My mother was heart-broken when he had informed her at the still tender age of seventeen that he had enlisted in the Royal Marines and, what's more, he had signed on for twelve years! This troubled her greatly, but it had been done and there was little she could do about it.

John, during his service, travelled to various world trouble-spots and saw quite a lot of action while serving his country. He completed this perilous undertaking but not without a certain amount of scarring to his inner-being. He held his cards close to his chest however, and never discussed anything that had taken place during those twelve years. It was as though he had no wish to remember the events of this cross that he had borne for so long; this undertaking of his at such a young age. Nobody ever intruded into any memories that he might have had regarding these troubled years. It was just as though this phase of John's life had never been.

The highlight in his life was in meeting a fellow naval conscript named Paula who brought stability back into John's life; a sunshine and gaiety that had been missing for so long. She was a joy to behold with her sparkling eyes and ready laugh, just the opposite in fact to John's seriousness and his inclination at times to be somewhat moody and, yes, volatile. She had got to understand this blight to his temperament but never took it personally. John would rather have cut off his right hand than harm Paula in any way, shape or form. Yet an incident soon after they married which demonstrated his volatile nature could have had very serious consequences.

⸎

After completing his twelve years of service John had obtained employment with a company, which entailed a five mile bike ride from home. As he cycled along on this particular day of the happening, he was pulling up close to the kerb at some traffic lights, when a car behind bore down on him, so close that he was forced up onto the pavement and crashed into a garden wall which caused him to fall heavily from his bike. He quickly picked himself up and, with a look of utter rage on his face, he charged over to the offending car. The driver, on seeing John's approach and noting the murderous look, quickly locked all the car doors and curled himself up in a defensive manner. He was absolutely terrified. There was no central locking on cars then but he managed to lock all the doors just in time.

"I'm sorry! I'm sorry!" he shouted as John tried to get at him by forcing one of the doors open. "I didn't mean it," the driver persisted as his assailant refused to give up.

The traffic lights changed from red to green but none of the other motorists behind moved, so captivated were they by what was taking place before their eyes as they watched this mad man in front trying to force entry into the car!

Sanity slowly returned to John then, after repeated hefty kicks at the vehicle in his fury at not gaining entry. He suddenly stopped, sweating profusely and breathing heavily, and the madness slowly disappeared from his face.

His actions towards this irresponsible driver who had almost mown him down would seem extreme to some. But had it not been for John's quick action in mounting the pavement to escape the car which had been bearing down upon him, he could very well have been lying at that time in the road, very dead.

He pointed a threatening finger now at this foolish, dangerous driver as he brushed the sweat from his face. "It's a good job you managed to lock those doors before I got to you," he told him, "or I wouldn't have been responsible for my actions," and he gave the car one final kick before he went to retrieve his bike, still lying on the pavement.

As John stood, still breathing heavily, composing himself, the offending driver stayed put. All the cars behind him passed on now and as they passed they sounded their horns and gave the thumbs down sign to the traumatized man sitting and clutching his steering wheel as he stared fixedly ahead, not moving. It was just as though he had been hypnotized, but he was undoubtedly pondering on the realisation that his life had been on a knife edge during this altercation with John. It is my guess that this foolish person never made the same mistake again.

⁓

John was a devoted husband and father within his marriage. He had no inkling however of the finer points of child rearing. Having a dental appointment on one particular day, Paula tentatively left the two children, John junior and Linda, in his care. After she had gone, baby Linda managed to make a terrible mess of her face with some chocolate that her daddy had found for her, and John was relating such to Paula on her return from the dentist.

"What did you clean her up with then?" Paula enquired of him, noticing the baby's scrupulously clean face.

"Oh, I found a damp cloth under the sink," John told her. "I cleaned her up with that."

Paula gasped at this. "That's the floor cloth, John," she told him. "It's been in bleach and everything."

But John was nonplussed on being told this. "She'll survive," was his only comment.

While baby Linda cooed and chuckled, displaying her mother's easygoing temperament, toddler John was a very different cup of tea, exhibiting a restless, volatile, nature much like his father, which proved very difficult to handle at times. Many times during the night his mother was up and down seeing to him as he stood rattling his cot and bawling his head off.

One particular night she said in exhaustion to John, "Could you see to him?" but John having no patience whatsoever with this, just chose to ignore his son's plaintive cries until, unable to stand it any longer, he shot out of bed. But Paula was there before him. "No, John!" she told him, as she plucked the youngster from his cot on realising that John's temper had got the better of him. "I'll see to him," she said, as she left the bedroom with the fretful toddler. She had been foolish to trouble John she told herself, as she once again took the initiative.

She endeavoured to understand this unfathomable trait in his personality, however, which reared its head almost always at meal times. John could not stand chatter at the table while he was eating. For some reason he needed quiet while he digested his food, with just the occasional word to Paula like, "The meat's a bit tough," or "This fish is nice." That was about the limit of conversation between them. The children, nonetheless, remained quiet while eating, and if they did forget and started chatting, they immediately got a warning look from their mother and stopped in their tracks. Whatever they wanted to say could be said later.

In spite of these idiosyncrasies of John's, these lapses in his personality, they were accepted in the knowledge that, all in all, they were a happy, well-structured family and that was all that mattered. Who's to reason why then, that in later years, the children having flown the nest and both entering into promising careers, Linda still with the engaging temperament of her mother, John junior the characteristics and handsomeness of his father, that their father would surreptitiously start to drink. He would suddenly during evenings, irrespective of who was present at the house, get up from his chair with no excuses and just leave the room. But you didn't question John. He was his own person. You just accepted that he didn't need to make excuses to anyone for his actions. That is how he was.

But it materialized, eventually, that John, in these later years, had become an alcoholic. Why? It's true that as a marine he and his comrades had been encouraged to drink the rum provided by their superiors. It quelled their nerves, especially in time of action, and smoking as well was encouraged. But as a family man John had no need to drink, although he did continue to smoke.

Was it that now, the children having flown the nest, John perhaps experienced a void in his life. He had been a devoted father and very involved with the children's lives. Did he miss their presence which now allowed him time, perhaps, to dwell on his earlier traumatic life? Who really knows why he had this sudden need to drink? Paula was to find bottles hidden away in various places around the house, but she kept her own counsel and said nothing.

It was inevitable then, that in time, the smoking and unexplained secret drinking took its toll and the children were to lose their loving but sometimes enigmatic father to a drinking and smoking related illness.

In life John had been very much his own person, notwithstanding that, in spite of his chequered past, he had been able ultimately to enter into a loving, stable relationship with both his wife and adored children. To make this enormous transition from the turmoil of his former years to the rational saneness of the latter, had taken exceptional strength of character, and that's what John had been – a very strong character – haunted, ultimately I believe, by the ghosts of his past.

Many, I'm sure, will fail to comprehend the implication of my referral to these 'ghosts of the past', but as I write this, my mind relives that day in Hoxton Market all those years ago, when as a small child I had witnessed my mother being almost badly burned by a careless punter in a pub which we were passing, as he threw his still lighted cigarette end through the open pub door which unfortunately landed on my mother. The incident had upset me badly and as I stood afterwards at the open doors while clutching a lemonade that had been passed to me while this foolish man ushered my reluctant mother inside for a conciliatory drink, it had been then, as I observed the other drinkers inside as they propped up the bar reveling in their nonsensical prattling with one another, that a sense of revulsion had enveloped me. "When I grow up, Mum, I'm never going to drink," I had informed her in a very serious tone as we later made our way to get the bus home, and that vow to my mother then and my lifelong aversion to drinking thereafter, could well have saved me from the path that John had taken when my own ghosts of the past visited me through a prolonged stressful period in my own life. To drink during that period had never entered my head.

Thomas Hardy, the famous poet and novelist, I know had experienced these ghosts on the death of his wife. Sadly his relationship with her had become estranged in the later years of their marriage, but as he sat holding her hand at the end, these ghosts appeared, causing him to reminisce on their former happy times together and he was able to put them to rest then by recalling the happy years and writing about them:

"I look and see it there, shrinking, shrinking,
I look back at it amid the rain
For the very last time, for my sand is sinking
And I shall traverse old love's domain – never again."

Then, as he recreated their first great romance:

"Woman much missed, how you call to me, call to me
Saying that now you are not as you were
When you had changed from one who was all to me
But as at first when our day was fair."

He goes on to picture her as she used to be, waiting for him at the station in her air-blue gown:

"Can it be you that I hear? Let me view you then
Standing as when I drew near to the town
Where you would wait for me – yes, as I knew you then,
Even to the original air-blue gown!"

In these poems about Emma, Hardy is rediscovering repressed sorrow and forgotten love. He is like an archaeologist uncovering thoughts and feelings that have been buried for a long time, bringing them to light, examining them; and in his writing them down then in poetic form a huge weight lifted from him, a cleansing of his soul took place, and he was able to lay to rest these ghosts that troubled him, causing him so much confusion and heartbreak. He was, at last, able to put paid to all of this negativity that had bogged him down.

There were times when he thought of the poems as a way of making amends to Emma – "The only amends I can make," he wrote. He was seeing her again in the place where he first met her and with which he always identified her, the remote coast of north Cornwall where the untamed landscape and the young woman on horseback with her hair flowing behind her had seemed almost exotic to him in 1870. Away from Cornwall her exoticism faded and after they were married they never returned there, for which Hardy blamed himself. More than anything, though, he was recreating his great romance writing for the first time, open and boldly, of "The woman that I loved so and who loyally loved me," restoring her to the Cornish cliffs where she had seemed to him to embody the spirit of the landscape:

"I found her out there On a shore few see,
That falls westwardly To the salt-edged air, Where the ocean breaks
On the purple strand
And the hurricane shakes
The solid land."

Finally, in his cleansing grief he wrote:

"Woman, much missed, how you call to me, call to me,
Saying that now you are not as you were
When you had changed from the one who was all to me
But at first, when our day was clear."

Hardy then, through his writing, was able to expel the guilt and grief that he felt on his wife's death. He was able to unburden himself and cleanse his inner-being which, in turn, enabled him to move on.

John, in comparison, was unable to do this. He was never a writer and still waters ran deep with him. He tended to be taciturn, private and not prone to expressing his feelings. If only, like Hardy, he could have spoken about the trauma in his youth, his years of serving in the marines, the fighting in enemy territories around the world, the killings and maiming that went on that he never talked about. Did all this ultimately come back to haunt him causing him to seek solace and release in the drink? Maybe he should have had counseling at the end of it all, as traumatized servicemen do today, but, knowing John as I did then, I realise that he would have looked on this as a weakness and a revealing perhaps of things too awful to dwell upon. "Best to forget," he would have told himself while not realising the damage to his inner-being. He would have stowed these unmentionable things, these happenings that were best left unsaid, in the recesses of his mind. But at what cost?

Goodbye, John.

ARTHUR

From deprivation to a slow climb up the ladder, to a modicum of affluence was the journey that Arthur took.

His aesthetic blond good looks were in keeping with his lighter character, which was in complete opposition therefore to John's swarthy attractiveness and more sombre mentality.

From grammar school into the Royal Air Force – leading to officer training, he somehow acquired the appropriate form of speech expected from those in that vocation, and he ultimately developed airs above his station, which, in the end, never actually came to fruition.

He met and married Beth, who lived in a very pretty part of rural Hertfordshire.

Beth was very elegant, and into the art of ballet, the only daughter of a rather quirky couple called Dot and Wilf.

The marriage produced a son, just nine months after the event, and Arthur was cock-a-hoop. "Come and see my son tomorrow if you like," said the telegram sent post-haste to me while I was living at that time in London; and it was quite clear, on my surveying this infant that he was idolised by all.

Deciding to leave the Air Force to settle into domesticity, the war having ended, Arthur attained office employment within a large chemical concern, but his aspirations for rapid promotion while there came to nothing. His character seemed to change at this point, perhaps because of his lack of acceptance of his failure to achieve advancement within the firm. Maybe he should have held onto the status of Officer in the Air

Force; but what was done, was done, and as time progressed, with little prospects of betterment, Arthur became cynical, disillusioned – regretting I think, his decision to throw up his promising career. And there were no further children for him and Beth, which proved to be another disappointment for him. Having come from a large brood himself, he would have loved for them to have increased their family, but this was not to be. This proved to be something of a disaster also for their one and only son who received endless attention, and repaid in kind by crying all through the endless nights. Arthur would spend unnumbered hours prowling around the bedroom with this howling infant, who would eventually decide then to lapse into a deep sleep just as dawn was breaking, leaving everyone exhausted.

Arthur with his adored son

Understandably, because of this, Arthur would go heavy-eyed to work each morning, tired, but victorious in the mistaken knowledge that once again he had saved the day, or night… But Beth was delicate, wasn't she? She needed her sleep, he would reason, having no regards to the toll that this unnecessary reasoning would eventually have on his own, future health…

He and Beth, like a lot of other newly-weds at that time, shared accommodation after their marriage, with Beth's forbearing parents, who doted not only on their first grandchild, while suffering without complaint the disturbed nights, but also on a lumbering old dog, Peggy.

Each evening, Peggy would recline herself on the rug bang in front

119

of the fire in the living room, blocking out most of the heat that came from its blaze with her sizeable frame. It really used to annoy Arthur that nothing was said to this soppy dog, and when Beth's parents were out of hearing range, he would make his feelings known to his young wife. "When we get our own place, Beth," he told her, "we'll have a proper dog, not some soppy thing like that!" indicating the lump sprawled out in front of them.

"What a spectacle" he remarked in disgust, as he noted the dog's unkempt appearance, with its long, tangled, uncombed ears, bloodshot eyes and obese pot-bellied frame, which was hardly surprising when one considered that the poor dog was never taken out and exercised, but would be just pushed out twice a day into the garden to do the necessary. And woe betide anyone who ventured unwarily into this domain; as her owners never gave much thought to the clearing up of the results of Peggy's visits. It was, as Arthur frequently moaned, "like walking through a minefield!" It never occurred to him at any time to do this distasteful task himself. "She's not my dog," he would tell Beth.

Poor Peggy, as she became aware that she was being talked about, would thump her tail heavily on the hearth rug, mistakenly believing that she was being spoken about in a complimentary way. It wasn't her fault that her eccentric owners had no idea as to the proper management of a dog; in fact, their plying her with sweets and biscuits each evening while relaxing with their wireless, the sound of needles clicking as Dot did her knitting, was positively cruel when you observed the evidence of her rotting teeth and spreading girth!

Came the time eventually however when Arthur did indeed obtain his 'proper' dog; like his bizarre in-laws, he had not the slightest idea as to the proper management of this prodigy of his and finished up taking it to a dogs' home, while acquiring a cat instead. So much for his grand ideas!

As was the habit in those days, during and after the war, Arthur smoked, as also did Beth. Following one particularly heavy social evening, with everyone puffing away, he complained early the next morning of discomfort in his chest, but assuming that it was a bout of indigestion after the somewhat rich food of the previous evening, he chose to ignore it. But, eventually, Beth was forced to call the doctor, the discomfort and pain having become more intense.

Arthur was then, protestingly, transported to the local hospital on the doctor's diagnosis of a heart attack!

"No! No! It can't be!" he proclaimed. "It can't be that!" he insisted. "There has never been a history of heart attacks in my family: it just can't be." But of course it was. He chose to forget that for some time now, he had been quite a heavy smoker...

"Is it serious?" he asked in a plaintive voice of the consultant, as this sober man made his ward rounds the next morning. He was hoping, of course, for a reply in the negative; some comforting words, perhaps; but the consultant made no bones about the matter.

"Of course it's serious!" he answered brusquely. "It's very serious," he told this naïve patient, who looked up at him with scared eyes. "And what's more..." the surgeon hadn't finished with his patient yet. "What's more," he continued, "unless you stop this disgusting habit, you'll probably find yourself back in here again before too long, and wasting my time." He put a lot of emphasis on the word "wasting", before he carelessly laid his patient's notes on the end of the bed and carried on to the next patient.

Arthur fell into a morass of despondency as he silently contemplated this disastrous happening to himself. "But I'm only forty!" he called after the consultant, as though that was a good enough reason for his not having had a heart attack.

"Okay," responded the consultant over his shoulder, as he flicked through the next patient's notes. "So stop the smoking then, and with any luck you won't be seeing me any more."

What a revelation for Arthur. He still didn't quite understand why this terrible thing had happened, believing himself to be immune from such things. "Didn't I pass the medical in the Air Force A.1?" he lamented to family and friends, including me, as we sat by his hospital bed that evening. I just nodded my head like the others but I remembered, as I sat there, how Beth and he had laughed their heads off not so long ago when they recounted to a gathering of friends in the house, how they had surreptitiously smoked at Beth's brother's wedding...

Ronald was to be married into the 'Plymouth Brethren' a very religious sect. In personality, he was the exact opposite to his skittish sister, revealing a taciturn, more serious nature. He quietly scorned unacceptable habits like Beth's and Arthur's smoking, although he made no comments. He was an academic like his father, but there the similarity ended. A big bumbling man, heavy of feature and loud of voice, this parent of his spent a lot of time blundering around the house, while shouting, "What's this, then?" and "What's that?" Nothing was ever to his satisfaction.

His large frame was topped by a mop of thick grey hair, through which his fingers raked continuously.

Ronald, in comparison, was more slender, bespectacled, quiet and unassuming. He showed a remarkable tolerance towards his bizarre, differing parents: his forceful father, and empty-headed, giggling mother, when she dallied around her 'enigmatic' first born.

His devastating news then to the family one evening that he was marrying Clara, his fiancée of whom very little had been seen, left everyone stupefied, and they sat with their mouths agape. No nervous giggling from his mother; no hand-shake from his gregarious father. Nothing!

"Well, I'm glad that you are all so pleased!" Ronald remarked. The wedding will be in two months and, of course, you are all invited.

He had stood bravely before them, coat draped over one arm, all ready to make a quick exit to meet Clara after his shock announcement and then he was gone, leaving everyone, for a change, with nothing to say. Then: "Has 'ee taken leave of 'is senses?" his father exploded. "Has 'ee gone quite mad! We'll never see anything of 'im if 'ee marries inter that lot. What are yer going ter do about it, Dot?" he boomed at his little horrified wife, as she stood with the teapot in her hand, having been in the process of pouring out more tea for everybody.

"Well, what can I do, Wilf?" poor Dot responded.

"You are 'is mother, ain't yer?" Wilf boomed again. "Yer must be able ter do something."

'ees twenty-eight, Wilf," his trembling wife told him. "I can't tell 'im what to do."

"Bloody 'ell!" Wilf shook his head in despondency. "That's it – that's it then. Why can't 'ee marry someone normal, that's what I'd like to know!" he almost shouted. "Once that lot get their 'ands on 'im, that'll be the end. You see if I'm not right; you see, that's all."

By this time, Beth's father was prowling around the room and tossing his head about like some demented parrot.

"What about this cup of tea I've just poured for you then?" his wife reminded him, as tears threatened to spill from her worried eyes.

"BUGGER the tea! BUGGER everyone!" Wilf bellowed, as he charged from the room, while slamming the door so hard the house fairly shook…

The dreaded wedding proved to be a painful process for himself, Dot, Arthur and Beth. The allocated day of Clara and Ronald's unfavourable union got off to a less than auspicious start.

"You're not bloody wearing that monstrosity are yer?" Wilf, still smarting from his son's shock announcement of a few weeks earlier, stood now, with one foot almost in the car that was to transport them all to the unpopular nuptials of this maligned couple. He looked in amazement at the apparition already sitting there waiting for him. He took in the ridiculous carbuncle that resided on his wife's head, while she in turn had sat with a smug expression clearly visible on her face, obviously believing that the hat to which he was referring would make a big impression on this husband of hers.

Her face had fallen then as she tentatively fingered this monstrosity, this very expensive item that had given her so much pleasure when she bought it. She had thought it very 'chic', in fact, little realizing at the time that it was rather heinous and not in keeping with her small stature and the rest of her attire, which had obviously been bought from one of the stores along the High Street.

"What's wrong with my hat, then?" she asked tremulously now, all her former pleasure in the buying of it seeping away.

"Because it's bloody ridiculous, that's what!" Wilf shouted. "Like some bloody spaceship ready to take off!" he told her cruelly, which immediately reduced the poor woman to tears. But the rage that Wilf had felt since he had been informed of his son's shock intentions had not yet abated. Insulting his wife since the incident, had been the only way he had found to alleviate this misery.

"Dad, don't!" Beth was fond of her father, but she realized only too well his shortcomings. One minute he could be hilariously funny, and the next quite cantankerous. Her guileless mother stood not a chance against this academic, changeable man. She often wondered how they came together in the first place, being such opposites.

"It's all right, Mum: you look lovely. Doesn't she, Arthur?" She gave her husband a discreet nudge. They had secretly had a good laugh, though, when Dot first showed them her very costly buy. "Er, yes, lovely," Arthur had said. "Lovely, Dot. It really suits you," he had lied.

His artless mother-in-law had given an excited giggle. "You won't mention it to Mr Brimm, will you?" she whispered to him in a confiding manner. Anyone who was not related by blood to her husband, always had to suffer this reference to Wilf as Mr Brimm, be they friend, neighbour, tradesman – whoever – it was always Mr Brimm this, and Mr Brimm that, as though he were someone quite important. But Arthur good naturedly accepted this bit of eccentricity from the little woman standing all of a quiver before him.

"I want to surprise him you see." Dot had giggled again as she crept from the room to hide this treasure, this very expensive item which lay within its elaborate box, as she carried it stealthily to its hiding place in the bedroom…

"Well! If **you** think it's bloody alright, you can sit with it then!" Mr Brimm told his daughter. He could be quite brutal at times. He was a whisky drinker, and as long as he was not denied his regular tipples he was a very agreeable man, much called upon by the British Legion, of whom he was a member, on the occasions of their socials, to go along with Mrs Brimm for the purpose of reciting some his hilarious monologues, and they got their meal thrown in for nothing. The scouts also asked this favour of him at their yearly jamboree, given in the local community hall. It was a joy to listen to his clever renderings of these well-known orations, and the laughter rang out loudly from the animated audience in response.

"He's so clever," his adoring wife would tell people, as they took their refreshments before the second half of the evening. He had of course had his whiskey before these uproarious performances, but on the occasion of the wedding, he had cautiously forgone this tipple. Wasn't his son marrying into a very religious sect? It would never do to turn up over-merry, plus the fact that he was expected to make a speech on this ghastly occasion. "Oh! Blast and bother," he said quietly now to Beth and Arthur, as they sat gloomily at the reception, finishing the sumptuous cold buffet served to them. The wedding service beforehand had been long and drawn out. It had been ages since they had had the opportunity to smoke, and their withdrawal symptoms were increasing by the minute.

"You will have to excuse us while we attend to a little matter, but we won't be long," Wilf imparted to his son's now in-laws as he, Beth and Arthur, arose from the table, eager to escape, even for a short spell from the suffocating, stilted conversation emanating from everyone. They had nothing in common with this religious lot, and would just be glad when everything was over and they could all go home, but their hosts now graciously reassured them as they made their tentative moves with ,"That's quite alright, Wilf, the speeches won't be for at least half an hour; don't rush." They were probably well aware of the purpose for this necessary temporary relocation of Wilf, Arthur and Beth, but they kept their counsel and turned their attention now to Dot, who remained sitting, still with her hat determinedly on her head.

"What a lovely hat, Dot," they enthused kindly to her, ignoring any negative thoughts they might have had.

"Don't worry, Mum," Beth had told her, during the journey to the wedding, her distress being very evident after being told by her husband that her hat looked like a 'bloody flying saucer!' "It's not a bit like a flying saucer," she assured her. "It's just, hmm, very nice. Yes, it's very nice. Men haven't the slightest idea about fashion," she had comfortingly assured her mother.

Once through the double-doors which led from the hall, Wilf, Arthur and Beth lost no time in seeking out an empty room; with a window. "Oh! What bliss; what a relief" they told each other, as they threw the window wide, so as to enable them to blow the smoke, (which had been inhaled deeply and divinely by them), in long spirals out of its welcoming gap into the abyss beyond.

They chatted and laughed as they surreptitiously stood around, chuffed that they could indulge in this unhealthy craving of theirs, with no one pointing a finger at them. "Ah! That's better – I'm not doing without my smoke as well as my bloody whisky, not for anyone!" Wilf informed his two compatriots, as they stood and wallowed in this much frowned-on pleasure.

Yes, it was a good laugh, and the details were related again and again to acquaintances and friends of the family with much mirth. The telling also of the untimely death of Dot's hat after the wedding had people fairly in stitches.

They had arrived home, exhausted, everyone just wanting their cocoa and bed.

"I'll just leave this here for tonight and put it away in its box tomorrow." Dot lay her treasured hat tenderly on top of the sideboard in the living room. "I'm too tired to do it tonight," she had told everyone, as they made their way wearily up the stairs…

Whether Peggy, their adored dog, retained a grudge with regard to being left all day while everyone went to the wedding, or whether she had just had a fit during the night, nobody could be quite sure, but the evidence of either happening lay on the hearthrug in the morning. Peggy had exacted her revenge while everyone slept, by sabotaging the hat!

How she had managed to reach it from the top of the sideboard in her overblown, elderly condition, no one knew, but the confirmation of this happening presented itself quite clearly now before them as they made an appearance the next morning.

At first, no one spoke as they surveyed this sacrilege of Dot's hat, and then: "Oh, Wilf! Look what she's done to my hat!" Dot cried.

Wilf stood unspeaking at first as he took in the massacre that had taken place while they had all slept, before a wicked grin spread slowly across his face. "Peggy!" he addressed the dog in mock concern as she thumped away with her tail on the hearthrug, believing that she had done something quite clever. "What have you done to that hat, you naughty gel?" he chastised her before he started laughing, and he laughed and he laughed. "Ah! Ha-ha, oh dear. Sorry, Dot!" And, "Ha ha," again, he uproariously chortled, before he suddenly then became aware of his wife's stricken face. She would never be able to afford another hat like that, the look plainly said, and Wilf stopped laughing now and repented as he said kindly to her. "Don't worry. Dot; I'll buy you another hat," he told her before going into fresh peals of laughter all over again.

But Dot wasn't pacified with this promise of Wilf's to replace her hat. "I suppose you're quite satisfied now!" she threw at him in a very vitriolic tone. "You never did like the hat, did you?" She burst into tears before hastily leaving the room. Her treasured association with her only son's wedding was ruined; torn to pieces. How could it ever be replaced? The hat was never mentioned in Dot's presence ever again.

Oh yes, the wedding in some ways had brought about a lot of laughter, especially in the telling of the secret smoking that had been very skilfully carried out, but I didn't hear any laughter now, as we sat by Arthur's bed. He had been told to 'stop it' and not to smoke again if he valued his health, but this was easier said than done, with the craving eating away at him as he lay in hospital. Oh no, there was no laughter now, just morose contemplation and, as I sat there, I stole a look at Beth sitting opposite me. I thought about how she had changed in the twelve years since marrying Arthur. While he had retained his good looks, Beth had let herself go. No longer was she the pretty petite ballerina with the lush dark hair and slender frame. Her slenderness had gone now, and she had become just – thin. She had allowed her hair to become straggly, and all the attractiveness had gone from her pert features... I felt dismayed then, wondering why Arthur stayed within the marriage. In my eyes it was a sin for a wife, or husband for that matter, to just neglect their appearance once they became ensconced in the partnerships with their spouses. I ruminated, as I sat there, while everyone chatted away, on the whole spectrum of the matter. Why did Arthur stay, why was he so faithful to Beth when he must have known how attractive he still was to the opposite sex with some of the female fraternity practically throwing themselves at him on occasions, especially when they viewed his wasted little wife?

"I just can't be bothered with the physical side of marriage," Beth had scornfully confided to me, not so long before. It had occurred to me then that she was very fortunate indeed that Arthur was still interested in her in that respect, but I'm sure that that occasion of which she had spoken must just have been a 'one off'. I was sure that no such thing existed between them at the present time. Had they been religious, I would have been able to convince myself that Arthur was making the supreme sacrifice of staying with Beth because of his marriage vows: 'for richer, for poorer; for better, for worse; to have and to hold, in sickness and in health,' the vows went, but there was nothing like that to hold him. Their marriage in church had not been for the religious aspect, but just for the glory of the occasion. No, it was nothing like that. I looked again at Beth while I contemplated all this. She was sitting beside her mother, and I couldn't help noticing how like her mother she was becoming. If you want to know what your wife will look like in future years, men are sometimes told, just look at her mother, and certainly this was very true with regard to Beth – she was beginning to very much resemble Dot, even down to the occasional nervous giggling, but not, I hasten to add, the empty headedness: you could never put Beth in that category. She was intelligent and astute.

It must be because of Craig, I told myself all the while. Arthur had always been obsessed with this young son of his…and the security of the family life that existed between him and Beth. She was a good home-maker. She made no demands of anybody and she exuded a pleasant personality. I realized that these things were paramount to Arthur. Goodness knows, he had had very little order in his life. I perceived then the flaws in his character; his moodiness at times; his unaffectionate nature; while Beth, like her quirky parents, had a warmness that always endeared her to people. I was sure then that this must have taken prevalence over everything else with Arthur. He would forego other pleasures to embrace what important attributes Beth did have to offer. Her nurturing of their precious son was very important to him. The relaxed home-life; the companionship; yes, even the closeness of her wacky parents; all these things combined together kept Arthur, I was sure, within the marriage, and on assimilating all these facts, I was able to bring closure then to my rambling thoughts...

"Just hurry up and get better," Beth was telling Arthur now. "We need you at home," she said, as she squeezed his hand. Yes, I was quite sure now of what kept Arthur within his marriage to Beth...

Craig, as he matured, proved to be a clever boy and attained a bursary to a public senior school, graduating then to university.

Money was tight for Beth and Arthur at this time, necessitating Beth to find some employment but they gladly supplemented their gifted son, of whom they were so proud, believing in a great future for him.

Unbeknown to them, however, was the fact that this treasured son of theirs, once at university, had become embroiled somehow with an unsavoury set of students. These students were, for reasons best known to themselves, completely opposed to the system. They were drinkers and not much good for anything. All talk and very little else, they blundered their way through their studies, just wasting government money.

The fateful day then when Craig had to confront his parents with the devastating news that he had failed his degree, caused the bottom to drop completely out of their world. No proud announcements to family and friends of their son's achievements; no graduation for them to proudly attend. Nothing!

"How could you?" his mother had said, while his father remained silent. One more smack in the face for Arthur, who had ultimately pinned all his hopes on his son, whom he was sure would succeed where he had so dismally failed.

Craig, however, pulled himself together, once away from this revolutionary mob at university. There would be no second attempt for him to gain his degree, no further support from his cash-strapped parents. He moved from home, which enabled him to stand on his own feet, and after a while managed to attain a modest success in his professional life, which took him for a number of years to Saudi Arabia. I personally thought this was rather risky, as he had drunk profusely with these undesirables at university. I immediately thought of the danger of living in such a place; the strictness of the regime there. Drinking of alcohol in this austere, abstemious part of the world carried horrendous punishments; how would he cope with this alone? But he, nonetheless, endured the austere system in this frightening part of the world, and stayed for several years before returning to England to pursue his career, and to marry.

Had he tolerated these years just to prove himself? Who knows, but the fact remains that he returned home a much more sober, responsible being, who went on to father three wonderful, bright and successful children. They attained the success that their father had initially thrown away.

Here, Craig and his family lived in a beautifully converted huge barn, which had been transformed into an elegant villa, way out in the country. The surrounding land boasted beguiling woods and running streams, through which Arthur and Beth, on their frequent visits, would exercise 'Brandy', the family's hulking dog: a 'proper' dog, in the caring of which, Arthur, all those years ago when he had owned such a thing, had failed miserably. "Come on, Brandy," he would call out to the dog, "let's make it five miles today." He was retired now. He could spend all day going through the woods and streams if he so wished.

Things in the end had turned out remarkably well.

CHARLIE

They say that behind every great man, there's a good woman!

Although Charlie wasn't a great man, far from it, in fact, it still took a good woman to set him on his feet and point him in the right direction.

The rheumatic fever that had made him so ill in his youth, and which had unfortunately weakened his heart, disqualified him from any of the armed forces that he was so keen to join, and he was bitterly disappointed.

He bummed around then doing nothing in particular while continuing to live at the family flat.

Mary came into his life and they were married. Brian, their baby son, was born in due course, and I remember him as a beautiful baby, with an equally beautiful nature. He rarely cried, but just smiled and gurgled all the time. His bluest of blue eyes complemented his blond curls. He was altogether a very handsome child.

Charlie was not the most appreciative of fathers however, and Mary tended to be of a very clinging nature and certainly not a good candidate for the auspices of a moody and pretty useless husband. This habit of hers got very much on Charlie's nerves.

"Oh, Charlie," she often addressed him, "what shall I do?" while at the same time she clung onto him and implored him with her eyes. "What shall I do?"

"I don't know, Mary," Charlie would reply testily. "Don't keep asking me what you should do – work it out for yourself." But poor Mary was unable to do this. What she needed was a man much stronger than Charlie, who seemed to scorn her attempts to lean on him. He was just unable to give her the love and support that she so sorely needed. If truth be known, it was he himself who needed to do the leaning. The situation between them was pretty hopeless, really, and the one big effort made on Mary's part to amend her inadequacy simply fell on stony ground, as far as Charlie was concerned.

Brian, the beautiful baby

Because money was in such short supply between the two of them, owing to her incapable husband's lack of meaningful employment, Mary had made a huge effort to supplement their income. Browsing among the shops in the High Street one day, she noticed a small card displayed in the glass door of a large department store requesting someone 'reliable' to clean the frontage of store early each morning.

Mary viewed the rather extensive façade before her, with a critical eye. Yes, it was rather grubby, she told herself as she stood there. She could make a big difference here. Give it a complete overhaul in fact. She got quite excited at the thought of the renovation she could bring about, so important for the store, she mused. Yes, so important, and she, there and then, bravely entered the imposing building to seek out the manager. If there was one thing that Mary was quite confident about, it was that she was a good cleaner. The flat that she had moved into when she married Charlie shone like a new pin, with not a speck of dust anywhere: oh yes, she was fully qualified to apply for this position advertised on the door; she had no qualms on that score…

Baby Brian sat bolt upright in his pram just inside the open doorway of the store the very next morning. He watched his mother as she, with a vengeance, tackled the grubby exterior. Mary wrinkled her nose nevertheless at the congeries of cigarette ends strewn around. "Look a' this, Brian!" she called to the baby in disgust. "Some people should be ashamed." Neither she herself, nor Charlie smoked, and she found this habit of other people's distasteful, but she staunchly carried on with a determined vigour until: "Will yer look at tha', Brian". She looked over at the baby again who all this time had sat contentedly watching his industrious mother. "Wha' yer think then? Don' it look lovely?" Mary viewed the frontage with complete satisfaction. She had done a really good job here but out of the corner of her eye then, she noticed the shop next door: a hairdresser's, whose frontage was in the same need that she had just administered to the store. It rather took the shine away from what she had done, being in such close proximity. Oh well, there's only one thing for it, she thought as she dashed back into the store to fill up her bucket with some fresh water, and she proceeded to scrub the offending frontage until she was quite satisfied that it fully complemented its neighbour.

Of course, the owner of the hairdresser's, when she came to open up later that morning after Mary had long gone with baby Brian, was delighted as she noticed the clean and shiny frontage to her salon, and arrived early the next day to query Mary. "It's awright," Mary assured her, "it didn't take me long; I just 'ad ter get some fresh water, that's all."

But the proprietor didn't let it rest at that. "Look," she told Mary now,

"I can't afford to pay you fer continuing doing it, much as I appreciate yer kindness, but if you'd like to pop in after you've finished every Friday, I'll do yer hair for nothing."

Mary was ecstatic as, on that first Friday, she proudly pushed baby Brian home, with not only several pound notes in her pocket, but a brand new hair-do into the bargain. She couldn't wait for Charlie to appear later in the day for him to see the new 'her' and to present him with the money; and as he eventually walked through the door, she stood purposefully in front of him, barring his way, with a huge grin on her face. "Well!" she said to him. Then, "Well!" She was sure that he must notice her new hair-do, but Charlie stood before her with an expressionless face.

"Well what?" he asked.

Mary pointed to her head, still grinning. "This," she told him. "What do you think?" But as Charlie failed to comprehend, the smile slowly left Mary's face; all the pleasure in the telling to Charlie of how she had come about receiving this brand new hairstyle, and the money she had earned that week just paled into insignificance. "It's awright," she said then. "It don't matter." She laid the hard-earned money before him and walked away. Disappointment emanated from her. She had given her all the day she tracked down the store manager about cleaning his frontage, her being rather timid by nature, and this was the thanks she got for her brave effort. Charlie, she told herself, was obviously dead from the neck upwards! She wouldn't bother him again.

It was inevitable then, that in the end, and to my sadness, Mary was to meet a much more caring man who was able to provide her with the love and protection she so badly needed.

Charlie continued his useless existence, on the break-up of their marriage, never bothering to keep in contact with his captivating son, and he just slouched around doing nothing in particular.

It was when he decided to do a spot of window-cleaning that he first met Pat, as she sat one day at her desk within the bank that employed her. She suddenly became conscious of a pair of eyes surveying her from the window. She got up from her chair and walked toward the owner of the eyes but Charlie averted his gaze on her approach.

"Will you be cleaning these windows weekly?" she asked him, in her pleasant voice.

"Yes, I suppose so," Charlie replied.

"Good," said Pat, "because they need doing every week."

She looked at him uncertainly, then asked, tentatively, "Would you like a cup of tea? I'm just going to make one." And that was Charlie's introduction to a good woman, just what he needed.

He was a fair bit older than Pat, but this didn't seem to bother her at all. In no time she had Charlie organised in a gently persuasive manner. She realised, of course, that he resembled a 'ship without a rudder' wavering through life with no direction or orientation. As she got to know him, it became clear to her that to a certain degree his life had been torn asunder, with his serious illness and the sudden loss of his mother, and the disruption of family life.

He hadn't the resilience of his older brothers to weather the hard knocks dished out to them and then to be left to fend for himself as best he could with no guidance from anyone; he was just the victim, really, of a fractured family.

What was very noticeable to Pat in her discerning way, however, was that 'Chas' as she was to call him, spoke in a quite well-modulated voice with no trace of the East End diction, and he was gifted with a good grasp of figures. What was he doing window cleaning?

In no time at all, she got him employment at the bank. They were married and Chas entered into the middle class world of bridge and horticultural activities. He was at one with his second wife. She was the rudder of his ship; his direction in life, the buttress that he had so badly needed. She gave him what he had been so unable to give to Mary, and she had brought the best out in him.

Contentment was their lot then, surrounded by a contingent of pleasurable friends for bridge, continental holidays and all that goes with a life of well-being.

Charlie had come home.

JIMMIE

Jimmie, the quieter more rational being of the brood, had survived evacuation at the onset of war, living with foster parents in Harpenden, a quite exclusive and pretty part of Hertfordshire. He lived but a few miles from where I was billeted but I knew nothing of this at the time. To me, he seemed to have just disappeared from the face of the earth, and it was quite some years before I had contact with him again.

He had been entirely happy with the nice people with whom he had lived: a childless, undemanding couple, simple in their lifestyle and quite thrilled to have Jimmie.

My father, soon after Jimmie had been allocated to these pleasant people, decided, probably in a fit of conscience, to visit his youngest son, and such a fuss was made of him on this visit he condescended to stay for the weekend. He excused himself, however, on that first Saturday evening, on the pretence that he wanted to explore the bewitching town through which he had travelled on his way to them. 'So full of character,' he had conveyed to these nice people in as refined a manner as he could muster, while leaving the cockney idiom behind.

The supposed visit of my father's to explore this town so bewitching, so full of character, was, of course, merely an excuse for him to quench his thirst in the first, most lively pub that he could find, and it didn't take long for him to be walking into a hail-fellow-well-met and uninhibited bar where he lost no time in seeking out kindred spirits.

He had noticed though, as he approached the town, that it sported a remarkably distinctive looking Fire Station right slap-bang at the beginning of the busy High Street and situated next to the lovely Rothamstead Park, which contained, among other amenities, of which I was much later to avail myself, an attractive outdoor swimming pool.

The fire station stood there now, shining like a new pin with its bright red and brass exterior, the brass so highly polished it glinted in the evening glow. My father, when he had first seen it earlier in the day, had been quite taken aback. How unusual to see a fire station so prominent in such an exclusive High Street, he thought to himself, and now in the lamp-light as he sought out a suitable pub, he came across it again, standing out and glinting still as it had done in the daylight earlier on.

He stood then, surveying it, noticing once again its pristine, shining prominence. It certainly didn't detract anything from the elegant town of Harpenden, so unique was it. Well! he thought. Wha' about that?

He became aware then, as he stood there, of some raucous laughter coming from within the pub opposite to where he was standing, on the other side of the main road. He turned towards the pub, sizing it up, noticing how large it was. He could see, through its windows, a long circular bar around which groups of animated men were clustered. They talked to one another in loud voices, each it seemed, trying to outdo the other with their strident tones, and then they would all laugh at some remark made by one of them, and the air around them was clouded by smoke from the cigarettes they puffed away at.

My father lost no time then, in making a bee-line to this source of hilarity, this smoke-pervaded bar, while patting his jacket pocket at the same time to check that his cigarettes were safely stowed there.

As he ordered his first pint, he was approached by a man who quickly made himself known as the fire station chief. He had seen my father, through the pub's large front facing window, as he stood there for those moments admiring his station.

"What did you think, then?" he asked him, while he gestured with his head towards this structure of which he was very proud: and that was what led to many pleasurable drink-filled Saturday evenings for my father.

His rather unsteady journey back to Jimmie then after his convivial 'night out' with the fire chief, had him entering the house at rather a late hour. His hosts had sat waiting patiently for him, their night-time cocoa being long forgotten, but my father, in his wily way, managed to excuse himself by putting the blame on his new found friend. "Just couldn't get away," he told them, and so it was agreed that in future he take the key so that these kind people could go to bed after their cocoa, instead of waiting up for him. They were probably conscious of the fact that my father was a bit worse for wear as he wavered before them making his excuses but, being the decent sort of people they were, they doubtless told themselves that he would, after all, be going home after breakfast the next morning, and, "How nice, Joe," they remarked, "to have become friends with our distinguished fire chief." That was the beginning of many pleasurable Saturday evenings for my father, meeting up with his new-found friend while they, between them, endeavoured to drink the bar dry. The fact that he saw very little of Jimmie didn't come into it, and he never checked on me living in misery just a few miles away: he just didn't have the time.

When Jimmie entered adulthood, he enlisted in the ground-force army, seeing quite a bit of action. The most gruesome spell of his enlistment was over a period of days when he and his comrades were consigned to the battlefield to pick up parts of dismembered bodies scattered around. As he related this to us, I felt quite ill, but Jim, as he was now known, brushed this aside. "Somebody had to do it," he told us as we all sat looking a bit pale around the gills.

In his eventual marriage, Jim was always a bit unsettled. His wife displayed a somewhat restless personality and never seemed to be able to stay for long in one place, moving from one house to another. Jim became a bit frustrated at this, and I expect it was a bit unsettling for their two children as well, but he, being of a quiet disposition and not easily fazed, accepted the situation with good grace.

The catalyst came when Elaine, Jim's wife, decided that they should emigrate. At this time there was a scheme being carried out by the government for people to emigrate to Australia. They were tempted then to throw in their lot, so to speak, during this bleak spell immediately following the war, and to venture to pastures new. Australia, being a relatively new country, needed new people, and so steps were taken to entice new blood to this place of opportunities. The long journey out by sea would be paid for by the government, for those resolute enough to take up this offer, and assistance given to families upon arrival. If, after a period of two years, it didn't work out for some, the Government would pay for the long journey home again, but only after two years, and not before.

Jim with Elaine

Another scheme was put into operation almost simultaneously at this time, whereby the government sent a ship-load of abandoned children to Australia to supposedly start a new life. These poor children had been put into orphanages in England during the war by their mothers on the pretext of hard-luck stories: husbands being away at war; no one to support them; their need to go to work etc., etc., and when these women tasted the freedom of earning good money in the factories and no encumbrances while they went out in the evenings to enjoy themselves, they chose to forget their offspring as they 'made hay while the sun shone' so to speak. Until some years later, when the war ended, employment in munitions factories ceased and husbands came home, then, and only then, did they remember their children. But it was too late: the children had gone. The government, being unable to contact these mothers who had made themselves untraceable, had sent these poor unfortunate youngsters to the other side of the world, and who could waste any sympathy on these spineless women who chose to forget their little ones, curtailing all contact with them? Could anyone offer sympathy to them? I don't think so.

Elaine, then, convinced by this lucrative-sounding scheme of the government, decided that they should take advantage of it, persuading herself that 'the grass would be so much greener on the other side of the fence'. Jim had been horrified at this. What about his job? What about the disruption to the children? However, Elaine was adamant, quite sure that this was what they should do.

A reporter from the local paper came to visit them. He had seen in the columns of his paper, 'Houseful of furniture for sale due to immigration'. He asked why this step was being taken by the family, and while Jim remained silent, Elaine proceeded to denigrate England. "We will be so much better in Australia," she told the reporter, and from that point on, with a single-mindedness, Elaine set the wheels in motion for the move.

The packing of various items that Elaine insisted on taking, proved quite difficult. Jim coped as best he could, but his patience ran out when trying to pack Elaine's knitting machine, which she insisted on taking. The steel rod that went up and down on the machine refused to stay within the packing case, so Jim did no more but went outside to the shed and got a heavy hammer with which he bashed the rod until it collapsed into the case.

The children were in fits of laughter about this but Jim simply told them, "Don't tell your mother. Let her just think that her machine was damaged in transit." And that was that!

After the family's long six-week voyage to Elaine's 'wonderland', she wrote to the family delighted at what she had found. "Everything is fine," she told us. "I'm sure that we will like it here."

We breathed more easily that she at last seemed to have found her niche. Just as well, we thought, as they were obliged to stay for two years before consideration would be given to the bringing of them back to England if things did not work out.

After a while though, we heard nothing and held our breath. Was it all going wrong? Yes, it did all go wrong and, after several months, there was a curt note from Jim that told us that they would be coming home when the two years were up.

How does one tackle a disastrous situation such as this? The whole debacle was enough to try any man's patience, and Jim was a very patient man. But there was a limit and, as they started on the long journey home, complete with Elaine's knitting machine, I believe it probably was the beginning of the end for both of them, as they coped once again with the stressful and complicated system of readjustment. Elaine had lost face now after finding that the grass had not been any greener on the other side of the fence after all, and coming back to the land that she had only two years previously so ruthlessly decried, made it necessary for the family's move back to be surreptitious. But, Elaine, to give her credit, had worked very hard while in Australia, and was very astute moneywise. With the help of her relieved parents on their daughter's move back to England, and with money she had herself managed to save during her absence, she and Jim were able to obtain a mortgage on a pleasant house in Chipping Sodbury, Bristol, while having both made strenuous efforts on their return to obtain employment so as to assuage their precipitous situation brought about by Elaine's discontent. Good! we thought as a family. Everything now seemed settled.

To our utter amazement, then, we learned of the split between Jim and Elaine. Had this after all, this sojourn to Australia and traumatic return, put paid to their marriage? It had obviously caused the initial cracks but we were shocked at the outcome and, anyway, Jim wasn't the type for divorce. His patient, forbearing nature surely would enable him to overcome the toils of marriage, but in this instance we were wrong. Now, children having flown the nest, Jim left Elaine to start a new life on his own, leaving their problematic marriage behind.

Contented with his lot then, and reaching retirement, he entered into the activities of the senior citizen brigade with huge enthusiasm: painting; rambling; computing: there was so much to partake of, things that a person has no time for during their working life. He maintained close contact with his grown children, spending lovely holidays at the chateau owned by his daughter and son-in-law in a beautiful part of France.

After a while further good fortune smiled on Jim when he unexpectedly became acquainted with a lady who he had known from a distance in the past. Ann had now been widowed for a few years but took solace in her bustling activities within the church. She wasn't looking for anything further as she was quite content, but an agreeable companionship sprung up between the two of them, while they each maintained their independence, and Jim was happy.

He had given his marriage, over a long period of time, what he could, before he had abandoned it. Who's to judge what is right and what is wrong in these matters? I believe that Jim's and Elaine's ultimate parting of the ways might have saved his life, his having being diagnosed on approaching retirement with a heart condition.

He now sustained a happy, rewarding lifestyle, free from the stresses that so encumbered him within marriage. He had endured these stresses until the children had flown the nest, but now he was free.

AUNTIE QUEENIE

What can I say about Auntie Queenie? She was one of three sisters, with herself being the eldest, then there was Sue and then my mother, Jane. An attractive businesswoman, church-goer and singer, what was she doing living with an unruly family like us, in our nondescript, shabby little house when, I'm sure, she could have fared much better?

I can't answer that, being too young at the time to not just accept that Auntie Queenie lived upstairs in her cosy little bedsit, just sitting most evenings, if she wasn't out singing with her choir or at a church meeting, to one side of her well-stacked fire listening to her wireless and knitting. Mostly, she ate out during the day but had in the room her little gas ring and other appliances should she need on occasions the odd snack or hot drink.

The room was somewhat cluttered, yet surprisingly tidy: a place for everything and everything in its place. The spacious windows at one end of the room boasted the prettiest curtains, set off by several attractive plants which adorned the windowsill, and large framed landscaped pictures hung from the freshly-decorated cream-coloured walls.

"Auntie Queenie…" I would say to her on occasions when I had managed to escape the carnage going on downstairs and sat at her feet sucking my thumb, "Auntie Queenie, when I grow up I want a room in my house just like this."

She would say nothing but go on knitting with a smile on her face.

Did Auntie, I have wondered, live purposefully with us to augment the precarious situation in which my mother found herself after the acrimonious split from my father? I doubt very much that my mother could have survived without this intervention. Certainly, Auntie had the best, the sunniest room of the house, but it needs to be borne in mind that, without the generous contribution towards the rental of our home, her sister would have undoubtedly gone under. Therefore, I have to assume that prior to the family's move from my father, some urgent consultation must have occurred between them regarding our survival, and Auntie made the ultimate sacrifice to leave her previous comfortable place of residence to move in with us.

One other thing that may have swayed her was her sadness at having lost her fiancé in the First World War. Like a lot of other women to whom this had happened, it had devastated her. Did, perhaps, living with us help to ease this sadness somewhat? Certainly one could not be indifferent to, or fail to become involved with, the hustle and bustle that went on in the house. She loved us children in her own quiet way, but this love in no way extended to my parents. 'Irresponsible' was the word she used regarding them.

My father especially she scorned. "A complete waster if ever there was one," she would lament, and her sister "a fool for marrying him when she could have done so much better." However she kept her own counsel and usually refused to enter into the fraught situation that existed between my parents. The old adage 'you made your bed, now you must lie on it' seemed to sum up Auntie's attitude to my mother. No messing about, just plain logic. So, when one day my father's younger brother came knocking at the door, cap in hand, pleading to be allowed to move in with us, she took the same attitude, on hearing the reason why.

Tom was not skilled and qualified as his brother (my father) was. He worked in a small factory making wrought iron implements. He sat on an assembly line with others, inspecting various parts before they were passed to be assembled for whatever purpose; a boring job to say the least.

One particular day a component was passed to him that should have been rejected further up the line. Tom took one look at it and shouted in a loud voice so that whoever was responsible should hear, "Who sent this bloody old rusty part down?" As he hollered, the other young lads on the assembly line laughed their heads off at his crude remark but, unfortunately for Tom, the owner of this small factory was sitting in his office with the door open at the time and heard everything. He got up and beckoned Tom to come to him.

"You know I don't allow swearing on the line," he said. He dismissed Tom on the spot. He was a Christian, you see, and made this quite plain to any youngster that he employed. "I don't permit swearing, coarseness or uncouth behaviour," he reminded Tom, who had been warned of this. He had gone home then and told his mother the bad news, but she didn't want to know.

"Yer can ge' out then," she had told him. "I'm not keeping you fer nothin." And so here he was, pleading to move in with us.

"How could you possibly do that, Tom? We're overcrowded as it is." Auntie Queenie showed him the door. "You knew the rules when you went to work at the factory. Anyway, why don't you move in with your brother? You can swear as much as you like there," she threw after him as he departed with his tail between his legs.

By today's standards, of course, what happened to my young uncle then would seem unbelievable in this present climate. No employer would be allowed to sack an employee out of hand as my uncle had been, but then, of course, things were very different, with mass unemployment, no unions and no government interference. If a man or boy was fortunate enough at that time to obtain employment, he held onto it with his life. My uncle made one mistake and he paid for it. Casual labourers, like himself, were two-a-penny and he should have known better.

Auntie Queenie had been off-hand when she sent him packing, but she had had enough to manage with my father, without having a younger version of him living with us. Being a church-goer herself, her sympathies were definitely with the employer. "Give to one, then you must give to the others, and what would that lead to?" she wisely informed us, as we stood in sombre mood watching the departure of Tom.

Later in life, when we children had departed, Auntie Queenie entered into a new companionable relationship with Rose, an extremely pleasant lady, who had, like herself, lost her partner in World War One. They moved in and shared together an attractive property in a much more prosperous area of London, well away from the dreariness of the East End.

Like Auntie, Rose was a businesswoman, so the two of them had a lot in common, both sharing a love of singing and amateur dramatics, and they spent hours tending their small back garden, transforming it from its former neglected state to something idyllic, with a little archway leading off from the small patio along a stepping-stone path to irregular patches of shrubs and flowers which skirted a small lawn: a little paradise in fact.

The transition for Auntie Queenie, from her former years of turbulence and strife with us, to the relatively peaceful existence of this new life, must have seemed a bit like heaven to her.

Today, of course, the cynics of this world would undoubtedly whisper behind their backs, 'lesbians,' but I don't think so, for we have to bear in mind that at this point in history, owing to the recent wars, men were in very short supply. Because of this, women were thrown very much together and I don't doubt that Rose and Auntie were just two of many who found solace in their predestined relationship.

As far as we were concerned, Auntie was now enjoying the happiness that had for so long eluded her. I'm sure, of course, that she would have preferred marriage, but this wasn't to be. After witnessing, for so many years, her sister's precarious survival within the matrimonial state, maybe her destiny was the right one for her, anyway. Who knows?

PART TWO

THE
TURBULENT
YEARS

INTRODUCTION

I pull no punches in Part Two of this book.

I relate within it my shattered life of living as a war-torn child with strangers in that completely unsophisticated era of the 1940s when people still had chamber pots under the bed; when laundry was done in the kitchen sink and put through the mangle before being loaded into a wicker basket and trundled up the garden to be pegged on a clothes-line, which extended the full length of the garden... a silent prayer would then be sent heavenwards that our inclement weather would hold off for long enough to enable this copious load to reach a modicum of dryness before being trundled once again back into the safety of the house.

There were no modern washing machines-cum-spin-dryers then to lighten the load of the housewife... no televisions to relax in front of and wile away tedious evenings.

There were no computers or mobile phones; in fact, few people even had an ordinary phone in the house; and to possess a car was a rarity during this era of which I speak, when modern technology had not yet invaded our simple way of living.

The telling of this awesome period of my life, however; the dangers and uncertainties that it afforded me; the ups and downs; the twists and turns of events; finally helped me at last to throw off the depression that had for so long lurked within me. But the anger that I had obviously harboured for all of this time came fully then into play as I wrote about those dire years when I had been forced to live with strangers and fell prey to their idiosyncrasies while I had been entrusted to their care during my formative years.

Revenge then became uppermost in my mind as the story evolved, spilling out against the perpetrators who had been so injurious to me. My sole aim was to expose them. I would use no pseudonyms for these people – to highlight them was my goal. Let them suffer as I had suffered, I told myself as the storyline unfolded.

Inexplicably then, as my pen flew unstoppable over the pages, an element of doubt invaded my ruminations. A hint of compassion crept into my subconsciousness and I became uncertain… What about the innocent descendants of those who were responsible for this bitterness within me? Should they have to suffer the guileful ways of their forbears? The matter then was resolved. Just three of these perpetrators have been named in the book and I know that they will stay silent. Was I right in taking this stance? The reader will have to decide for him – or herself!

THE JOURNEY

As I awoke that morning I had become conscious of the sunlight streaming in through the bedroom window, but it wasn't that which had awakened me, no, it was the banter going on in the next room. My brothers were calling to one another and laughing – that's what had pulled me from my slumber.

I slipped out of my bed to go to them. What was all this hilarity about? I was thinking as I padded to their room; it certainly made a change from the usual squabbling and fighting.

As I made this move towards them my mother's voice sailed through the air from downstairs, "Liz, come on. Come and 'ave yer breakfast." But I continued towards the boys.

On entering their room, their laughter and horseplay stopped as they turned to me. "Wha' do yer want, Liz?" they asked in a surprisingly kindly manner. They threw furtive glances at one another and as they did this, I felt a sense of unease because usually it was, "Don' come inter our room, Liz. Ge' out!" and I would be shoved unceremoniously out of the room. But there was none of this that day, just those mysterious magnanimous looks, and then my mother's voice sailed up the stairs once again, "Liz, will yer come!" so I made my way to her.

As I walked into our kitchen–cum-dining room–cum all-purpose facility, I pulled up smartly. I had noticed my Sunday coat and hat, which I usually wore for church, draped over one of the chairs; the chair with arms that my mother normally sat on. If one of the younger boys ever had the audacity to try and claim it he was soon, very briskly, tipped off! That was mum's chair – Off!

Why, I had stood there thinking, was my Sunday best attire draped over this chair? It was Thursday wasn't it, when my school gabardine mac should have been there? The mac that had been bought for me by my mother from the second–hand stall in Hoxton Market, but minus the belt, which the stallholder had promised to find for me but never did and, because of this, all my pride in wearing this article had gone and I had been left feeling bitterly disappointed, with my mother having to force me each school morning to wear it. Beside the chair holding my best coat and hat, stood our one and only small cardboard attaché case and on top of that reposed my gas mark in its box, which had fastened to it a long strap so that I could wear it slung over my head and around my waist.

I had stopped and looked at these things in surprise and threw a questioning look at my mother. Was I going somewhere? My mother noted the look. "Liz," she said, after giving me a quick glance before she diverted her gaze, "yer going ter the country for a few weeks. Ain't that nice?"

That was the first I knew of my extended sojourn into a life so utterly and completely foreign, so traumatic and, at times, so dangerous for me, that I sometimes wonder that I survived and came through it all.

"What about the boys, are they coming too?" I had asked her in a frenzied manner, but she was non-committal.

"We'll see," she just replied.

The war, having finally and irrevocably erupted, was to see a lot of children like me, plucked from the bosom of their families and dispatched to strange places, away from the imminent bombing of London. Most had been lucky enough to be taken in by responsible, kindly foster-parents, and were happy for the duration of the war but others, like myself, lived in the depths of misery, merely surviving by the skin of our teeth, owing to the hardship and deprivation imposed on us. Some never came through it at all, like the two young brothers fostered by a widowed farmer, for the implicit purpose of exploiting them to carry out some of the farm work, much too heavy for their tender frames. "Two young lads," he had told the billeting officer, "to help me on the farm." What lucky boys! But when, eventually, the school sent out alarm signals regarding the non-appearance over quite a long period of time of the youngsters, the billeting officer went post-haste to investigate, only to find them huddled up together in an outside barn, very dead! They had been worked and starved to death. With no woman around to see to their welfare, and the farmer finding them more of an encumbrance than useful, he had very conveniently just forgotten about them. In the chaos of the mass evacuation, they had been inappropriately placed, and forsaken. By the grace of God, I had ultimately come through, but why not those poor boys?

I stood on the platform now at the station. I was accompanied by an older girl who stood, like me, with her gas mask slung over her shoulder, and clutching in her hand a small attaché case, similar to the one that I held. Who she was, or where she had come from, I had no idea, but I was to learn later that this was a sister of mine being sent along to take care of me! She stood beside me then, listening intently to a harassed woman who was in charge of our small group.

"Now, hands up, my ten," this woman, whom I now recognised to be one of the teachers from the school, called out to us, and she checked that we all had our 'name' labels securely draped around our necks, along with our gas masks. "Now stick closely to me, all of you," she instructed us. "I don't want to get to Harpenden (our destination) only to be told that one of you is still standing on the platform here." She said this in a lighter vein with a grin on her face, in a attempt to quell the intensity of the situation, but although we all vehemently nodded our heads in response to this, we were all too confused by this dramatic step being taken in our lives, this sudden plucking of us from the imminent danger of the bombing that was to come, to appreciate her brave attempt at humour, and we trooped onto the train in sombre mood.

We hadn't been going long before one of the children complained of feeling sick! Our teacher cum-carer on hearing this, smartly whipped a bowl from a canvas bag that she had brought along with her and held it in front of this deathly white child. He obliging gagged into it while the others of us tried not to notice as we sat staunchly looking out of the train window. My sister, being one of the eldest, had had the unenviable task then of sitting with this bowl of sick on her lap until we arrived at our appropriate station. She had sat with a ram-rod straight back, head held high, as though distancing herself from this objectionable thing until 'Miss' finally took it off her and dealt with it. I remember little else of this journey that we undertook that day, only that we had all sat mute and gawping at one another until we reached our destination and had then stepped hesitantly off the train and onto a small bus that awaited us just outside of the station. This then took us to a school hall, acting as a sort of clearing centre, where we children, and those who were already there, sat and ate the sandwiches that we had carried with us. We then succumbed to a quick medical, performed by a sprinkling of doctors who sat at small tables dotted around the hall.

At the end of all this, we amazingly came face to face with our very own 'Nitty Nora', who had come on ahead of us for the prime purpose of examining all the children's heads for any livestock we might be carrying. A small number of children were discreetly stood to one side, obviously to be de-fleaed! The purpose of this clearing centre was for the allocation of children to various foster homes by people who had offered, or who had perhaps been persuaded, into entering the scheme.

My sister and I, having passed the inspection by 'Nitty Nora', sat quietly and unobtrusively to one side awaiting our fate! It was just as well that I had no knowledge at that time as we waited there, our small cardboard cases placed on the floor at our sides, the gas masks in their boxes on our laps, of the sadness and trauma that was to dig its talons into me over the succeeding years.

THE FOWLERS

As we drove into the drive of our prospective foster parents, I looked through the car window with astonishment. The large elegant house at the top of the drive, preceded by lush lawns, seemed almost like a royal palace to me and, as I stepped from the car, still holding on tightly to my small cardboard case and gas mask, I looked toward the front door, where our hosts Mr and Mrs Fowler stood, smiling. They welcomed us into their opulent home, while taking our coats on entering a large bright hall.

I stood entranced then as I took note. An elegant cabinet stood to one side of the hall with a telephone on it. Around the telephone stood an array of family photos, with smiling faces looking up from the frames; but it was the telephone that astonished me. I had no idea that people possessed such things. In the poverty-stricken area of London, which I had so reluctantly left behind that morning, we only had public telephone boxes for use in emergencies, like the need for a doctor or ambulance, or for the police, and these could be used only after a lengthy trek through a myriad of streets, before you found a functioning one.

My eyes darted now to a large fern in a pot, which dominated one corner of the hall, and I gazed at it in wonder. I had never seen anything like that, as with the carpet beneath our feet and the subdued wall lighting, which added further to the attractiveness of the hall. Where I came from, there was nothing lavish like this. There, you just entered a home via a damp, dark, narrow passage which led to the rest of the house. No carpeting, telephone or lighting, as they had here, nothing like that.

Where we now stood seemed almost palatial to me. These people are very rich, I thought.

Through my musing, I became aware then of a hand being placed gently on my shoulder. "Come on, Liz," a voice said, "come and have something to eat; you must be really hungry." I was guided with my sister through a door off the hall into a dining room, which boasted at one end, large patio doors. Beyond those, I viewed on the ground immediately outside, coloured flag stones, with corpulent shrubs in large containers dotted around, making this area awash with colour. Further on from the patio, well-tended lawns, bordered by flowers, lent further enhancement to the scene. A sprinkling of trees right at the top completed the extensive garden, but I noticed, nestled among the trees, a small wooden shack with windows, and its doors were wide open. I was to learn later that this was the Fowler's summer house, in which they often relaxed on fine days: Mr Fowler with his daily paper and Mrs Fowler with her knitting.

As my eyes wandered back then to the area just outside, my mind went into overdrive. The patio in front of us became our backyard at home, littered with the boys' five scooters, all toppled one on top of the other, and their wooden cart lay there also, on its side, exposing the hideous pram wheels affixed to the under carriage. A lopsided shed stood to one side of the yard, and this contained auntie's bike. No one was allowed to use this shed, only auntie. Her bike had come in very useful, many a time, for emergencies such as when the boys had gone out for the whole day on their scooters, while taking a picnic with them, and not returned. As night had followed day and there had been no sign of them, my mother had become almost hysterical and Auntie was dispatched hastily on her bike to alert the police! There was the occasion also when Auntie had to hurriedly fetch my father from the pub to come and discipline Joe, the eldest and the most unruly of the boys, after he had disgraced himself at the church film-show. Oh yes! there had been quite a few hair-raising occasions when Auntie had the call to speedily use her bike, and it took pride of place in the shed, unadulterated by the boys' more crude methods of transport, which languished in the yard outside, exposed to all the elements: rain, shine, frost or snow. No matter what, they stayed where they were.

There was no greenery to be seen in that back-yard, as there was here. No bushy shrubs or blooming flowers, or lush lawns but, even so, the thoughts of my brothers brought a dampness to my eyes. I remembered their roguish behaviour and insensitive rough treatment of me when we had been unavoidably thrown together during the preceding years; and their uncouth swearing which had rubbed off onto me, so that it had become an innate part of my vocabulary, and which was soon to reveal itself within my present circumstances. All of this, though, failed to stop the affection that I felt for them, so that I became distraught as I stood there deep in my reflections. I'd said not a word since we had entered the house, only being conscious of the Fowlers chatting to my sister in a friendly fashion.

"Come on, now," a kind voice said to me interrupting my distant thoughts. Mrs Fowler took my hand and sat me at the table. "You sit here, Liz," and my sister sat beside me.

I looked in awe then at the beautifully-laid table, at all the cutlery placed around: a knife, fork and spoon for each one of us; a serviette in its ring lying beside the knife and fork. In the centre of the table, stood a large glass jug filled with water. Glasses, tipped up on end, surrounded it. There was a small silver tray of condiments: salt, pepper and vinegar placed strategically in the middle of the table, flanked each side by ample china bowls with lids. These bowls contained potatoes in one, vegetables in the others. A tablespoon lay beside them for the purpose of serving each one of us with the amount that we required, with the meat already on our plates. Last of all, there was steaming brown gravy in a jug, giving off a delicious aroma.

As we sat eating, I noticed Mr Fowler dabbing at his mouth periodically with his serviette, and so I did the same. But I looked at all this grandeur before me with suspicion, and compared it to the meagre table setting in the kitchen at home, my mother dishing out each day from a big pot of stew at the cooker onto large plates, which she then passed to each one of us as we sat up at the long wooden table behind her. No need then for any fancy utensils, just one big pot containing the stew, which was made up of everything: potatoes, barley, vegetables, dumplings and everything else that my mother could lay her hands on. The almost total lack of meat made little difference to our enjoyment of this meal. The boys just gobbled it down with relish and then they would squabble over what was left on my plate, with me being very delicate and eating enough to hardly keep a fly alive. My mother would lash out in an attempt to control them. "That's right," she'd shout at them, "fight over 'er food; don't worry yourselves tha' she's no' even eating it!" Oh no, mealtimes there were nothing like the civilised ritual going on here, with the orderly correctness of, "Would you pass the salt, Dear?" from Mr Fowler or, "The meat is nice isn't it?"

Both of our hosts tried to jolly me out of my serious musing now, being concerned at my continued quietness. "We'll have a good day tomorrow eh, Liz? We'll be naughty and keep you off school so that we can all go to the park." They said this in a light-hearted bold manner, but with a chuckle. They were obviously worried at my lengthy silence and were trying to jolly me out of it. I became aware of this and entered into the charade with them. "Well, what do you think, then?" Mrs Fowler asked me. "Shall we be naughty and take the day off?"

I laughed as I replied to her in my awful cockney accent, "Too bloody right we will, an' all!" as I at the same time nodded my head in a knowing manner. They were the first words I'd spoken, and I was aware then of the shocked silence that followed, with Mr Fowler suddenly stopping in the process of dabbing his mouth with his serviette as he darted a shocked, surreptitious look at his wife; but I realised nothing of the gaffe that I had so innocently committed. What I had just said was an oft-quoted expression used by my cockney father, who on the rare occasions that he visited the family at home, often spoke in this manner, and I had simply emulated him, completely unconscious of the fact that I was within a different culture now where this form of speech was unacceptable. I was a proper little Eliza Doolittle in fact, but the shock to the Fowlers to hear such coarse language from one so young was profound, and it took them some weeks before they gently weaned me from the necessity of using common expressions like this in my normal day-to-day speaking. They had the sense to realise that it was the life that I had been born into which was to blame. There was no intention on my part to offend, I was just doing what came naturally to me. The Fowlers themselves were kind, intelligent, middle-class people; the proprietors of the then-famous 'Fowlers' black treacle', a well known commodity in the shops. It must have come as a terrible shock to them to have an uncouth cockney child, like me, planted on them but over the months that I was with them, they gently guided me to a more acceptable mode of behaviour, and it was to my lasting regret that in the end, just as I was blossoming into a pleasant agreeable child, they were forced to part from me.

"Would you like some water, Liz?" Mrs Fowler indicated the glass jug in the middle of the table, and at the same time poured water from it into a glass for me. Now this is a 'turn-up for the books', I thought to myself, as I remembered another of my father's cockney sayings. Water from the glass? At home, if we wanted water, we stuck our head under the kitchen tap and turned the tap on full. That's how *we* had our water.

I drank the water from the glass, demurely, right to the very last drop. Mrs Fowler was delighted. "You like water then, do you, Liz? Would you like another?" I nodded my head in response, and she poured me a second glass, which was a big mistake on her part because I later paid her in kind by wetting the bed, as she was to discover the next morning. "No more water for you in the evenings," she told me, as she removed the soaking wet sheets.

I suddenly became very tired now at the end of the meal. It had been a very long day. I was far from strong and, as I slumped in my chair, Mrs Fowler became concerned. She noted my deathly-white face. "I think bedtime calls," she said kindly. "We'll get the bath running."

I looked at her fearfully then. "We 'ad our barfs yesterday," I told her. "I don't need another one till next week," not realising that upstairs in this opulent house, a warm, modern bathroom existed. At home, in our shabby dwelling, our once-a-week baths were quite a performance, with my mother dragging this cumbersome tin bath from outside and into the kitchen, having heated up large saucepans of water on the cooker for this purpose. We went in one after another, but fortunately I went in first, as I was the cleanest.

Mrs Fowler laughed at me. "Liz," she said, "you'll have a bath every night here; but let's forget it for tonight shall we, and get you to bed? I can see you're very tired."

I felt great relief as she said this. Cor blimey! Wha' a good job the boys 'aint 'ere, I thought. They'd be 'orrified! Just to get them to bath once a week was a mammoth task for my mother.

I lay in bed then, watching with half-closed eyes, as Mrs Fowler tucked us up. She walked to the window then to draw the curtain, and I was suddenly wide awake. "Don'!" I said to her, "don' close the curtain; I don' like the dark." She conceded to this, but as she went to go from the bedroom, I called out in alarm again. "Don' shut the door," I called to her, "my mum never shuts the bedroom door at 'ome."

She turned and looked at me, "Alright, Liz," she said, kindly. "I don't like the dark or the bedroom door shut either."

The days that followed our rapid retreat from the imminent bombing of London to the relative safety of the Fowler's in the country proved to be a big upheaval in my life, the stress of which took its toll on my already delicate health. I soon succumbed to one of my regular feverish chest infections. My breathing became shallow, and Mrs Fowler, who I now called Auntie, became alarmed and sent for the doctor post-haste. She lavished every attention on me and seemed to enjoy having me at home with her.

I was a placid, uncomplaining child, whose only wish was to be loved and nurtured by someone. My former precarious living in a decrepit house, in one of the poorest parts of London, a house riddled with damp with no bathroom and an outside lavatory, coupled with the hazardous hours in the care of my unruly brothers, had made me a very forbearing being, grateful and appreciative now of the comforts and benefits of a warm house and the attention of these loving foster parents, who pulled me through this delicate phase of mine.

Cake-making, pottering in the garden with my foster parents and shopping most afternoons with Auntie became, for the next few weeks, while I was away from school recovering from my set-back in health, a pleasurable revelation to me. What a revelation! At one time, a few weeks prior, I had been a scruffy, coarse, East-End kid, who had only known the hardship of poverty. Now, though, I basked in my new life. I learned quickly the etiquettes of this higher society that I had come into, and, amazingly, I soon forsook my earlier existence. I had the intelligence to know which was best for me. I was aware also of the pleasure that Mr and Mrs Fowler, retired now with their family having flown the nest, got from their nurturing of me. I was like a second opportunity for them to cultivate a young being planted on them at a time when they had reluctantly, I think, relinquished all this.

Some two months after the mass evacuation, which had brought my sister and me into this new life, my mother decided to pay a visit. It was a blazing hot day that October morning when she had decided to come, and I sat in the shade on the front lawn awaiting her arrival. Even in this short spell of time of my being here with the Fowlers, I had changed. I was stronger and had become reconciled to my new way of living. I had stopped fretting for my former life, and so it was with no great emotion that I had received my mother that morning, when I at last saw her approaching me as she stepped onto the driveway of the house.

I almost failed to recognise her at first and when I did, I gasped in amazement. My mother was wearing on her person, an enormous fur coat which came almost to her ankle. It was buttoned up to a thick, bulky collar around the neck, so that her comparatively small head poked just above it. In one arm, she carried a rapidly-deteriorating bunch of flowers. She had had a long walk from the station in the day's unbearable heat, and she huffed and puffed now towards me, while bravely grinning from ear to ear, but I just continued to stare at her. The fur coat, I surmised, had quite clearly been borrowed from a neighbour just for the occasion, so as to make a good impression. In the penniless community from which I had recently come, the camaraderie among the people was prevalent. They would have shown concern for their neighbour's needs and, of course, my mother would have had no previous knowledge that this autumnal October day would be so blisteringly hot!

"'Ere we are then, Liz," she greeted me now, as she spotted me sitting there. "Gawd, don't yer look well," but disappointment clouded her face as she said this. "Ain't yer glad to see me?" she asked. I had made no attempt to get up and run into her arms, as she had expected. If the truth be known, I was a little ashamed of this ridiculous spectre approaching me. Was I already becoming, somehow, a snob? Would that be possible in one so young?

The Fowlers greeted my mother kindly, but there was no disguising the initial transient shock that registered on their faces as they noted her strange attire. She herself was a bit embarrassed then, as she handed over the wilted flowers. "I didn't know it was gonna be so 'ot,'" she explained, but she need not have worried. "Oh, they are lovely," Mrs Fowler lied. "They'll soon revive in some water," and she took the flowers from my mother like they were the crown jewels, before she handed her over to Mr Fowler for more kind attention.

Should I ever have the need to define the word kindness, I would hold up as an example the treatment that my mother received that day from my foster parents. Had she been the Queen she could not have fared better. They could have looked down their noses at her, derided what she wore that day, but they did none of this. In fact they did the opposite and treated her as an equal, and for that I will always be grateful.

Before my mother left, however, some very serious business had to be discussed with regard to my sister. "We're having great difficulty coping with her," my foster -parents confided. "She's reached an age when she needs firm handling," they added a bit tremulously.

My mother looked at them, puzzled. "Well, carn't you do tha," she asked in a slightly belligerent tone. "I've five boys at 'ome an' I 'ave ter be on at 'em all the time, an' no man to 'elp me."

The Fowlers remained calm. "Yes, we think you're marvellous," they told her," but we're grandparents now, and are passed wanting this sort of responsibility."

This was true. In fact, their young grandson lived with his parents just across the lane from where we were. Often I would play with Tommy. He was the same age as myself, and had his own little patch of ground in the back garden where we would dig and plant things. But on one particular day, he did something that stopped me going to him. I had arrived late that morning. He was digging furiously and when he saw me he scowled. "I'm sorry I'm late, Tommy," I started to say, but before I got any further, he, without a word, threw a shovel full of dirt straight into my mouth as I was still speaking to him.

In a shocked state I endeavoured to spit the foul stuff out and looked in amazement at him. He looked down and just continued digging, a little shamefacedly, while I, without a word, stood up and left him.

"Don't go, Liz," he had called after me. "Don't go; I'm sorry," but I left the garden and refused to play with him again. I suppose most children, having found themselves in the situation that I did, would have gone screaming to their mother, who no doubt would have resolved the matter; but, even at my age, I tended toward being a private, uncomplaining individual, who displayed an unforgiving nature to anyone who pushed me over the edge, and Tommy had done this to his disadvantage. "Grandma," he would come to the house and say, "will Liz come and play with me today? I've got some new seeds for the garden and I need her to help me plant them." But I resolutely refused.

"No," I simply said. I had cut myself off from Tommy, a necessary tactic I was to fall back on frequently in the ensuing years, it being the only way of me dealing with a situation that I could not emotionally handle. Tommy had cut me to the quick and the best way I could deal with it was to cast him to one side, to forget about him; and my foster-mother, in her wisdom, deemed not to interfere.

The conversation regarding my sister continued. I had been aware of the controversy surrounding her. She was five years older than myself, and was proving to be a bit of a handful to the Fowlers in all sorts of ways. Only the previous day, she had come home from school on a rusty old bike that she has found somewhere. She had sneaked it in through the back gate and propped it up against the summer house at the top of the garden. Unfortunately, during that night, there had been a heavy fall of rain and Mr Fowler was to find the next day, to his great displeasure, that the rust from the bike had transferred itself onto his newly painted house, the rust running in rivulets all down the front of it. What a terrible shock, his pride and joy defaced like this. It would all have to be rubbed down and painted again, but I had noted that this particular incident was not mentioned during the discussion taking place. Undoubtedly, my foster-parents realised that their set of values were completely different to those of my mother. She probably had 'five' rusty bikes leaning up against the shed in her backyard. She wouldn't see the relevance, only that the Fowlers were making a fuss about nothing; but this latest escapade of my sister's was causing serious concerns to our foster-parents as to whether they could carry on, and her ominous absence at the table with us now caused them further concern. Where was she?

My mother was in the process of leaving, when my sister burst in upon us. She stopped short when she saw who was standing in front of her, a look of utter surprise on her face. "Mum!" she exclaimed as she threw her arms around her, unlike the cool reception that I had given her earlier. "I forgot you were coming!"

My mother kissed her, then held her at arms' length. "What's this I've been 'earing about yer?" she rebuked her. "Wha' 'ave yer been getting up to?"

My sister chose to ignore this. "Are we comin' 'ome with yer, Mum?" was all she was interested in, but my mother brushed this to one side.

"Course yer can't come 'ome with me," she told my sister, sharply. "Wiv all tha' bombing goin' on, course yer can't come."

My sister clung onto her, crying now. "I don' wanna stay 'ere no longer," she wailed.

My mother stroked her head briefly, then, "Maybe it won' be for much longer," she consoled her, "but you jus' look after Liz, do you 'ear? Look after yer sister, or I'll ge' ter 'ear about it!" She said this in a much firmer tone, as she hurried away, no doubt relieved that her wayward daughter was now somebody else's responsibility, but her parting-shot as she went on her way had been to say over her shoulder to the Fowlers, "Anyway, if yer decide yer can't keep Barbara, then yer carnt 'ave Liz. They 'ave ter stay tergether!"

Maybe she thought that this would solve the problem they had discussed that afternoon: that, given the choice of keeping us both or losing me, the Fowlers would persevere with my sister, but as she had uttered those words, a coldness gripped me. No please, no, I thought, not realising that it wasn't through spite that my mother has said this to the Fowlers. I think that she genuinely, mistakenly believed that wherever I was to be, I needed the protection of my elder sister. How wrong was she!

I remember little of our eventual parting from the Fowlers, only that ultimately they were forced to call in the billeting officer, who had repeated to them those fatal words, "The mother stipulates that the two girls must stay together!" How could my mother have been so blind? Hadn't her first words to me when she came to visit on that blistering hot day in October been, "Gawd, Liz, don't yer look well?" Had she not seen how settled I was with the Fowlers?

My sister's wilfulness and immaturity at that time should have given her a clue as to how unsuitable she was for the caring of me, but now I was being wrenched from the very people who could have saved me from what was to come; being 'thrown to the lions', so to speak.

On reflection, as I ponder on this anxious period, I do wonder if perhaps a hint of jealousy on the part of my mother, my transference of affection from her to the Fowlers, could have been the reason for her stance. My cool reception of her at the first visit had been in contrast to that of my sister who had thrown her arms around her as soon as she saw my mother. Who could blame her for her resulting reaction?

My very necessary 'cutting off' mechanism came into operation at this time, the time of the removal from the Fowlers. It helped me to block out what was happening. It was my only method of dealing with stressful situations, and so I remember nothing of any kind words that might have been spoken to me then; no kisses or affectionate embraces given; nothing like that, but just me, sitting in our departing car, and looking through the vehicle's window at the Fowlers as they stood smiling tentatively while they waved us off. There were no tears from me, just a blank expression, and I didn't even bother to wave back at them. It was as though I had already cast off that privileged life which had been offered to me, where I had been so revered and loved. How could fate be so cruel one might ask? It was just as well I had no inkling then of what awaited me in the imminent, uncertain future; the fear and heartache that awaited me. Just as well.

HILL END

I remember little of the period between the sad parting from the Fowlers and the chaos that followed. My sister and I were being shunted from one unsatisfactory billet to another, until the resulting drama of all this eventually took its toll on my already delicate health.

I was once again admitted to hospital for a prolonged period of bed rest. My heart was a little weak, the doctor had told me, in a kindly manner. "But we'll soon get you well again," he had added in a jovial tone, as he took note of my frightened look.

Hill End was where I was to go. A large St. Albans hospital which was part psychiatric and part general, but now it had one complete wing taken over by the government for the treatment and rehabilitation of wounded servicemen. As the ambulance wended its way slowly up the drive that day of my admittance towards the hospital entrance, I found myself looking out through its side window. It was so reminiscent of that journey of mine, a couple of years earlier, to the London hospital, when the bells of the ambulance had been clanging urgently as it drove towards its destination with my being so very ill. This time there wasn't that urgency and the bells remained quiet, as I viewed the extensive grounds that we drove through where I noticed groups of men, clad in blue uniforms, wandering and conversing seriously with one another. Some of them were on crutches or in wheelchairs. Some had limbs missing and others were swathed in bandages. One or two of the men were smoking. There seemed a general air of solemnity around them as they walked the lovely grassland surrounds. There was no hilarity or smiles, nothing like that. All the wounded men talked quietly to one another in a serious manner.

I lay quite content in my hospital bed during those months of enforced rest, only being allowed out of it to go to the bathroom. There was some structure to my life once again. I wasn't as desperately ill as I had been in the London hospital; no treatment required, just plenty of calm and repose, so it was understandable that I actually revelled in my nice new safe environment. I was to remain in this idyllic situation for six months.

If the weather was nice, my bed would be pushed out onto the balcony and I could watch and wave to the wounded men and they would wave back to me. A teacher would visit the ward several times a week. I could already read fluently and she would enthuse over this.

"That's terrific, Liz!" she would tell me as I read to her. "Who taught you to read like that?" But I didn't know. I just couldn't remember a time when I wasn't able to read; it had just come to me. It was a natural gift that I had always had, which proved then to be my salvation really, having to spend all those hours resting.

Not every child, however, in the large ward was as compliant as me. In the bed next to me was every nurse's nightmare: a very naughty mischievous girl of about ten, who was always running off, or shutting herself in the bathroom, or pulling her newly made bed to pieces, anything to cause a rumpus! Her favourite trick was to look at the food brought to us, pull a face at it, then after making sure that no one was around, clamber to the head of the bed, open the window, which looked onto the grounds outside, and chuck the contents of her plate down onto the grass below! Of course, we all thought this was hilarious; it really used to brighten our day to see all sorts of things sailing through the air from the window: sausages, mince, fish, custard, rice pudding, all landing with a splat on the grass below. But one particular day, it all went pear-shaped. Two of the soldiers, in their hospital blue uniforms, happened to be lounging against the wall under the window. They were smoking and pointing to the food lying around when, suddenly, without warning, a whole load of spaghetti came flying through the air and landed 'plop' fair and square on their heads. The laughter from above stopped abruptly as we all darted back to our beds, while the culprit made a dash for the bathroom.

In the ensuing silence, we all looked towards the door leading to the ward, and sure enough, in a very short space of time, two enraged soldiers made an appearance with Sister, their heads covered in spaghetti. Needless to say, our fun and games came to an abrupt end when our erstwhile companion was sent home the very next day.

"I have quite enough to cope with," Sister had told the parents, "without the soldiers charging in here with discarded food all over their heads!" She didn't at all appreciate that it had livened up our days considerably.

On my eventually leaving the hospital, I was placed into some sort of Reception Centre. I suspect that the authorities were not sure what to do with me, and my sister seemed to have vanished into thin air.

I attended the nearest school, where it was my misfortune to come into contact with a cruel, sadistic woman teacher who seemed to take a delight in boxing my ears, even though she knew they had been damaged through measles which forced me, even then, to lip-read to a certain extent. She did this on several occasions, so that one evening at the centre, I had the most horrendous ear-ache which caused me to moan and scream for several hours, until I eventually lapsed into a fitful sleep. I can't remember any of the staff doing much for me. Maybe they didn't know what to do but at least I think they should have called the doctor, to give me something to alleviate the agony I was in.

My move from the centre in Harpenden to a billet in St Albans fared no better for me, and I realised before too long, the danger I was in upon being moved to this strange frightening place.

SCUM

I felt acute apprehension the moment I set eyes on my prospective new foster mother, Mrs Thrussle.

As I stood on the step of her front door, with my little cardboard case in one hand and holding onto the billeting officer with the other, we heard strange, high-pitched laughter coming from within. It seemed to go on rather long before Mrs Thrussel herself eventually made an appearance, and she stood looking straight at me as she sized me up and down while holding open the door.

"Oh, 'ere we are then." She tweaked my ear. "You're a nice little thing, ain't yer? Come in. Come in, then." She led the way along a narrow passage and into a room at the back of the house. The room was rather lacking in home comforts and, but for a window looking onto a small back garden, would have been rather dark as well.

Sitting around a table in the room were three young boys, looking very smart in their school uniforms. They nodded and gave me uncertain smiles as I put my small case on the floor and just stood looking back at them.

"I'm just about to get some tea," Mrs Thrussel told the billeting officer, "so you can leave 'er and get going if you want."

The woman needed no second telling, and she cheerfully went on her way with a "Goodbye then, Liz; be good."

I studied Mrs Thrussel as she popped in and out of the kitchen, placing cups and plates on the table in the room where I sat at the table with the boys. I studied her with a discernment that is probably unusual in one as young as I was then. I felt wary of her; wary of her continual laughing as she bustled about. She looked sideways at me with her small piggy eyes. "You'll like it 'ere with us, won't she, boys?" The boys just nodded. They didn't seem to have much to say about that, but Mrs Thrussel chatted on. However, almost immediately I didn't like her. I didn't like what I saw. "We 'ave some good fun don't we?" She pinched one of the boys on the cheek, and he looked half-smilingly at the others.

What she considered 'good fun', I was to find out about the very next day, and although I didn't realise it at the time, the knowledge was to come to me much later in life that I had been billeted with the female equivalent of a paedophile, but I was then completely innocent of such matters. Of course the manic laughing that the billeting officer and I had heard on the doorstep, pointed to the instability of this dangerous woman with whom the boys and I were trapped, and I slept restlessly that night because I was frightened; afraid of what was to come.

I didn't have long to wait when I heard her manic laughing through the front door again, as I returned from school the next day. I saw her face appear fleetingly at the window when she heard me knock. She dragged me in, shutting the door hurriedly, and as I walked into the back room, I was amazed at what confronted me. The boys were in a half-dressed state, their trousers down; but on my entrance, and seeing the shocked look on my face, they hastily attempted to make themselves decent. However, this crazy woman stepped in with, "NO! Don't pull 'em up; we were just 'aving some really good fun then. Come on, get them down again." And as she pulled their trousers down, laughing maniacally, she called out to them, "Who's got the biggest cock then? Come on get 'old of it. No, Danny, don't try and hide it." And she instructed the other two, "Get his trousers down, and pull his cock out. Let's see 'ow big it is. Ooo! Look," she whooped; and "ah ha, ha ha!"

This disgusting behaviour of hers in trying to get the boys to molest one another, carried on until the totally confused youngsters were sweating and exhausted, and I realised that my fear of the previous night had been completely justified. This was a mad woman, if ever there was one, completely and utterly mad.

"Alright," she'd call out at last, "put them away now and we'll 'ave some tea. We'll 'ave some more fun another day, eh?" The boys lived in complete fear and confusion, not knowing what to do about this frightening situation.

This unstable woman would sometimes be visited in the evening by a young couple, Terry and Eva. They would sit chatting with a cup of tea on their laps and their talk would suddenly become stilted with innuendos and, as they glanced across to where I sat quietly reading, fear would grip me. I would become conscious then of my breathing becoming shallow. What were they up to? What were they planning? Inevitably, I hadn't been in this mad house long before I lapsed into my former delicate state. Overcome by anxiety, my heart gave out again and my pronounced struggling for breath alarmed Mrs Thrussel so much, she was forced to call the doctor to me.

"She must have plenty of rest, and lots of quiet," the doctor told this strange woman, who looked at him intently with her piggy eyes, as she took instruction from him. He wasn't to know, of course, that the state I was in was brought about purely by terror, as he patted me on the hand when he left. "I'll come back and see you later on in the week, shall I?" he said with a reassuring smile. But in the following days, as I lay resting in the bed upstairs, I would suddenly hear the same piercing laughter when the boys were home from school and the usual fear would grip me as I contemplated what was going on downstairs.

One evening, as I lay in the darkened bedroom with just a lighted candle flickering on the table beside me, I heard the door being quietly opened. Mrs Thrussel entered, closely followed by Terry. She pushed him into the bedroom.

"Terry's come to see 'ow you are," she announced, while giving him a meaningful look, before she sidled back out of the door. "Go on," she had urged him, while giving him a shove. "Go on," she repeated. Terry came towards me, a wide grin on his face, and I felt a cold clamp of fear grip at me. Had he come to molest me, I thought; but even if he had, there wasn't much I could do about it: I was too weak to put up any resistance.

He came and sat beside me on the bed and almost immediately the grin disappeared as he realised how ill I was, and had been for several days. He sat looking at me, his mouth slightly agape. He took in my feebleness and my struggle to breathe and a scared look came over his face.

"Liz! You alright are you?" he asked me hesitantly.

"Yes, Terry; I'm alright," I answered weakly. He took my hand and to my surprise I noted a sudden rush of tears come to his eyes, as he summed up my frightening debility.

"You'll be alright, Liz," he said, trembling, as he stood up and backed away. "You'll be alright." He didn't seem to know what else to say, and his face, as he looked down at me, was full of remorse.

"You'll be alright," he said once again as he lingered at the door. "I'll come and see you when the doctor's been again, shall I eh, Liz?"

"Yes, Terry," I said. I closed my eyes and gave in to the overwhelming tiredness that engulfed me, as my fears subsided; but Terry and his girlfriend never did come to the house again.

If he had come that evening with the intention of molesting me when I was so ill, his sense of decency had obviously taken over, and for that I shall always be thankful.

Fortunately, my stay with Mrs Thrussel, with the piggy eyes and maniacal laugh, was cut short in the end after a heated discussion occurred one day between herself, the billeting officer and the parents of the three nice grammar school boys.

It was quite obvious from what was being said between these people that the boys had been brave enough to disclose to their parents what had been going on in that dangerous house.

"You'll be very lucky if I don't report this to the police," the billeting officer spat at this depraved woman, who had been intent on bullying these nice boys, who had in the end, been brave enough to speak up, thank God!

"We was just 'aving a bit of fun, weren't we, boys?" But any attempt by this perverted woman to exonerate herself was quickly cut short by one of the fathers.

"Fun, you call it? That seems a very strange way to me of having fun. I think you need to get yourself sorted out, madam, before you get yourself in real trouble. In fact I happen to be a solicitor and if I wasn't so snowed under with all the younger solicitors been called up, I'd take you on for what you were doing to my son, make no mistake."

The boys were helped by their mothers to pack their belongings, and my little cardboard case was also packed for me as we all prepared a hasty retreat from this frightening, mad woman. As we made our way to the front door, I hesitated and pulled back.

"What is it, Liz?" the billeting officer asked me. "Have we forgotten something?"

"I want to say goodbye to Sammy," I told her. "In the garden." I pointed through the window. It had been just a week ago that Mrs Thrussel had taken us all to the pet shop, a little way from the house and along the main road that we lived on.

"Look at this," she said, grinning at us, while she pointed to two attractive young puppies in a large cage on show just inside, on the other side of the window. The floor of the cage was covered in sawdust, and in each corner a large, heavy bowl of water and dog-meal stood for the puppies to eat and drink. One of the puppies bounded up to us as we looked through the window at them. He pawed at the cage, trying to get us. The other puppy lay quietly watching.

We laughed at the antics of the bolder of the two.

"Shall we 'ave 'im?" Mrs Thrussel asked us and, as we nodded our heads, she marched into the shop. She bought the delighted puppy, but as we were about to walk out with him, I tugged at her sleeve.

"The other little one is going to be so lonely on his own," I said, sadly.

Mrs Thrussel stopped short at my remark and shot a look at the other little dog sitting quietly watching us, as his former companion twisted and squirmed about in her arms. She stood contemplating the situation for a moment and then, "Oh alright, we'll take 'im as well," she said, taking her purse out once again.

When we got back to the house, with me holding and cuddling the timid little one, Mrs Thrussel produced a tin of corned-beef. She hadn't the faintest idea on the management or feeding of dogs, never having had one before and after the corned-beef had all gone, mostly eaten we noticed by the more robust puppy while the other just sat and watched, she didn't know what to do with them. She found a cardboard box and lined it with newspaper.

"We'll put them in this," she said, "and we'll put them to sleep overnight down in the cellar, as it won't matter too much if they tiddle down there."

We carried them down the steps and left them, much to the indignation of the one we decided to call Sammy, the noisy one of the two. He cried and whined for a long time. He didn't like being deserted like this, but from the other one we heard not a peep, and in the morning when we went to retrieve them from the cellar, we found him cuddled up to Sammy, quite dead. He had obviously been taken from his mother too young, which would account for his previous listless, delicate state.

Now I stroked Sammy, who was chained to a kennel in the back yard. His tail wagged furiously as I fondled his ears, and even as young as I was, my thoughts were that the puppy who had died had been the lucky one. He had escaped the life that Sammy now lived, just chained up for hours on end in that tiny garden. At least the little one, my young mind reasoned, would be happy in heaven now.

Mrs Thrussel looked on, tight-lipped and silent as we all left the house. I was glad to be shot of this unbalanced, dangerous woman, as I'm sure were the boys, who I never saw again. I believe they were taken by their parents back to London. Better they risked the carnage going on there than remain in the hands of a paedophile!

Thinking back later in life, when I became more mature, old enough in fact to discern more clearly the situation in that household, my mind's eye pictured Terry, sitting on the bed with me when I was so ill. I visualised again the sudden rush of tears to his eyes, coupled with the sad remorseful look that came into his face, and I remembered that he didn't come again with his girlfriend to Mrs Thrussel's after that night.

Basically I think, deep down he was a decent chap, who somehow had become intertwined with this evil woman, but when it had come to the point of carrying out a perverted act on a small child such as myself, his sense of decency took over. Maybe this had pulled him up short and opened his eyes to the downward slope that he was sliding down. His non-appearance again at that perilous house seemed to suggest this. What an amazing escape I'd had!

THE LANES

As we walked into the spotlessly clean house, a woman, who immediately reminded me of a penguin, shook hands with the billeting officer accompanying us. My sister had reappeared on the scene and stood beside me once again. I don't know where she had been, but here she stood now, a bored, resigned look on her face.

The house we entered was situated bang in the middle of a large council estate called 'Dellfields', and the woman who greeted us turned now to walk into the kitchen for the purpose of offering our deliverer a cup of tea. I realised then, as Mrs Lane walked back to us, why she reminded me of a penguin. The large bust on her persona stood way out in front of her, dipping then to a surprisingly small waist, followed abruptly by an enormous backside: all this supported upon amazingly slim legs and nimble feet; but if you viewed her sideways as she walked, her head jutting forward, there you had it, the uncanny likeness to a penguin!

No refreshment was offered at that point to my sister or me, as the billeting officer gratefully downed hers in the immaculate front-room where we all sat, until we became aware of a small group of resident children unashamedly gawping in curiosity at us through the window. I expect it was the car which had brought us, drawing up outside, which had at first drawn their attention to something going on. Only really important people had cars in those days, the early days of the war.

Mrs. Lane shooed the children away, as the billeting officer took her leave and then ushered us, with our small amount of luggage, to the bedroom. "Come down when you've unpacked," she said, "and you can 'ave some tea." We lost no time in doing this because we were hungry. On entering the room downstairs, we found that a little man was already seated at the table. This was Mr. Lane, as small as his wife was large!

My sister and I had placed in front of us then a plate containing a slice of bread cut into four portions. A scraping of margarine and a thin layer of jam had been carefully smeared on the bread. A small home-made fairy cake sat on one side of the plate, and all was eaten by my sister and myself in a minute.

We heard the front door slam as we sat there and into the room bustled a tall, well-built boy of about fourteen years, who regarded us with interest but didn't speak as he sat down on the opposite side of the table.

"Oh! Come on' Peter: you're late again," his mother reprimanded him, as she tottered in with a plateful of steaming hot dinner which she plonked before him. "Where did you get to this time? I've had to keep your dinner hot for ages."

Her son just got stuck into his meal and ignored his mother.

"Peter," she said now to him, "I asked you a question. Where have you been?"

"Nowhere," he responded. But his mother continued to nag him until: "BE QUIET, WOMAN!" he shouted at her now; then: "WHY DONT YOU JUST GO AND JUMP IN THE LAKE?"

The lake he was obviously referring to was situated in the picturesque park at Verulamium, just off the central part of St. Albans. It was large and beautiful with swans and ducks swimming with other wildlife, and resting on the little islands in the middle of the water. Trailing willow trees had been placed strategically around its perimeter, together with smaller trees and greenery. All in all it was astoundingly beautiful. To one side of this sizeable lake, one could walk over the little bridge to a boating and paddling-pool where a small cafe served ice-cream and refreshments to families picnicking there.

Roman ruins within the parkland were of great interest to the many visitors and tourists, but the lake, with all its attractiveness, was the main attraction. This obviously was where the son was inviting his mother to go and throw herself.

I looked up from my now empty plate in shock. I couldn't believe how this boy spoke to his mother. There was no way that my brothers back home in London would have dared speak to our mother like this because, if they did, my father, or even Father Joseph from the church, would soon be summoned to sort them out.

Mrs Lane appealed to the boy's father now, the little man sitting opposite us.

"Tony! Are you going to allow him to speak to me like that?" she pleaded with him; but he was obviously as frightened of his son as she seemed to be: he was just a sparrow in size, compared to this arrogant youngster sitting with us.

"Peter, don't speak to your mother like that," he ventured, after giving it some thought; but he might as well have saved his breath, as his son replied that he could go and jump in the lake as well! And there it ended: nobody uttered another word; just the sound of his older sister snivelling was heard as she sat beside her father. She was obviously as cowed by her brother's outbursts as her useless, ineffectual parents were.

I sat with my eyes downcast while all this was going on. Another madhouse, I was thinking.

STARVATION

The word 'starvation' was certainly operative when it came to mealtimes at the Lanes'. Breakfast each morning for my sister and myself consisted of a small bowl of cornflakes, and when I say small, I mean probably a tablespoon carefully measured into the dish, and on a plate at the side of the dish lay a thin slice of bread with a scraping of margarine and jam, finished off by a cup of tea, so weak you could almost see the bottom of the cup. I do wonder sometimes whether my liking for a decent cup of tea, and my lifetime addiction to butter spread really thickly on my toast in the mornings, dates back to this deprived time of miniature portions at the Lanes'.

My sister, on the first morning, had looked across the table in surprise at Peter, who had graced us with his presence at the table on time, as he tucked into a plate of egg, bacon, fried-bread and fried potatoes, with a mug of real-looking tea at its side. I had also looked, mouth agape, but Mrs. Lane soon put us in our places. "You needn't look at Peter like that," she told us, "he's a growing lad and needs his food." She placed an affectionate hand on his shoulder before sitting down to likewise portions herself. "Anyway," she continued, "you will get your free school dinners, won't you?"

This fact was just as well, as it soon became evident that our wartime rations of eggs, bacon, meat, etc, were used solely for the consumption of Mrs Lane's obnoxious son, to keep his strength up, and of course, his mother as well.

Teatime for us, in the house, consisted of more or less the same as breakfast, without the cornflakes: one slice of bread, cut carefully into four – presumably to make it look more; one small fairy cake; and the usual cup of weak tea. While Peter got bigger and stronger on our rations, and certainly more vociferous when telling his mother to "GO AND JUMP IN THE LAKE, WOMAN!" I, over time, became thin and listless and, but for our school dinners, probably would have just faded away.

I particularly remember one occasion, as I walked to school, when I passed a very old lady. She smiled at me in passing, as I observed her walking stick and stooped stance. It occurred to me then that I wouldn't at all mind changing places with her. Because she had smiled at me, I thought, she must be happy, so obviously she wasn't hungry as I was. No, I wouldn't mind at all I mused, as I continued on my way. It didn't bother me that if I did change places with her I would be old, but I wouldn't be hungry, I thought; that was the most important thing.

My reasoning over this, points, I think to just how desperate I was at the time. A few days after this incident, my sister had been called down from the bedroom late one night by Mrs. Lane. Sometime later I was also called down and sat on a chair, while I was told that my mother had died. She had been ill in a London hospital when a bomb had exploded nearby. A large pane of glass at the head of my mother's bed had fallen on top of her, injuring her badly. She had never recovered, and had passed away.

As Mrs Lane told me of her death, with my sister quietly sobbing, a shred of humanity obviously touched her and she asked me, "Would you like a nice cup of hot chocolate, Liz?" She had been battling all day with the task of imparting this awful news to us, and now that she had succeeded, she was obviously filled with remorse. But much as a hot chocolate, a rare treat in this stingy household, would have assuaged the hunger that gnawed away inside of me, I wanted nothing from this woman, who could allow my sister and me to starve while her spoilt, objectionable, overweight son consumed our food rations.

No, I wanted nothing from her, and so I simply looked at her, and said, "No thank you, Mrs Lane."

Soon after the death of my mother, my sister reached the age of fourteen when she promptly left school and started work in the offices of a large electrical company called E.A.C. meaning: Electrical Apparatus Company.

She was soon to meet Freda, a lovely sunshiny girl who, on realising how unhappy my sister was living in a half-starved state at the Lanes', managed to persuade her own mother to allow her friend to move in with them. "She can share my bedroom," Freda had told her mother, and my sister, who needed no second invitation, had soon moved her few belongings from that miserable house where we were both so unhappy, and gone to live with Freda, leaving me to continue my gloomy experience alone.

From that point on, as I spiralled into a morass of misery, I withdrew into myself. I discarded all emotions and ceased my nightly prayers: the prayers I had been taught at Sunday school.

"God always answers prayers," my teacher had told us children, but now I thought, what is the point? I had prayed for my mother when I just knew that she was ill. I had prayed that she might get better, so that she could take us home to London to my brothers, and yes, even the bombing! Being perhaps killed by a bomb, I reasoned, was surely preferable to the misery that I wallowed in now, slowly dying, I told myself, from hunger; but here I was, deserted and in a state of helplessness. What had I got worth living for? I just accepted that nothing was ever going to be any different – yes, I would probably soon die of hunger, I told myself.

Amazingly, I just carried on in my almost anaesthetised state, the hunger within me being virtually brushed to one side and forgotten. I had always been frail – now I was just a bit more frail.

During this long Second World War, that was causing so much misery for me, an influx of American soldiers suddenly made an appearance in England. They had entered the war after the bombing of Pearl Harbor, and now they seemed to be everywhere.

The soldiers were billeted in various buildings dotted around the town, which had been taken over by the government for the sole purpose of housing them. T hey lost no time then in entering into the social life of the young-set. The dance-halls were packed with their breathtaking appearance. Their modern, smart, uniforms left the English soldiers, with their drab, nondescript attire, completely in the shade. The girls flocked after them, and even Mrs. Lane's dull, colourless daughter, Peter's sister, managed to acquire one for herself. When she brought him home one evening, her delighted mother flapped around, offering him refreshments and congenial conversation, while her small, insignificant husband sat in one corner of the room, his ear pressed to a little wireless set whose battery was obviously running down, with weak transmission coming from it. I would be sent on the errand tomorrow. I sat thinking of carrying the quite heavy, dangerous thing, which contained acid, to the appropriate shop for replacement.

"Hold it carefully," I would be told, as I gingerly carried it in a strong bag. "Don't tip it, whatever you do." I didn't really need this warning. I was well aware of what I was carrying- it might as well have been a bomb!

"And how long are you in England for, then?" Mrs. Lane questioned her daughter's thin, gawky soldier, who without his showy uniform would have looked nothing.

His reply was so indecipherable with it being uttered in an American hillbilly accent, that nobody was any the wiser; no matter, here was perhaps a future son-in-law for Mrs. Lane, whose daughter couldn't take her eyes off him, even though he spent some of the evening, conversation being seemingly beyond him, picking his nose. There was no way that any young girl, unless she was truly desperate, could possibly fancy him, but then this girl, Peter's sister, was I imagine, quite desperate!

Christmas came around, and a false hilarity invaded the house. This gaiety was obviously what was expected at Christmas and someone had put up a tree, of sorts, in the lounge and some crackers were dotted around. But considering that I was still hungry for the most of the time, I didn't feel like entering into the spirit of things and just sat quietly.

"Oh! here they are," called out Mrs Lane, as a sudden knock on the door announced the arrival of her elder married daughter with the two grandchildren.

Mwah! Mwah! Mwah! She kissed the little ones as they entered. "Come and see what Grandma's got for you," she said, as she guided them towards the tree where little packages were dotted around, all in sparkly paper. "Can't have your presents yet though," Mrs. Lane told them, "we must have our Christmas dinner first." She bustled around, laughing and winking her eye at her younger daughter standing to one side with her hillbilly boyfriend, still picking his nose in contemplation of the scene in front of him. "Come on, you two love birds," she told them gaily. "Stanley, you sit here beside your 'beau'." She couldn't believe the good fortune smiling on the family at that time, with an expected engagement in the offing. She pinched his cheek playfully as she seated him. Anything that she could do to hasten this event, would be done, but as I looked then at Stanley, I wondered who he reminded me of. Oh yes, now I knew: he reminded me of the dopey one in the Laurel and Hardy series. Oh well, there's no accounting for taste, I thought, as I sat down with the others.

With exaggerated flourishes and gestures, Mrs Lane served up our Christmas meal. "We'll pull the crackers later," she told us, "when we have our cup of tea."

I got the usual small portion put onto my plate, while Mrs Lane's daughter looked on in concern. "Is that all that Liz is having?" she asked her mother, as she stared unbelievably at my plate.

"Oh, Liz doesn't eat much," Mrs Lane told her daughter, while I sat silently. I wished with all my heart that I was given a choice. Her robust son might need enough food to 'stuff' his face, but so did I, as my skeletal frame indicated.

"You should take her to the doctor," her daughter persisted, but this was just brushed to one side. The subject was closed as far as Mrs Lane was concerned.

"She'll live," was the only comment she made. "Now who's for seconds?" she asked, while indicating with a wave of her hand the Christmas fare still left on the table; but her invitation didn't include me, obviously, and I kept my mouth shut.

"Here you are, Liz, a present for you." I looked in surprise at Mrs Lane's elder daughter as she proffered a gaily-wrapped present to me with one hand, while balancing a cup of tea on her lap with the other.

I took this offering with a thrill. I had sat watching everyone else undoing their presents – the grandchildren especially who had a pile each – but I had been given nothing and so I undid this unexpected gift with excited anticipation. But as the Christmas paper fell away under my eager hands, my glee was soon replaced by bitter disappointment, as I looked down on a book which contained pop-up pictures of fairies and castles; a book, in fact, suitable for a much younger child, and of no interest to myself.

"Oh! How kind, how kind. What do you say, Liz for that lovely present?" Mrs Lane urged me, indicating with her eyes, for me to do the expected thing to her eldest daughter. I, of course, thanked her very much but did they not realise, I sat thinking, that I was now ten years of age: an avid reader already of the classics, such as Louisa Alcott's 'Little Women', 'Joe's Boys', etc. I had read all of them. I had shed tears over Black Beauty and been fascinated by Treasure Island. I had read most of the children's classics in fact, and now, here I was staring in disappointment at a toddler's book: all princesses and wands and castles which swam now before my tear-filled eyes. I quickly brushed the tears away, should anyone notice, while I retained a fixed smile on my face, then I laid the book to one side.

What did they think I was: a dunder-head? I was thinking to myself, as I started for school a few days later, the book held firmly under my arm.

"Oh, that's nice," Mrs Lane remarked to me as she saw me out of the door, "taking that to show your teacher are you?" What she never did know was that as soon as I walked into class that morning, I dumped the book into the nearest waste-paper bin. That's what I thought of the book – rubbish!

185

As I endured my stay at the Lanes', getting thinner and relying solely on the school dinners for nourishment, I became apathetic and listless. I was sick of the Lanes: the fat mother; the ineffectual father and daughter; and Peter. But something happened one day that shed a new light on Peter. I remember the incident quite clearly, as though it were yesterday. He came rushing into the house one day, really excited. "Quick, Liz," he called to me, "come to the shed: Puss is having her kittens. Quick! or you'll miss them being born."

'Puss' was a stray cat who had wandered into the garden. Because of her unkempt condition and her advanced pregnancy, it was obvious that someone had disowned her and the, as yet, undisclosed soft side of Peter had come to the fore when he had announced his intention of caring for her. His love for this mangy cat as he fed and groomed her, was in complete opposition to his mother's stance.

"You can't bring that into the house," she had told him. "It might even have fleas," she said. "Put it in the shed: I won't have it in the house," she repeated.

"Alright, woman," Peter had retorted. "I'll make it a bed in the shed," and then once again, in no uncertain terms, he had invited her to just "GO AND JUMP IN THE LAKE, why don't you?" And yet there he was on that special day, watching with a tender look on his face as 'Puss' gave birth to five tiny, squirming kittens, already being nudged about by mum and being licked from top to bottom as she cleaned them before they then found their way to the milk-bar.

"Cor! Look at that, Liz," Peter said, as we both watched in wonder. He whispered sweet endearments to 'Puss,' as she purred loudly at his approach. He had fed and seen to her needs; he really seemed to love this scraggy thing lying before us.

"Wow!" he said to me now, "five kittens. What are we going to do with them when they are ready to leave their mother? Oh well," he said then, as the cat scratched his chin, "we'll worry about that when the time comes, as long as they don't get into the house with old 'fancy knickers' in there!"

As I trundled home from school, I swung my school bag around and around in deep thought. I was, as usual, hungry, but I went to look at 'Puss' and her still squirming kittens before I entered the house through the back door. The house was empty! No Mrs Lane pottering around the kitchen; no one at all at home.

I looked around and took stock. In her methodical way, Mrs Lane had left everything all ready for the preparation of tea, and I noticed the sliced bread already on the breadboard, the margarine and jam beside it.

I looked longingly at the bread and marg. Who would know, I thought, if I quickly had a couple of slices? But I hung back, knowing that she would somehow know and I'd be in real trouble; so I went back out and wandered along the street looking for someone to play with, but no one was around. They were probably all in enjoying their evening meal, the thought of which made me even more hungry.

I despondently sat down on a wall to wait for someone to come out, but no one appeared, and as I wearily stood up to go back to the house, back to temptation, I was surprised to see Peter coming towards me. He had obviously got home early from school.

"Liz," he said as he reached me, "have you been to the house?"

"Yes I have, Peter and your mum's not in; but I never touched anything," I said quickly, looking unnecessarily guilty as I contemplated how tempted I had been to eat some of the bread.

He thought about this for a moment and then gave a little laugh when he realised what I had been getting at.

"Oh, hungry are you? Well you needn't have worried because Mrs Fancy Knickers has obviously gone into town, so she won't be back for a while yet. Come back with me will you, Liz?" I took his outstretched hand and walked with him back to the house.

"Lay with me on here will you, Liz?" He pointed to the settee in the living room, and I did as he asked. He lay beside me and put his arms around me, then kissed me on the lips.

"You know I love you, Liz," he whispered as he proceeded to cuddle and fondle me.

I lay very still, knowing that we shouldn't be doing this. The one thought on my mind was that Mrs Lane might make a sudden appearance, and this is exactly what happened! Although Peter had been confident that she had gone into town by bus to do some shopping and wouldn't be back for a while, his mother suddenly came into the room with a neighbour who she had been visiting and with whom she had stayed for a cup of tea.

"What!" she said, as she saw us lying together on the settee. " What's going on here?" she demanded. Her mouth gaped open in complete shock.

Peter quickly slipped off the settee. "Well, where have you been?" he shouted back at his mother. "I found Liz here sitting on the wall outside, and she's hungry; she's always hungry," he informed his mother. "You don't give her enough to eat." He very cleverly placed the ball squarely in her court, thereby taking the onus off himself.

Mrs Lane gasped at the crafty cleverness of her son in his attempt to transfer the guilt from his shoulders onto hers, but for once she stood up to him, probably egged on by the thought of the neighbour standing by her side, taking it all in. This would spread about like wildfire now among the other neighbours in the street. His mother squared her shoulders now as she stared fixedly at her objectionable son, and she did likewise to him, as he had done to her.

"Well, if we're talking about Liz always being hungry," his mother spat at him, "who is it who gladly eats her rations? That's never bothered you very much." This was fast becoming a battle of wills, and Mrs Lane seemed to be winning this time; but Peter stopped her in her tracks.

"You do as well," he retaliated. "That's why you're so fat!"

Mrs Lane gasped at this, and took a short intake of breath. "If only your father was here," she said, "I'd get him to sort you out."

Peter laughed at this. "He couldn't sort a fairy out," he ridiculed her. He was determined to have the last word as he shoved his way past his mother, emitting loudly, "OH GO AND JUMP IN THE LAKE, WOMAN!"

He rushed out of the room slamming the door so hard as he went, that the whole house seemed to reverberate.

Needless to say, the rest of my stay with the Lanes was quickly curtailed. The incident with Peter and me on the sofa, could not be ignored. Who's to know, had we not been discovered in that comprising situation, what might have happened; what might have followed on from the kissing and fondling.

"You'll be going to another billet tomorrow," Mrs. Lane coldly informed me the very next day. "We don't want you here any longer," she sniped, as though everything was my fault. "And perhaps you'll get more to eat wherever you go," she informed me, in a sarcastic manner. "Anyway," she continued, "if you've been that hungry here, you should have told me, not Peter." She spat this out in a spiteful manner. She certainly hadn't wasted any time in arranging my removal. The shame of this whole disgraceful episode of the previous day with Peter – the shouting and insults that he threw at her in the presence of her neighbour – rankled deeply with her, yet at breakfast she had still served him bacon, egg, fried bread etc, items of food that had never passed my mouth since I had been with them, so I was glad that I would be going. I had hated this house with the fat mother; the loud-mouthed son; the useless ineffectual father; and gormless daughter with her equally gormless American boyfriend. This woman must have known how hungry I had been while living with her. If it hadn't been for the 'free' school dinners, I'm sure I would have undoubtedly just slipped away. Yes, I was glad that I would be leaving that hateful household. Surely anything would be better than – or rather, nothing could be worse than – how I existed here. Yes, I was truly glad that I would be going.

There was just one thing that saddened me about the move, and that was the realisation that I would not be seeing Miss Jeffries again, as I would be too far away. Dear Miss Jeffries, my Sunday school teacher who, on suspecting my circumstances with the Lanes, with not being given enough to eat, always filled me, at the end of Sunday school, with generous portions of cake together with a very large mug of milk.

"Don't be afraid to eat as much cake as you can, Liz," she would urge me, " – it will only be thrown away otherwise."

Not realising that this was just a ploy for the purpose of sustaining me somewhat, I readily obliged, and ate my fill.

189

At my last meeting with Miss Jeffries, she had come and sat with me. The class had finished and I had my refreshments before going home. She smiled at my obvious enjoyment as I downed the last dregs of milk and she took my hand then:

"Liz," she said, looking earnestly at me. "Liz, have you been saved?" I was somewhat taken aback by this and looked blankly at her as I thought: saved – saved from what? But I didn't want to show my ignorance, so I simply replied to her, in the same reverent tone that she had used to ask me this question, "No, Miss Jeffries, I don't think I have."

She smiled, and patted my hand. "Then we shall have to do something about that next week, shall we, Liz?" I readily agreed to this, even though I had no idea of what she was talking about.

Now… I thought, as I packed my little cardboard case once again in the readiness for the move; now, I mused in an abstracted way, I shall never know what it was that Miss Jeffries wanted to save me from! Dear Miss Jeffries – how I would miss her. She had been the one beacon of light shining in my miserable existence; the one ray of hope that had helped to sustain me.

MUM

Once again I found myself standing and clutching tightly onto my, by now, well-travelled small cardboard case, on yet another doorstep, standing with yet another 'billeting officer'.

As usual, there had been not much to pack into the case: just a few outer clothes, together with a brand new nightie provided by the welfare, with my having grown out of the old shabby one that I'd worn since my evacuation from London.

"You can't wear that any more, Liz" the billeting officer had said to me the previous day, as she viewed the nightie. She had held it against me. "Look at that," she said. "Right above your knees, and almost falling to pieces! I'll get you another one from the stock." She had promptly gone and then returned with an old-fashioned flannelette monstrosity, with long sleeves.

She noticed the disappointment on my face, as I looked at this 'old granny' thing.

"I know that it's not very modern," she had quickly said, "but think how warm it will keep you in bed. And you can just tuck the sleeves up and shorten the length with a few stitches until you grow into it – you're growing so quickly" she added, as she attempted to extricate herself from this travesty.

It was true that I had grown in height, considering the starvation diet I had been on over the preceding months but girthwise, I had remained stunted, with my teeth appearing to be too large for my haggard face. I vowed not to wear this horrendous garment, which was in fact promptly replaced by my new foster mother, after she and the whole family laughed their heads off on seeing me in it as I had sat drinking my cocoa before retiring on that first night.

"You can't wear that!" my new foster mother had expostulated "that's for a little old lady, not a child – I'll take it back to the welfare office and get it changed; take it off and just wear your knickers in bed for tonight."

Here we stood now uncertainly before the front door of this new foster family, my coat slung over one arm.

A hairbrush – which I had forgotten to pack into my little case – protruded from the coat's pocket and, in my nervousness, I pushed it more securely back in. That was the one thing I must not lose, with my hair being quite long at that time and needing frequent brushing to prevent any tangles from taking hold.

As the billeting officer timorously knocked at the door, she gave me a sideways look to make sure that I presented a clean and tidy appearance. She had briefed me in the car regarding this new billet.

"Liz," she had said, "I hope you will be good at Mrs Owens' where we are going." I listened intently to her as she told me that it was where my sister was living now.

"We have gone to a lot of trouble to persuade Mrs Owens to take you in, as she hasn't got a lot of spare room, with her already having two grown-up sons, quite apart from your sister and Freda, her daughter," she told me. "So I hope you'll fit in and won't be any trouble, as I'm sure you won't," she added, while giving me an encouraging smile, knowing full well that I had never been guilty of this in the past.

"It's so difficult to get billets," she added almost to herself, "but I know you will be well cared for at Mrs Owens," she continued, "although, of course, she's not young anymore; in fact, she must be getting on a bit; so be as good as you can, Liz, will you?" She said this light-heartedly while continuing to smile at me, and I promised her that, "Yes," I would be good. It wasn't in my nature to be anything else. I'd had to conform for so long now that I took the line of least resistance to any situation. I had no rights not to conform!

The door swung open then, to reveal a fairly elderly woman with iron-grey hair done up in a bun on top of her head. She smiled at us as we stood there, while showing rather ill-fitting false teeth, which tended to slip around as she spoke. She stood, completely enveloped in a large, spotlessly clean apron, and looked as though she herself had been scrubbed from top to bottom, with not a blemish in sight. She exuded a completely no-nonsense stance but before she uttered a word to us, her eyes had shot straight to my very short gymslip which, much like the nightgown, I had completely outgrown, so that now it rode way up my thighs!

"Oh dear," she exclaimed, straight away before even inviting us in. "We will have to do something about that!" she said, indicating the offending garment. "What if you have to bend down in front of the boys? You would show all of your knickers! No, we can't have that." But then, without further preamble, she ushered us into the house with: "Come in, come in anyway: all the family will be home soon from work, so I can't hang about because they'll be hungry and expecting their meal on the table. Good Lord!" she said to me then, almost in the same breath, "is this all you have?" She took my little case from me and looked incredulously at it, while clicking her false teeth at the same time. "So this really is all she has?" she asked the billeting officer, unnecessarily again. "We will have to do something about that, wont we?" She stood in thoughtful pose for a moment, then:

"Perhaps we can at sometime make you a couple of things out of some dresses of mine that no longer fit me; we'll see." And Mrs Owens did indeed put a lot of effort into doing this during my stay with her, causing me extreme embarrassment at some time in the near future.

My first evening meal with the Owens was a happy yet enlightening experience, as six of us: me, my sister, Freda, Mrs Owens, Norman and Lou (Freda's brothers), all sat eating together a basic, but fulfilling meal.

Norman, the elder of the brothers and the more friendly hailed me with, "Wotcha, mate! You coming to stay with us, then? Who knows how we're going to fit you in." Everybody laughed at this, but then a very strange thing happened. Mrs Owens, in the middle of the laugh, suddenly fell asleep, her head almost drooping into her dinner, and her ill-fitting false teeth almost slipping from her mouth.

Nobody seemed to take too much notice apart from Norman, who exclaimed "Oh Gawd, she's off again," and he banged his knife on the table. "Wake up, Mum" he told her, until his determined banging brought her around.

While I sat, not understanding the episode, everybody else just carried on chatting as though nothing untoward had happened, but it left me feeling very unsettled. Nobody had bothered to explain to me that Mrs Owens suffered from a condition that caused her to just fall into a sleep without any warning, and this was to happen time and time again but, after a while, I came reluctantly to accept it, just as the others did.

It became apparent to me in quite a short space of time why Mrs Owens had agreed to take me in to live with the family. I was to become a forbearing companion to her for her lonely evenings, when she was left by herself after the family had sailed forth on their various activities.

"Bye, Mum," they'd call to her as they headed off. "Isn't it nice that you've got Liz now for company in the evenings?" And I was left to play endless games of cards with Mrs Owens and to listen to her unremitting episodes of her earlier life with 'Daddy'.

"You know, Liz," she stated one evening. "Lou is so much like his daddy." She had just waved to his departing back, as like the others he made his exit through the door. "A very serious character is Lou, and Daddy was just the same." She went over to the sideboard on saying this and picked up a large, framed photo. "Here's Daddy," she said in a reverent voice, showing it to me while lovingly holding on to it. "See the likeness, Liz?" she enquired of me.

As I looked at this portrait of 'Daddy' I perceived a grave, unsmiling replica of all three of his offspring, especially, yes, especially of Lou, with his looks of disquiet and his unfriendly manner.

I observed how 'Daddy' displayed on the photo a large Roman nose which seemed to dominate his whole face; yet had he smiled this would have detracted from the overall close attention that one paid to this unfortunate feature of his. Norman and Freda had, to a certain extent, inherited their father's features, but because of their sunny dispositions – they smiled a lot – this blight, this facet of the nose, was minimised and one found oneself looking instead into a pleasurable attractiveness. But Lou, on the other hand, because of his more sombre nature, did not display the same charisma as his brother and sister, and so this dominant feature was more obvious in him.

Mrs Owens replaced this photo now, with a sigh. "We do miss him you know, Liz," she said in a hushed voice. But then, in a business-like manner, she commanded, "Come on then, let's get on with this game of cards," as though it had been me who had caused the interruption in the first place.

These boring, incessant evenings with Mrs Owens playing cards, and listening to her reminiscences of her earlier life with 'Daddy', seemed to continue indefinitely, but one evening my ears pricked up when she confided to me how this former husband of hers, 'Daddy', was a 'cut above the rest'! Oh Yes.

"You know, Liz," she divulged to me that night, right in the middle, again, of our game of cards.

"You know, 'Daddy' was a very honourable man: you could trust him implicitly. Yes, *implicitly*, Liz," she said with some force, to make quite sure I understood. "When I tell you, Liz.." she said to me then, the game of cards once again having been forgotten for the moment… "When I tell you how I had to be on my guard ALL the time when I was young, with some of the whippersnappers I kept company with; how they would, while we were in the cinema, spread their overcoats across our knees, almost as soon as we sat down, but I knew what they were after, Liz," she told me vehemently. "I knew what they were after; I wasn't daft you know. I knew, oh yes! Not like dear 'Daddy'," she finished lamely, as she thought of him. "He was too honourable, Liz. He was an officer in the Army you know," she informed me with pride. "That sort of carry-on would have been beneath him. He knew how to treat a lady," she finished, in a dream-like state now as she thought of Daddy.

I had sat listening to her with my mouth agape. I hadn't the faintest idea what she had been talking about; what she had been insinuating. I was just eleven years old and completely naive of such things.

"Do you think those whippersnappers might have been after your sweeties?" I asked of her now, after giving it some thought. She looked at me aghast. "What!" she expostulated. "What are you talking about, Liz? Don't be so daft!"

I should explain that in those days of my childhood, knickers with a pocket in them were fashionable for small children, and when I was a little younger, and still at infant school, I loved this little garment with the secret pocket and I would make a great display of lifting up my dress and rummaging around to find the hanky I kept there, or even a few little sweets that I had secreted away. But, of course, once I started junior school, I would have been a laughing stock had I displayed such a thing. I wondered now, after having listened to this strange episode of Mrs Owens, were these knickers fashionable in her young day and she then had perhaps, like I had, kept sweeties in her pocket. Was this perhaps what those young whippersnappers were after? I could think of no other explanation.

Mrs Owens gave me a look then from under hooded eyelids. I think she realised that she had gone a bit over the top with me: I was, after all, still very young.

"Just forget what I was talking about, Liz" she said quietly to me. "You'll understand one day, when you're a bit older," and she scooped the cards up in her hands. Then, "Let's start that game again," she said, completely dismissing the subject.

Mum, in her indomitable way, I found, loved people coming to the house, be they dustmen, coalmen, the milkman; she didn't care. If she could catch them, she would. Cups of tea would appear and these tradesmen would be expected to stop in their duties for a while, and listen to all that Mum had to tell.

The men were wonderfully tolerant with her, and accepted with good grace the kiss she would bestow on each of them before their eventual departure. "Cheerio then, Mum," they would call, as they sped on their way; and even the young insurance man, who called one evening a week, even he was not exempted. Almost as soon as the poor man had entered the house, Mrs Owens would clutch at him, and steer him to one of the ancient armchairs in the room. A cup of stewed tea, that had been brewing in the teapot while standing on the fire-hob all evening, would be put into his hands, and then he would have to sit and listen patiently to Mum's tales of worry and woe, and he would gratify her politely with: "Well I never, Mum" or, "Is that so?" while every now and then, he would endeavour to make a move. But this wasn't allowed until Mum had told him everything, and so this poor man just had to sit and suffer before he could claim the small pittance on a policy that she had taken out with his large, well-known, and reputable insurers. "Who knows that one day you mighten set fire to the house," she had told the family, when she had first made this transaction. "Have another cup of tea before you go," he was eventually instructed. It didn't matter that this beverage was by now absolutely black because it had sat for so long on the hob!

It came as no surprise then, when this poor young man stopped coming. In his place, a much more mature man started to make an appearance, and he had no compunction regarding etiquette. He would just take the money, refuse the stewed tea, and shoot out again with, "Sorry, too busy to stop." He didn't hang around.

"What a rude man!" Mum would throw after him. And she would instruct me, while he was still within hearing, "Empty the pot, then, Liz. That's a waste of a good cup of tea." She said this pointedly, in as loud voice as she could muster. He wasn't going to get off completely scot free.

This demand of Mrs Owens to be in intimate contact with all sorts of people, though, was extraordinary. I had never in my short life then, or have I since, ever come across a person with such an outstanding need.

Nobody who visited the house was allowed to escape from her affectionate clutches, if she could possibly help it. This compulsion of hers for touching and communicating with everyone was, to put it mildly, quite bizarre, and one event that really stands out in my mind, when she truly came into her own, was the day of the Co-op lady's visit. "Come in, come in," she had told this lady, as she at the same time rushed to put the kettle on for the inevitable cup of tea. But then she stopped in her tracks as she took note of the pale face and tremulous movement of our visitor. She took her by the arm then, as she guided her to the one and only comfortable chair. "What is it, darling?" she asked her with concern. "Are you not very well?"

The Co-op lady attempted a brave smile as she timorously negotiated the chair. "I'll be alright in a minute," she told Mum. "I just got up feeling not too good this morning, but I expect it will pass off."

Mum looked at her doubtfully, and became even more concerned when the poor lady began to quietly cry, the cup of tea trembling in her hand.

"You shouldn't be out: you should be in bed," Mum told her. "Yes, well I'll get the bus home after this cup of tea," our not-very-well Co-op lady told her through her tears.

"Oh, we'll do better than that," Mum said with determination. "Liz, you look after our lady, while I get a car to take her home." And this is just what she did!

In her hurry, before she dashed into the street, she had forgotten to take off her all-enveloping overall, and as I viewed her through the window while she rushed along the pavement, I noticed that she also still had her slippers on. But, true to form, in an amazingly short space of time, she reappeared with a young man, who entered the house wearing a very surprised, questioning look on his face.

Mum lost no time then in assisting our Co-op lady into his car, with the words, "And I don't want to see you until you are completely better. The Co-op won't go broke if you just have a couple of days in bed." With that, she planted a goodbye kiss on her cheek, and for good measure, she gave one also to the bemused driver!

When it had materialised later that day, at the evening meal, what Mum had done – how she had persuaded this young man to respond to this act of mercy – everyone had, as usual, fallen about laughing.

She had apparently half-run, she told the family, to the main road at the bottom of our street, and she had then positioned herself in the middle of it, and waved her arms until the first car came along, which contained the young man. He had no option but to stop, or run her down! She had then, without preamble, jumped into the front passenger seat and had commanded the astonished driver to "Please come to my house – just up the road there – to assist our very unwell Co-op lady."

After an amazed silence from the family, as everyone digested this unbelievable episode, picturing Mum standing in the middle of the main road, still in her apron and slippers, and waving her arms about, Norman was the first to speak. He made some cryptic remark to the effect that "It was just a wonder that you weren't mown down in the process!" and of course this had brought forth fresh bursts of laughter. But Mum had reproached him with, "Norman, don't be so cynical," and then she had appealed to Lou, who had meanwhile just sat, looking horrified. "Lou," she said, "what do you think?"

"Well," he had answered, after giving the matter some thought. "I'll tell you what I think, Mum. I wouldn't have gone dashing into the middle of a busy main road, putting myself in that much danger, but I would definitely have escorted the young lady to the bus stop." He smiled as he said this: a damsel in distress was right up Lou's street. He liked the ladies, even in spite of his humourless disposition.

Mum was somewhat placated by this, though, and turned then to the girls, as she told them in a conspiratorial manner, "I expect the poor lady had her monthly 'wotsits', you know what I mean!"

"Oh! That's right, tell us all the gory details why don't you?"

Norman rounded now on his mother. "There are some things you know, Gel, that are private, as I've told you before, which us men don't wish to know about." He laughed then. "You really do take the biscuit sometimes, don't yer?"

Mum squared her shoulders at this. "Oh, it's alright for you men: you don't know what suffering is! And don't keep using that common language, Norman – calling me 'Gel'; what would…"

"I know, don't say it: what would Daddy say, if he was here?" – Norman finished the sentence for her.

Lou had heard enough: this rough way of speaking from his brother also got on his nerves. He refused to acknowledge, as we did, that it was all part-and-parcel of Norman's make-up to enter into this sort of dialogue with his mother, just for the purpose of teasing her and livening things up a bit.

"I have to go," he said, rising from the table. "I can't keep my scout group waiting." But he pointed a portentous finger at his mother before he left us. "Don't do anything like that again, or you might get killed next time," he warned her.

I loved this banter that went on each evening around the table: Norman and Freda with their sense of fun, and Lou in, complete contrast, with his pronounced, inborn seriousness. Obviously he was very much like his late father, 'Daddy', who, as Norman always maintained, still ruled the house from the grave.

THE BAKER BOY

Wally, however, was Mum's very favourite, with this outstanding need of hers to get close to people. He was the baker boy, and he would breeze in through the back door each morning, with his bread-basket slung over his arm, and grinning from ear to ear.

"Where are you, Mum?" he would call out as he entered, and if she wasn't downstairs, he would hurry over to the stairwell door and holler u the stairs, "Are you up there, then?" Mum would come hurrying down to plant a noisy kiss on his cheek, and then another, as though she hadn't seen him for ages, even though it had only been yesterday. He would pick her up then and swing her around, and they would fool about, laughing and almost toppling over.

"What will it be today, Mum?" Wally would then ask her in a high-pitched voice. "One or two loaves? White or brown?"

"You know it's brown, Wally, you rascal," she would reprimand him. The family often pleaded: "When can we have some nice, crusty white bread for a change?" but Mum knew best. "I know what is, and what isn't, good for you," she would tell them; and that was that, as far as she was concerned. The fact that she herself was unable to enjoy this lovely bread that the family had requested because of her loose false teeth, was kept discreetly to herself. If she couldn't partake of this pleasure, why should anyone else? was probably her innermost reasoning......

Even though Wally was nineteen, his voice, amazingly, had never broken, which is why everything he said was so high-pitched, like a

201

young boy; but this never bothered him, and it certainly never bothered Mrs Owens; in fact, in spite of this she had secret designs on him for Freda.

"Are you joking, Mum?" Freda said in horror when her mother divulged this to her one evening. "A baker boy!" she said, incredulously, "whose voice hasn't even broken. Do me a favour, will you? I'd have to be pretty desperate to marry him. Why don't you marry him yourself, if you're that keen." We all laughed at this, as we imagined Wally walking up the aisle with his bread-basket over one arm, and Mum clinging on to the other; but Freda was really affronted and sulked for a while after this comment from her mother. She wasn't that hard-up for a boyfriend, and even if she was, Wally would be the last on her list......

Fortunately for me, while I was at the Owens', there were respites from the long boring evenings playing cards with Mum, or listening to her accounts of her times with 'Daddy', and this was when the girls decided together not to go out after their day at work, but to stay in instead.

On one of these welcome evenings with them at home, I sat quietly reading, and as I read, I suddenly became conscious of a lovely sound coming from the front room. I realised that this was Freda singing, as she accompanied herself on the piano. I lay down my book and went unobtrusively to her, and I quietly sat, and then curled up on the settee as I listened, enthralled by her beautiful renderings of Ivor Novello songs.

'Shine Through my Dreams'; 'My Dearest Dear'; 'I Can Give You the Starlight' – all his ballads sung exquisitely by Freda in her spell-binding voice, and I floated into another world as I listened, until she suddenly became aware of me.

"Hello, Liz," she said, then. "How long have you been sitting there?"

"Can you sing some more, Freda," I just asked her. She laughed at this, but before she could reply, Norman came bursting into the room.

"Geroff that piano, Gel," he said to Freda, "and let's 'ave something a bit more lively: you're giving me the collywobbles listening to that." He flicked through the Novello album until he came upon something more to his liking. "Ah! This is better," he said to himself. He proceeded then to thump away on the piano, after shoving Freda unceremoniously off the stool, and he went into a loud rendering of "DON'T put your daughter on the stage Mrs Worthington! D-hon't put your daughter on the stage!" And then, "My car will m-e-e-t her, but her mother came to-o-o! It's a two-seater but her mother came to-o-o!"

As Norman continued to thump the notes out while he sang, Freda and I went into fits of laughter, but then a voice sailed forth from the kitchen. "Norman! Will you stop that racket; whatever would Daddy say if he was here?" Mum had considered Norman's raucous singing as an affront to her ears, and even Lou came into the room, looking immaculate in his Scout Master's uniform, before he went off to his troop, to see what all the noise was about. He hadn't the same sense of fun that Norman had, and was quite taken aback, but we just carried on laughing.

"I wish Daddy would stop trying to rule this house," Norman said now, mocking, as he relinquished the piano stool.

How completely different these two boys were, though, in character, I sat thinking now, as I took note of Lou's look of disapproval at his brother.

Norman, like Freda, was a bundle of fun and very popular with everybody, who found him a delight to be with, but Lou was a very different cup of tea.

A lovely girl would several times a week visit the house to supposedly see Mum. She was, I remember, a young supervisor of 'British Home Stores' in the town. She would pop in around teatime, and mum would embrace her and put a cup of tea in her hand.

As everybody arrived home from work, they were equally pleased to see this pleasant young person and would chat away to her, but as Lou entered the room he would stop short and glare at her.

"And what are you doing here – again?" he asked her rudely.

She would immediately be on the defensive. "I've come to see Mum," she would tell him, "not you," and Mum would back her up.

"Don't speak to Linda like that, Lou" she would tell him. "She's come to see me, that's all." Lou would smirk and just sit down for his meal. He knew better, of course, and so did we. We knew that she had been sweet on Lou for some time, but he didn't want to know about it. So, it was all the more surprising that he did eventually end up marrying Linda, so perseverance, as far as she was concerned, did pay off in the end, and Mum's delight, of course, knew no bounds.

But, to get back to Norman, with him being so different from Lou, and his cynical amusing remark about his late father the evening of the piano episode that he wished Daddy would stop trying to rule the house, there was a certain amount of truth in this statement of his, because 'Daddy' was always exerting his presence from the grave. Just the previous evening, it had become evident in a somewhat amusing way, with Norman, of course, being the perpetrator. Unfortunately, though, it backfired onto me!

We had all just finished our evening meal and Freda sat quietly reading a book. She started to laugh to herself, and in the end Mum said to her, "Freda, what are you laughing at?" Freda said nothing, but then she quietly laughed to herself again. "Freda!" Mum said to her once more. "I asked you, what's so funny in that book?"

"You wouldn't want to know," Freda said, tantalizingly, to her mother; But this got Mrs Owens all the more intrigued.

"Tell me, Freda!" she insisted, as her daughter continued her mirth; and we all by now had our own ears pricked to what was going on.

"Oh, alright," said Freda. "I'll read it to you, but you won't like it," she told her mother. This only got us all the more interested, as we sat urging her with our eyes. We listened carefully then while she read it out: "As the young man got up to open the door for this attractive lady, he accidently farted; then, as he quickly sat down, he inadvertently farted again!" Freda went into another paroxysm of laughter, as did all of us, but Mum went into a state of shock.

"FREDA!" she admonished her daughter now. "Freda, how can you read stuff like that! What on earth would Daddy say if he were her?"

"He'd probably have a bloody good laugh" said Norman, who was laughing the loudest.

"I just don't know what this world's coming to," Mum said, in a state of trauma now; and, as she collapsed onto a chair, her head drooped forward and she went into one of her 'sleep' episodes.

"Quick, Liz," Norman called to me. "Go into the kitchen and get a wet flannel for Mum." I shot out and returned with the flannel, while still laughing but, as I handed it to Mum, she somehow managed to swipe me across the face with it before she actually lost consciousness, as though it had been all my fault. From that day on, I was very wary of her, and the family weren't too pleased at what she'd just done. "You do that to Liz again and you'll have me to deal with," Norman told his mother when she came around. He was the eldest of the family and at times had to use this status with his mother, but in no way did I hold a grudge against Norman for this unintended gaffe of his. He had been a stable influence in my existence at the Owens', and I loved it when most mornings he would say to me at breakfast, "Well, how are we today then, Mate?" I loved him for this, but Mum always chided him with, "Norman! Speak properly. Don't keep calling Liz 'mate': it's common."

And Norman would nod his head at his mother. "Yes, alright, Mum," he'd say. "I know what you're going to ask me now: 'What would 'Daddy say if he were here?'"

THE DANCE SESSION

Dancing among the young set during the time I was at the Owens', was very popular, and so, some evenings were great fun, as the furniture in the large living-cum-dining room was all stacked up against the walls, or removed elsewhere, so as to make space for dancing to records on the gramophone. Freda, Barbara, Norman and Lou would invite their friends in and they would dance all evening to the popular tunes of that time. I was allowed to stay up and join in the fun, and I loved every minute of it.

Towards the end of these evenings, I would help Mum to make jugs of hot chocolate for everybody when they were all becoming thoroughly exhausted. What lovely times they were. But Norman came to the fore again on one of these occasions when an 'old–time' waltz was inadvertently put onto the gramophone. Everyone looked in amusement at one another, but before the record could be changed to something more modern, Norman dashed across the room to his surprised mother and without further ado, he pulled her to her feet and clasped his arms firmly around her.

"Come on, Gel: let's be 'aving yer," he said in that common way that so annoyed his mother. "This is more your era," he told her, and he dragged the poor, protesting woman across the floor with a flourish. With one arm around her waist and his other rigidly holding her right arm pointing straight out in front, he whirled her around and around, while he at the same time pumped this outstretched right arm up and down, up and down, in time to the beats of the waltz!

He gasped out the words of the tunes as they danced, and each time they reached the ends of the room, he would yank Mum's outstretched arm smartly down to his thigh, as he negotiated a complicated turn for them, before straightening up again, when he would stick his head high in the air and making, a concentrated effort, once again strive to reach the other side of the room.

"Norman! Put me down, put me down!" Mum was yelling at him. And "O-o-o!" as she did her best to avoid his clumsy feet. But Norman was having none of it, and continued with this undignified carry on.

Lou stood watching this debacle going on between his brother and mother with distaste. He was an excellent dancer himself, and didn't appreciate this lowering of standards. He and Linda were both skilled in this art and, while she stood with us, laughing at this carry on, Lou just stayed silent, a disapproving look on his face. But our laughter increased even more, as Norman and his mother stumbled once again past us for the last time of this crazy waltz, and negotiated just one more complicated turn. He twisted his head towards us, and mouthed over his shoulder, away from his mother's hearing, "Oh dear! What would Daddy say!"

As this never-to-be-forgotten evening neared its end, and to this day, I don't think that I have ever seen anything quite so funny, John, our recently widowed neighbour, who had come in to spend the evening with us, made a request to Freda.

"Before we all go home, Freda; would you sing to us?" he asked her. We had all suspected for some time that John had an intense liking for Freda. He had heard her lovely singing through the adjoined walls of our two houses many a time and was obviously very attracted to her, but he had a grown-up family, and one of his daughters was almost Freda's age. We were all aware, however, of the attraction between these two and, as Freda sang now, the atmosphere became electrified while they threw secret glances at one another. But Mrs Owens wasn't at all pleased. She had sat eagle – eyed, taking it all in, so that the following day all hell had been let loose.

"Don't get any designs on my Freda," she had told this neighbour as he departed. "She happens to be spoken for," she added.

Although Freda had heard what her mother had said, she kept silent while she saw all her friends off. Mum, by then, had gone to bed, but she lost no time the following morning in tackling her.

"And WHO..." she asked her mother at breakfast, "...WHO am I supposed to be betrothed to, then?"

"Well..." her mother stuttered. But now she squared her shoulders, and she said defiantly to Freda, "You could do a lot worse than Wally" and as Freda gasped, she added, "you know what a lovely boy he is."

"Oh-h-h!" exploded Freda now, in exasperation. "Oh-h-h we're not on that again, are we? When are you going to stop interfering in my life?" and with that she flounced from the table. But her mother was determined to have the last word. "Just remember," she threw at her daughter's departing back. "Just remember that you're still only eighteen, and you couldn't marry anyone, anyway, without my permission until you're twenty one: just remember that. It's your voice he's in love with, not you," she finished, cruelly.

Poor Freda, what had she ever done to deserve such scorn? She was a beautiful person with this spell–binding voice. ... "Her daddy had a fine voice," Mrs Owens had informed me one day. "He sang in the Abbey choir, you know, Liz," she told me. I didn't refute this at all. Freda must have inherited her lovely voice from someone, and it certainly wasn't her! The rendering of those lovely songs by Freda on that certain evening, as I had sat curled up on the settee, remained with me always, and whenever I hear them, even today, a picture of her comes into my mind.

I often sing Ivor Novello lyrics myself, having been blessed with a reasonable singing voice. His songs, I believe, will never die; unlike some of the transient rubbish that is churned out today.

With regard to Mrs Owens' cruel remark to Freda of the last evening, when John next door had so obviously shown his affection for her, I begged to differ. "It's your voice he's in, love with, not you," she had spat to her daughter, but Freda's voice alone wasn't what drew people to her. Her singing was a great attraction, yes, but her outstanding personality went way above that. I do believe that at one time, an agent was interested in promoting Freda, but her irregular features went against her, mainly her uneven teeth and slightly asymmetrical nose, neither of which would present a problem today, with all the cosmetic surgery available.

Freda was born before her time, I believe. Had she come onto the music scene today, I just know that she would have been a resounding success, so outstanding was her talent.

My time at the Owens' dragged on. I was starved of congenial companionship because the grown-up family all had their own outside interests, and I started to become somewhat depressed. My health started bothering me again, and as I attempted one morning to get out of bed, I slumped back on to the pillows. I was consumed by a debilitating exhaustion. I was aware of all the activity going on upstairs. "How much longer are you going to be in that bathroom, Lou? I'm bursting my breeches 'ere!" – this from Norman, who always left getting up until the last minute, and then went through the house like a whirlwind, so as to not be late for work. The others would be already downstairs, enjoying a leisurely breakfast, and the smell of burnt toast wafted up the stairwell where the door had been left open for Norman's rapid descent. He would then just grab a slice from the table as he dashed through on his way to catch the bus. "Umm, someone's burnt the toast again," he would throw back over his shoulder, as he hurried away.

"Norman!" his mother would call after him, but she needn't have bothered, he would do a repeat performance the next day, and the next.

Dear Norman. But as the smell of the burnt toast infiltrated my nostrils, I felt nauseated and just lay very still while the nausea washed over me. I was way too weary to move anyway, and then I felt that ominous pain below my ribs – yes, I had once again come down with pleurisy, the very serious illness that had hospitalised me in my infancy. I remembered, as I lay here now, how my five brothers had at that time been in and out of the bedroom, as I lay then, waiting for the ambulance, and how they had each held my hand, and told me: "You'll soon get better, Liz; in 'ospital, you'll see. And how Arthur had placed a little packet of my favourite biscuits in my hand. "From Mr Evans, Liz," the kind owner of the small grocery store, where Arthur had worked part-time after school.) "Yer've always liked those, 'aven't yer?"

Mum shot into the bedroom now. "Why aren't you getting up?" she shouted at me, but then she took note of how ill I was. "Oh," she then said. "Freda!" she called down the stairwell to her daughter. "Could you come up here for a minute?" The two of them surveyed me as I lay there, so still.

"You should have the doctor," I remember Freda saying to her mother.

"How can I?" Mrs Owens replied. "It costs half–a–crown to call him in, and I just can't afford it." This statement of hers, regarding finding money for my welfare, was inconceivable, considering she had managed somehow to find enough money to take me to the pictures with herself a few days earlier to see a film that was showing at the local cinema. "Have the day off today, Liz," she had said to me. "We'll go and see that film on at the Gaumont Cinema, that I fancy.

My schooling didn't matter that much to her. Freda had of course gone to grammar school, she informed me one day. "But there's not much fear of you going there," she had told me. "You have to be quite clever to go to a grammar school you know." As it turned out, she was right. I was, in the end, allocated not to a grammar school, but to a commercial school, because of my English ability.

As we had hurried along the road on that day of our visit to the cinema to catch the bus, which was imminent, we actually passed the school–board lady, who was undoubtedly visiting a recalcitrant pupil absent from class, but this didn't bother Mum. "Hello!" she called out, as the woman passed us on the other side of the road. "Just going to the pictures," she informed the startled lady.

"Mum!" I hastily whispered to her, "that's the school–board lady."

"I know" she replied to me in a nonchalant manner, and then, increasing her stride, she just said "Come on, or we'll miss our bus." And now, here I was, desperately ill, and she couldn't afford half–a–crown to call a doctor to me!

After almost a week of agonising pain and fever, and just being assisted by Mrs Owens each day to use the chamber–pot from under the bed, which I needed very little as I ate nothing, and drank very sparsely,

I began to slowly feel better. I opened my eyes one day, after a more restful sleep, and who should be sitting beside me, without his bread-basket, but Wally, and he grinned at me from ear to ear.

"Trying to frighten us all to death, are you, Liz?" he joked with me. "Beginning to feel a bit better now though, are you?" His face took on a serious look as he showed his concern. I nodded my head at him.

"Wally!" I then said in surprise, "you haven't got your basket!"

He laughed heartily at this. "I'm not here to sell you bread, Liz" he chortled. "I've come to see how you are!" and then Freda came in and sat beside us. I thought she looked a bit tearful about my condition, but Wally took her hand as she sat down. "She's feeling better at last," he told her quietly, and I was surprised to notice that Freda didn't pull away from him... and there was something else... what was it? Yes, that's it, that's what it was! Wally's voice had broken, so that he now spoke manly; much more manly. He wasn't a boy anymore: he had left that behind. Is this what had brought Freda round to reciprocate the fond feelings that Wally, for so long, had obviously had for her? I very much hoped that this was the case. They were two very dear people and truly deserved one another. Yes! I fervently hoped that they would be together... and, eventually, they were.

My illness had kept me from school for almost a fortnight, so I was pleased to go back to see all my friends once more, but I had been left very fragile now, and as I walked into class, the teacher took one look at me and led me by the hand to the headmaster, who questioned my suitability for being there.

"Should you be here, Liz?" he asked me. "You look very pale and thin; shouldn't you still be at home?"

I replied hastily in the affirmative. "I'm a lot better," I told him. "I want to be here at school." But I could see that he wasn't satisfied with this, as he peered at me over his glasses. He took me by the hand and walked me back to my class.

"Liz must lay in the rest–room each day after lunch," he told my concerned teacher, "until she gets stronger. She should also have double her milk allocation to build her up a bit," he said, looking at my wasted

211

frame; and I must say that that was what I needed for quite a few weeks. Convalescence was what I really should have had, but this was the next best thing.

On reflection on my serious illness, however, I realise now, that to come through it without more-serious consequences was indeed a small miracle. To go those days without anything very much passing through my lips must have rendered me quite dehydrated but because I was so ill, it went unnoticed. In theory, I should have been hospitalised and put onto an intravenous drip to prevent this danger of dehydration and I can well understand now, why neglected children of today can just quietly die through lack of responsible protection, but I was meant to come through, to live my life… My reasoning often asks, why? I could have slipped away quite quietly at that time! But it wasn't meant to be.

This serious illness, however, did not prevent a daunting happening occurring to me just as I was getting back to normality and feeling much better. I had got up for school on that morning in question, feeling decidedly groggy. I wanted no breakfast apart from a cup of tea.

"You look white this morning, Liz" Mrs Owens remarked. "I hope you're not going down with another chest infection." She said this with concern, but I assured her that I would be alright. I didn't want to stay off school, but once again I found myself in the rest-room.

"You mustn't come to school tomorrow if you're no better," my teacher had told me, and so, there I lay in the rest-room in agony with these terrible stomach pains I had kept quiet about.

On getting home from school that day I had to run urgently to the toilet. It was freezing cold in there, being outside the house, and I sat shivering as I tried to cope with the waves of pain going through me; but then, as I wearily stood up, I was horrified to see blood on my undies. I rushed indoors to Mrs Owens. "Had I got appendicitis?" I asked her, while I almost fainted with pain and shock! She looked at me quizzically now, as I stood trembling unsteadily on my feet.

"Why, Liz," Mrs Owens said, in a disbelieving voice. "It can't be, surely." She said this almost to herself. "You're only just eleven years old;

surely it's not that already, is it?" she asked me; but I had no idea what she was talking about.

"Come lie down here on the sofa and I'll get you some pain-killers," she told me kindly. "I'll get Freda to have a word with you when she gets home." From that point on, for the remainder of the afternoon until the girls did arrive home, mum would periodically stop what she was doing, as she prepared the evening meal in the kitchen, and she would peep at me from the door, presumably to ascertain that what had gone on before was still the case. When at last the back door opened and Freda made an appearance, she was literally grabbed by her mother and shoved in to the corner of the room, where a hurried conversation took place, while furtive glances were thrown in my direction.

Freda took a long intake of breath through her nostrils as she sat with me then, her hand holding mine; an intense look of serious concentration emanating from her features.

I had noticed on occasions, that she often employed this idiosyncrasy of hers, when in deep thought, and faced with this difficult task before her now, it came fully into play.

"Liz," she began, and she paused then while her mother placed a cup of tea silently, onto her hand, as though this might sustain her daughter somewhat.

"You know, Liz," Freda started again, and went on to explain to me, as best as she could, the full intricate details of this phase of my life into which I had entered, albeit rather early, but her troubled face brightened then as she imparted to me that when I married, it would help me to have children. "That's a nice thought, isn't it, Liz?" she said radiantly. She took my hand again. "Join the club, Liz," she said, as she got up, having done her best with regard to this very difficult undertaking that she had been given.

Once Mrs Owens got over the shock of my very early entry into maturity, she was cock-a-hoop', and couldn't wait to announce to everyone at an appropriate moment, when we were all at the table for our evening meal that: "Liz has today entered into womanhood!" She thought she was being very modern in making this, for me, very embarrassing statement, and was surprised at the shocked silence that followed. The family just suddenly stopped eating, and the cheerful chatter that had gone on faded away as everyone just stared at their plates, taking in what had just been disclosed, with this shock announcement bestowed upon them in this sudden manner.

"Did you hear what I said?" Mum was very disappointed at this reaction from the family. "Liz has…" she hesitated here…" Well don't you know what I'm talking about?" she asked, much to everyone's discomfiture.

"Yes, we do know," Norman spoke up now. "We're not daft, Mum. But there are some things that are private." It was unusual for the eldest son to be so serious, and his mother was rather taken aback at this unsmiling stance that was being taken by Norman, but she refused to be intimidated by what he said. "Oh, come on," she expostulated, "we're not living in the dark ages now, you know – don't they give sex education in the schools these days? It's not a taboo thing now, like it used to be."

Much to our amazement then, Freda, who up until this point had listened intently to this banter between her mother and Norman, suddenly burst out laughing, and then she laughed again. "What's so funny, Gel?" Norman asked, as he lapsed back into his common way of speaking that so annoyed his mother.

"Yes Freda, what is so funny?" Mrs. Owens was somewhat relieved, now that the subject was taking a turn for the better and she actually permitted herself to smile as she asked her daughter this question.

"Alright," Freda conceded, when her laughter subsided, "I'll tell you. Yes, Mum," she nodded at her mother; we did have sex education at school, and the rotters left it all to poor old Miss Arkwright to tell us."

"Well? What's so funny about that?" Mum asked.

"What's so funny?" Freda replied. "Well, I'll tell you Mrs Owens: Miss Arkwright was a spinster, about eighty, and she had a moustache! The poor woman was so embarrassed, she could hardly breathe in the telling, and we all sat there sniggering knowing that we could have told her a few things that she didn't know about." Freda went into fresh peals of laughter, while her mother gasped, "Freda!" The rest of us joined her in her mirth, excepting Lou, who got up then and left the table. He'd heard enough: he hadn't smiled once through all this heated discussion, but his sister had certainly 'saved the day'. T hat was Freda for you: ever optimistic. She always refused to be bogged down by controversy, and in this latest incident, she had rescued me from acute impending embarrassment.

THE MIDNIGHT INTRUDER

Mrs Owens was not to be silenced on this delicate matter, however, and repeated this indiscretion of hers when my father made one of his rare appearances a few weeks later: on a Saturday, when all the family were at home.

She had kindly invited him to have a mid-day meal with us, before he then took me out; and as he and I rose from the table for this purpose of leaving the family to visit the shops in the town, before he started his journey home, she came right out with it. "Oh," she said. "While you're in the town, Mr Bone, would you mind taking Liz to a chemist and buying her some sanitary-towels, because she's, er, she's started her... you know what she's started don't you?"

Once again, there was this horrified silence around the table, as my father took in what was being said to him like a bolt from the blue, and he fixed her then with a sharp meaningful look. "Was that really necessary?" the look clearly said. He delved into his pocket and drew out a bank note. "I think that's more for a woman to do, Mrs Owens," he remarked, as he passed the note to her. "Here, that should see her alright for a while."

Mrs Owens felt a bit embarrassed herself now, as she realised her blunder. "Well, I can't afford to buy them," she justified herself, putting the onus on my father, as though he begrudged giving her the ten pounds for my very necessary needs. "I only get so much for Liz, you know, and it doesn't stretch to extras like that."

"What a stupid woman," my father remarked to me, as we left the house. "Has she no tact at all? There's one born every minute you know, Liz," he told me laughingly, trying to lighten the situation, as I walked self-consciously along the street beside him. "And right in front of those two young men, as well" he said, almost to himself. He shot me a concerned look, then, "Liz," he said, "if you ever get worried about anything – *anything!*" he emphasized, "don't hesitate to get in touch with me. You know that I'm usually in Harpenden at the weekends staying at Jimmie's, don't you?"

I nodded my head, not really realising at that time to what he was alluding, but he did seem very worried regarding my situation: my living with this elderly, tactless woman, who could so brazenly disclose in front of her two young, unmarried sons, the most intimate details of my delicate condition. Only much later did I realise to what he had been hinting at, this man who walked beside me; who up until that point in my life had had little contact with me. His heavy drinking had alienated him from the family, until my mother's death, when he attempted to make amends, albeit rather late; but there was nothing lacking in his concerns for me at that moment in time – nothing, as his facial expression so clearly intimated. He was truly concerned for his daughter... very concerned.

Mrs Owens' revealing all to her sons at that time; her utter and complete indiscretions before two rapidly maturing young men in the full throes of puberty, were indeed to have consequences. Maybe the woman with her own old-fashioned values had inadvertently thought the boys were pure and strong and could rise above any temptation that would come their way, but one of them had not been capable of this. His mother, in her foolishness, had obviously stirred up an awakening in him and, so it was, that a few nights later I was aroused from a deep sleep. I wasn't sure what had disturbed me, but as I opened my heavy eyes to the half light of the room, I was completely astonished to see Lou kneeling beside the bed. I gasped in surprise. "Lou!" I said, but he quickly put his hand over my mouth for me to say no more, and he put his finger to his lips. "Sh-h," he said quietly. "Sh-h!" And he then turned around and quickly went out of the room on all fours.

At breakfast the next morning, he had already left the house, and I thought no more about the incident but, of course, I realised that he had been wrong to be in my bedroom. I was sleeping in the tiny little box-room on my own at the time. I knew that had Mum been aware of this happening during the night, she would have 'floored' her son, as big as he was, being very puritanical herself, but she alone was to blame for this incident, I'm sure. She should have used some common sense, and not been so naive as to think that her revelation to all and sundry regarding my menses would have no consequences. Yes, as my father had remarked to me, she was "Stupid! Liz – one born every minute." He obviously had realised the danger of this woman's insensitivity, and he was to bring this home to her when later when I was compelled, in desperation, to do something very dangerous – not that I was ever touched by the boys, apart from this one lapse of Lou's, but the whole consequences of the situation that I was in, drove me to act very unwisely at a certain time in the not-too-distant future; and, in my naivety, I wouldn't, of course, have realised what could have been the consequences of my actions

My early maturity brought with it an imbalance of my stability! Where before, I had been compliant, happy to go along with the flow – I now became a bit unstable and would break down, crying in class. I wasn't sure why, but my teachers paid no heed to my distress. They obviously knew of my situation… Mrs. Owens would have made quite sure of that. I was still at junior school, after all, and the only one in the whole establishment to enter in to maturity so early. I just wasn't ready for it. "Why can't you do P.E today, Liz?" the boys would ask me, but they weren't as dumb as they made out to be. They knew exactly what they were about, and I would tell them hotly to mind their own business!"

On one particular morning, however, during music, the young Welsh teacher, Mr Evans, played his violin for us. It was a very nostalgic piece that he played, and he looked through soulful eyes at me all the way through the rendition of this melancholy composition.

I had this awful urge to laugh at his puppy-dog eyes drilling into mine, but I managed to control my mirth until we got back to class, when I then exploded into quiet laughter, and I laughed and laughed. "Mr

Evans was in love with me," I told myself. How funny, how absolutely hilarious – I could not control this quite maniacal convulsion that took hold of me, making my shoulders shake and my eyes water as I sat back at my desk, aware of the curious stares thrown in my direction by the other children and our teacher. They must have thought I'd gone quietly mad, but they said nothing, but then the same thing happened a few days later, when the headmaster announced in morning assembly that the doctor and nurse would not be coming after all that day for the 'General Well-being' examination of us children – it would be on Friday instead.

We were aware then, on this announcement from the Headmaster, of a loud gasp from the boy who stood next to me. "Oh no!" he called out in disgust to the Head, "have I washed my feet all for nothing then?"

There was a general outburst of laughter at this, but I went beyond everyone else, and as the laughter from the others subsided, I still laughed uncontrollably. I could not stop, even had I tried. Once again the tears flowed from my eyes and my shoulders shook, as this maniacal mirth took control of me. But this time, everybody gawped at me, as I was led away by an understanding teacher. Yes, their sustained stares told me, I had obviously gone completely mad!

THE HIDEOUS DRESS

I became quite aggressive in this unstable phase of my life, which in normal circumstances would have been quite alien to my usual complacent nature – so much so that my teachers became quite alarmed. My temper knew no bounds at times and it came to the fore one day when I was taunted by a rather spiteful girl right in front of Alex, a rather dishy boy who had asked me to be his girlfriend, and always pigeon-holed me to partner him in the country dancing, much to the envy of the female fraternity of the class. But this particular girl, unlike the others, who would sometimes gently tease me about this, was always scathing in her remarks to me regarding him and me, and on one particular day, her nastiness knew no bounds.

I had come to school that Monday morning, already feeling mortified by what I was having to wear.

Mrs Owens, true to her word of when I had first moved in with the family about making me a few garments to supplement my handful of clothing with which I had arrived at the house, had spent the weekend industriously cutting down and altering one of her dresses that she no longer wore, with the purpose of fitting me out in it. She cut and tacked and sewed all weekend until she was quite happy that she had got it right, and she was very pleased with herself.

"Come on, Liz," she had said to me on that morning. "Put it on," she encouraged me, "and I hope you appreciate that it's taken me all weekend to make you this." She nattered on as she helped me to struggle into it. "Well?" she said at last to all and sundry.

Freda and the boys stood aghast as they surveyed the spectacle standing in front of them.

"What do you think, then?" she asked once again. "I've done a good job there, haven't I?"

Freda was the first to break the silence. "You can't send Liz to school in that!" she told her mother in alarm.

Mrs Owens was very affronted at this. "Why not?" she enquired of her daughter, in a very annoyed tone. "Don't you realise it's taken me all weekend to make that for Liz?"

"You shouldn't have bothered," Norman chipped in now. "Nobody should even be seen dead in that!" he slipped out of the door quickly then; he was already late for work, and so, there I stood in this monstrosity of a dress, whose shoulder-line came halfway down my arms, and pockets that should have been just below the waistline reposed glaringly on my hips.

"We'll find you a belt to give you some shape." Mrs Owens bustled off upstairs and came down with the item, but it didn't do much to take off the hideous appearance that I presented as I stood forlornly there. "Ah! That's better!" she assured me, but I wasn't convinced, and as I dragged myself unwillingly to school that morning, I was full of dread.

As I entered the building, I didn't have long to wait for things to happen.

"Oh! Ha ha ha," my adversary, the spiteful, jealous girl shrieked, as she looked in shocked amazement at the comical appearance, once I'd taken off my coat. "Oh! Ha ha ha ha. I don't believe this!" she was shouting out to everyone as she pointed at me. "Just look at Boney!" She never called me Liz; I was always 'Boney' to her, my surname being Bone.

Everyone turned to look at this peculiar sight standing uncertainly there and I noticed that Alex was among them. But he wasn't laughing: he just stood looking very embarrassed.

Suddenly, a rage consumed me and a fist shot out involuntarily and made contact with my abuser's nose. Blood spurted everywhere, and one of the children ran to get a teacher.

"I'm not sorry," I sobbed to this sympathetic lady, as I sat with her in the rest-room; the headmaster having been summoned to sort out the furore.

"She was making fun of me," I told this nice teacher, as she sat surveying the hideous dress that I had been made to wear to school that morning.

"I understand, Liz," she was telling me, kindly.

"And I hate being in this school anyway!" I spat out.

"Where would you like to be then, Liz?" she coaxed me gently, as I calmed down.

"I'd love to be back with Miss Noble," I almost whispered, as I thought fondly of the headmistress back at the infants' school I attended before coming to the juniors.

"And what was so special about Miss Noble?" this patient teacher said now, as she smiled at me.

My thoughts went back to this treasured school where I had been so happy. Where I happily wore the undergarment with the secret pocket in it, and no-one laughed when I sorted this pocket out to retrieve my hanky or to find a sweetie to suck, and Miss Noble kept Rusty, her dog, in her office. He would lie obediently in his basket under her desk and sometimes we would be privileged to take it in turns to take Rusty around the playground to stretch his legs. "Come and let me know if he does a 'whoopsy'," Miss Noble would tell us, and if this did indeed happen, we would rush excitedly back to her office and then pull up sharply at her door before announcing in a serious tone, "Please, Miss Noble; Rusty has done a whoopsy in the playground," whereupon she would hurry out to see to it.

I wouldn't care too much, I thought at that moment, that Alex wouldn't be there. He can't like me any more, anyway, I told myself, after what I'd just done. Only boys got into fights like that, didn't they? giving one another bloodied noses. But my benefactor laughed now as I finished telling her where I would like to be, especially the bit about Rusty. "Welcome to the real world, Liz," she said. "Oh that we could all stay in that stage of our lives: it would be so much easier…"

I found myself later that morning being escorted home by the welfare lady to tackle Mrs Owens about sending me to school in that hideous dress. "Do you think you could find something for Liz that fits her properly?" she asked Mum in an icily polite tone.

Mum stood there gobsmacked, as she took in what the welfare lady had said to her. It was bad enough to have had her morning interrupted by this completely unexpected visit, but as she had stood on the step of the front door that morning to be confronted by the two of us, with me standing there in that awful dress, her mouth had gaped open so that her loose false teeth, which for most of the time slipped and slid around anyway, almost fell out! She knew instinctively then as she viewed the dress afresh. It dawned on her just how ghastly it looked. She realised at that moment what we were there for, but she wasn't going to be browbeaten by this hoity-toity woman standing before her now in the living-room of her own home, oh no! "I'll have you know that it took me all weekend to make that dress for Liz, because when she first came to me, she had practically nothing!" Her hand went up involuntarily to her mouth as she said this, with such force, and putting such emphasis on the word 'Nothing', that had she not, her teeth would probably have shot out onto the floor.

The welfare lady, realising the tactics Mrs Owens was using, in an attempt to extricate herself from this awkward situation, decided then to take a less-aggressive approach.

"The thing is, Mrs Owens... let's sit down and take the weight off out feet, shall we? And a cup of tea would be nice," she added, smiling now, as she attempted to reason with this offended woman. She followed Mum through into the little kitchen, and as the two of them stood supping hastily-made tea, me having been somewhat forgotten in the living-room, I listened to the continued discussion between these two through the open door.

"The thing is, Mrs Owens," the welfare lady continued, "I believe you have a daughter yourself; is that right?"

"Oh, Freda you mean? Yes, that's right," Mum answered, "but of course, she's grown up now, you know."

The conversation between them was taking a more congenial turn now – the beverage they held in their hands obviously taking effect, helping them to take a more rational approach to this prickly subject.

"Oh yes, Freda is grown up now and working – in a very good job, I might add," she informed my benefactor. "And call me 'Mum'," this lady was told, much to her astonishment. "Everybody else does, don't they, Liz?" Mrs Owen shot her head around the door as she asked me this, whilst nodding her head vigorously.

The welfare lady accepted this rather unusual invitation, albeit with some surprise, but she was, no doubt, beginning to realise that it was better to try to stay on the right side of this animated woman rather than on the wrong side, and so she took full advantage of it.

"Er... well, Mum," she started hesitantly; but then with a forced camaraderie she said jovially, as she at the same time touched Mum on her shoulder, "Well now, come on, Mum – be honest – would you have sent your Freda to school in a dress like that?" They both as one looked toward my pathetic form. She forced herself to laugh a little as she asked Mum this. Might as well go the whole-hog she was obviously thinking, but Mum wasn't that bothered and, without even considering the question she, quick as a flash, shot back at the welfare lady, "Oh, there would have been no need for that because, you see, my Freda went to grammar school, where everyone wore uniform; and anyway, Daddy made very good provision for all of the family. Not like poor Liz, who came to us with practically nothing, just the bare essentials!"

At this point, the welfare lady decided to abandon this wasteful topic of conversation: she was never going to win with this woman, however much she tried. She briskly brought the matter to a close, then. "I'll take Liz to the welfare clothing store," she told Mrs Owen. "They'll provide her with a nice skirt and blouse for school, but we mustn't waste time," she said, so anxious was she to get away from Mum. Her time anyway was precious: there were other children who equally needed her care.

As we made our departure, Mum threw her arms around the poor woman's neck and kissed her. It was as if they had been lifelong friends. "You're so good to Liz," she told her, as we then got on our way.

What a relief! I was returned to class with no more being said and, as I stole a sideways look at my tormentor, sitting very quietly now with her red swollen nose and tearful eyes, I thought to myself: 'Who looks stupid now, then?' My eyes swept uncertainly to Alex, sitting over the other side of the class. He smiled secretly at me and my heart fairly burst with joy. 'Alex still likes me,' I told myself. 'Oh! He still likes me.' How lovely that I was obviously still his girlfriend. I could still be his partner in country dancing too. I hadn't lost him after all.

Although after this serious incident I made a real effort to control my aggression, something happened a few weeks later when it stood me in good stead.

I was running during morning break with a small group of children from the playground back to the classroom to pick up a ball that we had forgotten to take out with us. As we ran along the hall, a voice boomed out at us: "And where do you think you're going, then?" We stopped in our tracks as we were confronted by the caretaker, a somewhat shifty character who I had always noticed never looked anyone squarely in the eye when they spoke to him. We stood uncertainly now, looking at him as he scowled at us. We were not sure what to say but then his eyes alighted upon me, and he drew me to him and he enfolded his arms around me. "It's all right," he was telling us now, as his scowl changed to a smile, showing his unkempt teeth. He clutched at my very-well-developed bosoms and held me close to him as he said this, but it wasn't all right as far as I was concerned. I objected to his slimy manhandling of me and I could smell his stinky breath wafting over my shoulder. I instinctively then, in a flash, lurched forward almost double and, at the same time, shot my heavily-clad foot backwards, straight into his crotch. He staggered back against the wall behind him and he groaned loudly.

"You BITCH!" he called after me as, with the others, I ran back into the playground. "Wait till I see your teacher," we heard him say.

We were all a bit traumatised over what had just happened and stood looking silently at one another. I was particularly worried that I would be in further trouble, but this grovelling man... this bit of scum... said nothing to anybody, of course. If he came across me at any time after this misconduct of his, he would just give me that certain look, and I in turn gave him an equally certain look that told him that I knew that he would keep his mouth shut over what had happened. I wasn't completely stupid, young as I was.

I had been very tempted at that time to confide in Mr Bates, our then class teacher, about this unmentionable episode that had so bothered me, and which had brought my aggressiveness to the fore. My trust in Mr Bates had been complete since an incident which had taken place within the classroom a few weeks earlier…

For days, Mr Bates had got us making coloured paper chains and big silver stars to decorate our classroom for Christmas. It had been lots of fun, if somewhat messy, and one boy in particular seemed to have more paste on *him* than any of his paper chains.

Mr Bates had looked in amazement at him. "Tom!" he had said, "I do believe you have more paste on you than on any of your decorations! I think perhaps we had better stick you up instead." We all laughed heartily at this and so it was that, as he had stood that morning holding onto a stepladder, all ready to hang the decorations, we were all in a very jovial mood.

"Now who doesn't mind going up ladders?" Mr Bates asked us children, as he stood with his foot on the bottom rung of the ladder to keep it steady. "There's quite a few chains to hang, so who doesn't mind heights?"

Several of the children clamoured around him. "Me, Sir! Me, Sir! I don't mind," they said. But Chloe pushed herself forward. "Can I, Sir? I did bring that big, silver bell, didn't I, Sir?"

Mr Bates hesitated at this bit of blackmail. "Well, I would rather one of the boys…" he started, but Chloe insisted and he reluctantly gave way. "All right, but be careful," he instructed her, as she quickly clambered up the ladder and then, too late, he realised his mistake as loud laughter broke out in the class.

"Whoo-hoo!" and "Ah-ha-ha" everybody screamed. "Look at Chloe's frilly knickers!" Chloe didn't bat an eyelid though; in fact, she just laughed herself and tantalisingly went a bit higher.

"Oh, Sir! Look! Look!" the delighted boys were calling as they continued to laugh. But Mr Bates kept his eyes averted and looked staunchly downward while holding firmly onto the ladder.

"Now, now, boys. Stop that," he told them, completely embarrassed, and he instructed Chloe while still looking at the floor. "Chloe, will you come down now, please? I think one of the boys should go up the ladder..." That decent man had refused to look up at Chloe's knickers and that's why I respected and trusted him. And so, when this creep of a man, the caretaker, had violated me that day, I thought seriously about confiding in Mr Bates. "Tell him, Liz. Tell Mr Bates," the other children had urged me, but at the last moment I had lacked the courage. I'm sure that had I spilled the beans, with the other children as my witnesses, this unsavoury character must surely have got his come-uppance; by my hesitation and eventual silence, though, I had let this disgusting man off the hook and probably given him the opportunity at some later date to assault some other unsuspecting child who, in all likelihood, would do the same as me, and stay silent. One can only hope that the caretaker was eventually caught in the act, but usually this type of misfit of society would be too crafty and clever for this ever to happen, unfortunately.

ESCAPE!

Time dragged by at the Owens', with the endless boring card-playing sessions and the listening to Mum's unremitting reminiscences, 'Daddy' being the main topic. But these evenings were interspersed with Freda's singing. What a joy it was to me; it certainly alleviated some of the misery I suffered. But I was becoming desperately unhappy and disillusioned with my lot. My happy disposition was gradually being eroded away. I was becoming very sullen and one day this fact showed itself when Mrs Owens came from the living room into the kitchen with a cup of tea for me. "Here you are, Liz: that's for you," she told me. "Drink it up before it gets cold then," she urged me now, as she noticed the surprised look on my face. We'd finished our meal a while ago, but I did as she asked before putting the empty cup in the washing bowl before me. She then looked at me with a smile hovering around her mouth. "Did you enjoy that, Liz?" she asked me.

"Well, it was all right," I replied. In actual fact, it had tasted horrible. She burst out laughing now, and I could hear the others behind her in the living-room laughing as well.

"That..." she chortled, as she held her ill-fitting false teeth in. "That... " she began again, "he-he, ha-ha... was the grouts from everyone's cups. I'm glad you enjoyed it," and she fell against the wall while holding her side, consumed with mirth. But I didn't see the funny side of the joke. She knew I liked an extra cup of tea but this was disgusting, repulsive, in fact, especially drinking *her* grouts. I felt I might have been contaminated by this obnoxious brew that the family had conspired to create for me and I held my throat now and gagged! This caused the family to laugh even more, but as Mrs Owens observed my disgust, she became annoyed with me.

"Oh, come on, come on. Where's your sense of humour?" she spat at me. "Miss High-and-Mighty, that's what you are!" she told me, as she walked from the kitchen.

I stood, feeling I had reached a new 'low'. It was bad enough that I had recently been given the task of going around each morning with a bucket from bedroom to bedroom to empty the chamber pots from under each bed, (the lavatory being outside, as some were in those days), and now this!

My state of mind as I sat with her that evening for the inevitable game of cards, which lay now on the table at which we sat, was sombre.

"Oh, stop sulking, Liz!" Mum reprimanded me. "Let's get on with this game. We'll play pairs tonight, shall we? That keeps us sharp, you know," and she spread the cards face down all over the table.

I tried to enter into the spirit of the game, as I forced imminent tears back, but my heart wasn't in it. And then the inevitable happened: Mum drooped her head and went into a deep sleep. 'Oh, not again!' I thought. This was obviously going to be the pattern tonight: me just sitting there waiting for her to wake up so that we could just carry on, with another long, boring evening ahead of us. Why should this happen to me? I asked myself, while everyone else was out enjoying themselves. I visualized them as I sat there: the girls going merrily off that evening to a 'hop', which was held at the local community centre. They had taken ages to get ready after their hurried evening meal. "You do the washing-up tonight, Liz," they had told me in their haste, "and we'll do it tomorrow – and the day after," they added, as if to console me.

There had been a lot of giggling going on upstairs from the two of them, as they prepared for the much-looked-forward-to weekly event and they were calling out to one another. "Oh yes, wear that! It's lovely." And then from Freda: "I'm not so keen on the colour of this lipstick now, since I bought it, but it will have to do; I can't afford another one just yet.

And so their chatter went on until they emerged looking quite lovely: my sister with her naturally blonde hair curling round her shoulders, and Freda looking radiant, her face wreathed in smiles.

I looked in envy as the two sailed out through the back door smelling strongly of eu-de-cologne. "Don't wait up," Freda called to her mother.

I fully understood why the girls were so excited as they made their way to this Friday night 'hop'. Only a couple of weeks had gone by since they had been pressurised into taking me with them, when Mum had been unwell and had stayed in her bed for a few days. "Take Liz with you," she had pleaded with the girls. "She can't sit here all evening on her own."

The girls had looked doubtful as they had considered this request. "She's really too young," Freda had said, "and it's very late finishing."

But Mum counteracted this with, "Well, as it's a Friday, it won't matter too much because she doesn't have to get up for school tomorrow."

I was cock-a-hoop when the girls reluctantly took me along. "You'll have to sit in a corner, Liz," Freda told me, "because you're really too young to be going at all." But I didn't care about that – that didn't bother me. Just being with the girls and the sense of freedom I felt was fantastic. What a night!

The sound from the noisy band inside the hall wafted through the air before we had even reached the doors, and the excited babble of the young dancers as they thronged into this electrifying place greatly added to this completely happy atmosphere. There seemed to be hordes of them pushing their way into the hall; it was just as though they couldn't get in quickly enough. Some of the girls clung onto their American soldier boyfriends' arms as they shoved their way inside. The English soldiers standing around the edges of the hall wearing their drab battletop uniforms, stood hardly a chance against these Americans who strutted about looking very handsome in their military-style garb. There was far more mystique surrounding them than our poor dull-looking soldiers could ever boast of. There was, however, a good camaraderie amongst these two differing sets of servicemen with their glaringly contrasting uniforms. No rivalry existed between them. Everyone was at the dance to enjoy themselves and to forget about the war for a few hours while they were able to, the war – in its fourth year – being at its height.

From my seat in the corner where Freda had placed me, having literally managed to smuggle me in among the deluge pouring through the doors, I sat pop-eyed at the frenzied dancing going on in front of me. No-one had lost any time in getting onto the floor to dance in a completely animated fashion to the jive that started the evening. Over the men's shoulders the girls went and through straddled legs they were pulled! This way and that way they danced, with arms and legs flailing in all directions. It was as though their lives depended on it – the rock music from the band getting louder and louder by the minute!

In no time at all, it seemed, the end of the evening came. Everyone had had their fill of pop, served from the small bar at the back of the hall which had done a roaring trade all night, quenching the thirsts of the frenzied dancers. Through the air now came the melodic strains of the 'Last Waltz', and the couples took on a seriousness in their movements as they listened, mesmerised by the singer's melancholy words of Vera Lynn's "Goodnight, Sweetheart – See you in the morning… Goodnight, Sweetheart – when the day is dawning." They danced closely to one another as they swirled around the floor.

To my surprise, then, I became conscious of my sister gliding past in the clutches of a very regal-looking American. He was gazing tenderly into her eyes as they past, and I felt a bit apprehensive. She was, after all, just sixteen. But I needn't have worried because I listened to her conversation with Freda on the way home. She told her that the American had been quite honest in revealing that he was, in fact, married, but he had the need for a girlfriend in England – would she consider it? With reluctance, my sister had replied that she could not. Girls then did not enter into illicit affairs as they do now. There was too much at stake at that time, anyway, with babies being born out of wedlock unacceptable. No, no – as sad as she felt, my sister, with great reluctance, had had to spurn this would-be lover.

… as I came rudely back to the present, the whole, sad, debilitating situation of me sitting in this dreary room, playing these dreary card games with Mum, hit me full on. Was this what my life was going to be now? I asked myself: just placating this elderly woman through each long, boring evening? I felt downcast; trapped! What could I do? I thought, as I looked wildly round the depressing room, lit only by economically-dim lighting. It was as though I looked for a means of escape! I could stand this no longer – no! I decided to end the game rapidly, while she was out of it. I looked quickly at her sleeping form before I then turned over and sneaked a look at each down-facing card, so that when I awoke her, I would know where the pairs were. By cheating like this, I could bring this utterly spiritless game to a quick end, and then perhaps she would let me go to bed, where I could read my books.

"Mum! Wake up!" I implored her then and she opened her eyes.

"Oh! Where were we?… where were we?" she said in a daze. "Oh look, Liz, let's call it a day, shall we? I'm extra tired tonight." She threw me a guilty look, as though at that moment she realised how hard it was for me.

"Come on then, up those apples and pears (stairs)," she told me cheerfully and I at once went to my bedroom. But I was in a strange mood now. I think it was that I'd reached the end of my tether at last. I sat on the bed, contemplating escape. I couldn't stand this life anymore; I just had to get away from it all. Why should I be treated like some general dogsbody while everyone else enjoyed life? I thought. Did no-one care about me? I suddenly caught sight of myself then in the little mirror by the bed. What I saw there didn't improve my frame of mind at all. The face that looked back at me was made to look hideous by the ungainly hair surrounding it. Another one of Mum's innovations was the cause of this ugly and not very presentable hairstyle. She had just chopped my lovely long hair right off. "Let's do away with all this," she had said as she brandished the scissors inches from my face. "Short hair will be so much more manageable," she had told the family as she had hacked away a few days previously, and now look at me! I sat thinking, as the tears started falling. I look absolutely ridiculous with the length on one side of my face being shorter than the other. That, then, was the straw that broke the camel's back!

I found my little purse, which still had some birthday money in it, and I just sat there on the bed with it clutched in my hand until I heard Mrs Owens' footsteps come lumbering up the stairs and then her bedroom door opening and closing. I slipped stealthily off the bed and hastily down the stairs to the back door, which I closed behind me very quietly. I felt free! Free to walk away from my misery. I felt no fear, no remorse, as I made my way to the bus stop at the bottom of the road. I caught the last bus into the town, where I hoped to get a connection to Arnos Grove train station, and then I would be well on my way home into London. I breathed a sigh of relief as the bus started up. I tried to ignore the questioning look from the conductor: it was ten o'clock and rather late for a young girl to be out.

With minutes to spare, I was soon jumping aboard the bus in the town that would take me where I needed to go, and once again, I ignored the questioning look from this conductor as he handed me my ticket. I turned my head to the window. I spoke to no-one: I was only interested in getting home. It was nobody else's business. My mind had been made up and I had acted upon it!

THE STRANGER ON
THE TRAIN

A hand shook my shoulder now; I had without realising it gone into a deep sleep during the long bus ride.

"Come on, Miss. Arnos Grove." The conductor gave me a concerned look. "Are you all right on your own?" he asked me kindly.

"Yes, I'm all right," I assured him, as I quickly alighted from the bus, but now, as I stood there on the pavement, I was suddenly afraid. It was completely dark!

I had forgotten about the nightly wartime black-out rule in Great Britain, in case of enemy aircraft flying overhead – indeed, in the distance, I heard the eerie wailing of the sirens warning people to take cover before any bombing started, and even the departing bus, I noticed, had suddenly turned its lights off.

As I stood then, in my fuddled state, completely disoriented by the pitch black and not knowing what to do or which way to go, I became aware of voices in the distance to one side of me and I turned towards these voices, which sounded light-hearted and jolly, interspersed with laughter. Coming up to me, was a group of young people. One of them walked a bit in front, while holding a torch and as they reached where I stood, the torch was directed full beam onto me. Everyone stopped then, looking in surprise. A little kid was the last thing that they were expecting to come across obviously, and then one of them spoke. "Hello. What are you doing here all alone at this time of night?" The young lady who addressed me stepped from the crowd now and approached me.

"I've run away," I told her, quite brazenly. "I'm looking for the railway station to catch a train to Old Street. My relief at making contact with these people gave me back my confidence, and I felt quite safe now in revealing my daring escapade to this friendly lady. She gave a small gasp though, as she thought about what I had just told her, but she unhurriedly took my hand then, just as one of the boys came back to us from the group, which had quietly moved on.

"Come on, Janet! Come on, we'll miss a lot of the dance if we don't get there soon. Come on now," he pleaded with my good Samaritan, as they passed me.

"Look, come with us; we're going past the station," she told me now, and we hurried to catch up with the group.

As we reached our destination, Janet turned me to face her. "Look," she said, "don't speak to any strangers. You shouldn't really be out on your own." I could see that she was unhappy about leaving me but the others were calling out to her again, as they continued on. "Come on. Come on, Janet!" and she reluctantly left me there.

I seemed to sit on the platform then, waiting for the underground train to Old Street for a very long time. I sat and shivered; partly from cold and partly, I believe, from fear. I was the only one on the platform and the train coming in would be the last that night.

As it pulled into the station, I saw nobody in the carriages. I threw aside any misgivings that I might have had as I had sat there shivering and I entered into what I thought was a vacant carriage. It was only as I sat down and the doors closed behind me that I became aware of a man sitting almost opposite to where I was. He look at me unconcernedly as though he had been expecting me but he said nothing and I just averted my gaze from him, bearing in mind the danger of speaking to strangers.

"Old Street! Old Street!" I heard a porter call out at last from the platform, as we rumbled into my destination, and I smartly shot through the doors as they opened, away from any prying eyes.

I left the station hurriedly and I walked along the High Street in what

I hoped was the right direction for home, but with it being so dark, it was difficult to know for sure. And then my heart lurched, as I heard footsteps behind me. I dodged quickly into a shop doorway and stood very still, my heart pounding in my chest as I peered into the darkness. I could just make out that it was the man on the train. He walked a few steps beyond me and then he stopped and looked back. He had seen me! He came to where I was. "Do you know where you are going?" he asked me.

It seemed such a reasonable question that my fear dissipated and I answered him. "I'm not completely sure," I said.

"Where is it you're hoping to get to, then?" he asked.

I told him the name of the block of flats that I was making for and also the name of the street they were in. "Yes, I know the flats," he said now. "Look, take my arm and while I take you there, you can tell me why you're out all alone at this time of night." I accepted his offer, quite unafraid now, and as we walked along, I poured my heart out to him.

"I'm really sorry," he said, after listening to what I had to say, "but by running away, you've put yourself into a lot of danger. You won't do it again, will you?" he asked me. "Just find someone to tell if you're ever that unhappy again. Look! Here we are." He pointed to the block of flats in front of us. "Now run across the square to them and I'll wait here a bit until I know that you're all right. Don't stop for anything," he said. "Just run straight there."

My feet seemed to grow wings as I tore across the quadrangle and up the five flights of stairs to safety.

To say that my brother Charlie, who was then living in the flat alone, was surprised when he finally came to the door in answer to my incessant banging, would be the understatement of the year.

"What on earth!" he started, as he looked down on me standing there. He dragged me inside. "What are you doing here?" he demanded of me. "Do you know what time it is?"

"I've run away, Charlie," I said, breaking down and crying with relief now that I was safe.

He made up a bed for me. "Tell me in the morning," he simply said, as I tearfully tried to explain to him. "I'm dog tired," he yawned. "Whatever it is, we'll sort it out tomorrow."

I can't imagine what must have happened back at the Owens' when my disappearance was discovered the next day. I know that my father was urgently summoned from Harpenden, where he stayed some weekends with Jimmie's foster parents. He got great pleasure out of staying there with these nice people, and an added bonus was that he had found an amicable drinking companion in the fire station Chief, who also liked a Saturday night tipple in one of the delightful pubs situated in the town centre. They had many a pleasant evening putting the world to rights, but my father was, of course, careful to moderate his drinking while staying at Jimmie's. At least he had the common sense to do that, in view of his heavy drinking in former years.

He was summoned hastily, my sister had eventually told me, and then he had had to listen to Mrs Owens' tirade of "What a thing for her to do! I've done a lot for Liz you know, Mr Bone. I did all I could to make her happy."

"Well, you obviously haven't been very successful," my father had told her, as she continued to grovel to him.

"Let me make you a cup of tea, Mr Bone." Considering Mrs Owens had never had a good word to say about my father in the past regarding his drinking, she was certainly doing her utmost now to ingratiate herself to him, but my father wanted none of it.

"Yes, all right: I've heard it all before," he told this frightened woman, as the family stood uncertainly to one side, and saying nothing. "Let's just do something about it, shall we?" Have you informed the welfare?" and that is why the very next morning, Charlie and I confronted two very official-looking ladies on the front doorstep of the flat. They were enormously relieved to find me safe and sound and, as Charlie invited them in, they spoke kindly to me over a cup of tea.

"Well! I must say, we're very glad to see you safe, Liz," they said, smiling in a friendly manner. But then a seriousness crept into their voices. "What was it, Liz? Why did you have to run away like that?" Don't be afraid to tell us: we won't be taking you back there. Was it one particular person who you were running away from?" I didn't really understand the implication of that certain question then, as I do now. I had been a rapidly-maturing girl and two young men had been living at the house: were they in any way responsible for my running away? But I can say straight away that no, that was never the case. In fact, I loved Norman: he had been like a big brother to me. Lou, of course, had made that one mistake when I awoke to find him kneeling beside my bed that night, but I don't think he had touched me. I hadn't been kept hungry or anything like that at the house, so what was it that drove me to do such a dangerous thing? I can't really answer that. I think that it had been a culmination of events over those last few years that had brought this about. A sense of desperation had enveloped me if you like, so I simply told these two ladies that I had been unhappy, and they just had to accept this.

That very same day, much to the relief of my brother, who would not have known what to do with me, I was taken back to St Albans in a nice car. I had been assured, once again, that I would not be taken back to my former billet, but was taken instead to some sort of Reception Centre, where I stayed for some days. I loved it there. All the staff were very friendly. I had my own little bedroom, and I was made a great fuss of, there being only a handful of children at the centre. But then my world fell apart!

"Liz," called one of the staff cheerfully one evening as I sat reading a book in the lounge. "Liz, we've found a lovely family for you to go and live with. We'll take you to see them tomorrow, shall we?"

My face dropped a mile. "What?" I said, not quite believing what I had just heard. "I can't go from here. I like it here. I'm happy. You can't just take me away, can you?" Tears sprung to my eyes. I was terrified. I had felt safe for the first time in a long while. Why would they want to send me away? Hadn't I suffered enough? And now they wanted to move me on again.

"Look, Liz, don't cry. We're not sending you away. We would love to keep you here; you're certainly no trouble." My hands were clasped then as it was explained to me gently that I had been here merely to be assessed. It was usually the troublesome children who stayed on there, but that wasn't the case with me, and a really nice family had been found to take me in. "They have a daughter the same age as yourself," I was told. "You'll love it, Liz." And I just had to accept that that was how it had to be; there was nothing I could do about it, and my father's visit to me at the Centre hadn't helped matters. "What a dangerous thing to do, Liz; to run away in the middle of the night like that," he had said to me. "It's just a wonder that you're still with us... but it's all right, it's all right," he said quickly then, as he took not of my crestfallen face. "Whoever that man was, though, who saw you safely from the station to the flats – I'd like to shake his hand. You could have so easily come to harm, you know; a young girl like you..." his voice suddenly trailed off as he said this. "But it's all right, it's all right. I understand why you did it... I understand," he finished.

In retrospect, now, when I think about the carefree life my father had lived, which had caused his alienation over the preceding years from my mother and the family, I realise that his heavy drinking had left little finance for his own flesh and blood. My mother had been forced to look to our local Catholic church for support, to exist at all, during those dire days of the 1930s Great Depression, and right up to the time of that dangerous escapade of my running away in the dead of night to get home to London, he was still getting the most from life. I saw very little of him, even though for most weekends he was just a short bus ride way in Harpenden, staying at Jimmie's, whose foster parents, a childless couple, had very kindly offered the hospitality of these short breaks to my father when he visited from London. He had quickly taken advantage of this charitable gesture, while at the same time he took the opportunity, on the pretext of going into town for an evening meal, to spend each Saturday evening drinking with the Town's Fire Chief in a well-frequented pub within the centre. As I have related, he had quite accidentally made the acquaintance of this Fire Chief on his very first visit to Harpenden, and they spent many a weekend evening drinking together. But, of course, my father had been clever enough in his wily way to control his drinking for just that one night to enable him to negotiate the considerable walk back to Jimmie's, where, fortunately, the foster parents would have already gone to bed, having by that time had their nightly cocoa. Nothing must spoil these very pleasant weekly jaunts, he realised this, and was astute enough to cause no offence with regard to this matter. But in the meantime I, the youngest of his brood, continued to suffer from his neglect. I had had no mother to protect me. How could he demean me then for what I had done? "It's all right... it's all right," he had told me. "I understand why you did it... I understand." But it had been a stranger who, in the end, had saved me. I can only think that this must have been some kind of guardian angel, the way that this man had suddenly, mysteriously appeared; and then, just as quickly, disappeared. He had given me the protection that my father should have given, but in my father's selfishness, he had foregone his responsibility, the drink being more important to him. And once the crisis of my running away had passed, his usual pleasantries took precedence once again, leaving me to cope with my entailing life as best I could. The state welfare would look after me, just as they had always done, he had probably told himself.

AUNTIE, UNCLE, MARION AND ME

The car journey was uneventful, as I sat silently contemplating the move to another billet. I gazed, unseeing, through the car window, while the woman accompanying me did the same. No words passed between us as we made the short journey to Beresford Road, where my next foster family lived.

By now I had become almost completely inured to my unsettled existence, moving around to uncertain, dubious places and not questioning it anymore, so that when we pulled up outside a very neat-looking semi, its windows showing pretty lace curtains I, without further ado, just got out of the car. As usual, I carried my few belongings in my rather ancient-looking cardboard case, and I placed myself with my chaperone on yet another doorstep.

Nothing in particular was going through my mind at this time. I was rapidly becoming unwillingly conditioned to the disturbing aspects of my life – this unpredictable, capricious, endurance – and so I managed to distance myself then from what had to be. Indifference had, in the course of time, set in and perhaps this wasn't a bad thing in its protection of me – the uninterest and resignation of what fate now had in store for the future.

Both my imminent foster parents were at home on the afternoon of my arrival but it was just the woman, who I was to call Auntie, who greeted us at the door.

"'Ere we are then," she trilled, as she ushered us in: her nervousness quite apparent. "'Ere we are," she repeated, as though she wasn't sure what else to say, and she fluttered around us as we stood, ourselves uncertainly, in the hall. "Awer Marion will be home soon," she told us in a pronounced Hertfordshire accent – not 'our' but 'awer', and I was quick to notice this flawed diction of hers.

"Well then, well then... Bob!" she called out, almost in the same breath; she's arrived – Liz is 'ere!"

A distinguished-looking man appeared quite unhurriedly then from the front-room, which was just to one side of us. "'Ere we are then," he just said as he stood there.

Auntie broke the silence now. "I was just saying that awer Marion will be home in a minute – ain't that right, Bob? In fact, 'ere she is now!" A loud ringing of the bell announced their daughter's arrival, much to the relief of Auntie, as she bustled her in. "'Ere we are then... 'ere we are." It was as thought the vocabulary in the house consisted of just these three words: 'ere we are'.

As I was led upstairs to the bedroom by Auntie and Marion to deposit my things – the billeting officer having gracefully declined the cup of tea that had been offered to her – "I'm afraid I can't stop," she had said. "I have another delivery to make you see," she told us, as though it were parcels from the post-office and not children that she was delivering. I looked back for an instant to where Uncle stood... was still standing, a serious, thoughtful expression showing on his face. He watched our ascent of the stairs contemplatively, as though he had doubts about whether it was a good thing to be taking in this stranger, who might perhaps cause a disruption of this tight and secure little unit, but he said nothing. "She'll be all right," Auntie had remarked to the billeting officer as she had, with some relief, shown her out, emitting nervous little laughs all the while. "She'll be fine with us, as long as she's good, you know what I mean?"

No wonder Uncle looked apprehensive. He and Aunty obviously doted on Marion, their one and only, which was so evident when she had made her appearance home from school. Was I a threat, he was probably thinking, to their comfortable little 'clique'? And why wouldn't he be worried by the arrival of this intruder who had recently run away from her former foster-home in the dead of the night! But it was a happy little group who sat around the table for tea, once I had left my few belongings up in the bedroom which I was to share with Marion, whose excitement of acquiring a sister was very noticeable. "You choose which bed you'd like, Liz," she had told me, as we had sorted out our sleeping arrangements.

"'Ere we are then." Uncle, seeing how happy his daughter appeared, was in a more relaxed frame of mind. He smiled at me now, as we sat at the table for our evening meal, and I discerned how like him in features Marion was: the same nose, the same mouth, the same captivating expression of pleasure. In comparison, Auntie was quite ordinary with her blunt features and no-nonsense hair, but there was a oneness between her and Uncle which was quite noticeable to me: the way her hand lingered on his shoulder as she asked him, "What will it be, Bob: poached or scrambled eggs." So different from what I had left behind those months previously at the Lanes', where the ineffectual father was a nonentity within the family. Here the situation was in complete reverse, as I was to find over the coming months. Uncle certainly took precedence here as head of the family, that was quite obvious.

"What sort of a week have you had then, Bob?" Auntie asked him, once she had finished attending to his needs.

A smile slowly crept around his mouth as Uncle considered this question and, as he flicked his serviette out and tucked it under his chin, he pondered on his answer. Then... "I'll tell you what kind of a week I've had, Lucy," he said, laughing now. "I'll tell you that it's been quite hilarious being with those builders 'oo'er renovating that derelict house..." Although these two people spoke to one another in lapsed grammar, I realised they were of middle-class, with Uncle being a professional person, but both had retained a strong Hertfordshire dialect from their humble origins.

"What 'ave they been up to now, then?" Auntie asked.

"What 'ave they been up to? Well, I'll tell yer – they almost killed old Tom – that's what they've been up to." Uncle held his side with laughing then, while his wife looked at him aghast.

"What?" she said. "Whatever did they do then, Bob?"

"I'll tell you what they did, Lucy... I'll tell yer. You know how old Tom likes every now and again to go and sit on the lavatory and have a crafty fag, don't you?... you know, I've told you before..."

"Yes, I know," said Auntie, in a wide-eyed fashion. "What's that got to do with it then?"

"Well, I'll tell yer – you won't believe this, but I'll tell yer just the same. Oooh..." Uncle was laughing so much in the telling of this that he went into a paroxysm of coughing, but then he wiped his eyes on his serviette to make the supreme effort of controlling himself.

"Lucy," he continued, "those men – tom's work mates – knowing that Tom was due for his illicit fag had, unbeknown to Tom, tipped some paraffin down the toilet so that when he dropped his fag-end between his legs into the pan... he was blown clean off the lavatory! Oh-ho, ha-ha-ha," Uncle hooted with laughter once again, while Auntie looked at him in a state of shock.

"Bob!" she cried, "how dangerous! Is he still alive, then?"

This only served to make Uncle laugh even more. "Yes," he blustered, "but you should hear what he called the others!" He burst into laughter once again.

Although Auntie laughed with him now, she gave him a warning look. "Bob!" she said, in earnest... then looking at us two girls to see what our reaction was, she gently reprimanded him with, "Should you be telling me this in front of the girls?"

But Uncle wasn't bothered. "There you are, girls – just don't try having a fag while you're sitting on the lavatory-pan!" Marion and I laughed along with him but I was doubly pleased because it came to me than that Uncle had accepted me – his cautionary look had gone, and as I realised this, I perhaps laughed the loudest. I felt more secure now that I had become one of this tight little clan.

Life with the Finches proved once more to be yet another catalyst in my life. A well-ordered way of living prevailed in the home: "Now, Liz, this is how you do it," I was told on the first weekend of my stay with them. You get the water in the bucket but not too hot, though!" Auntie warned me. I stood listening to her as she went on to explain the intricacies of cleaning the bathroom, which would be my job every Saturday morning. "We all do our bit here, Liz," Auntie told me, and this will be yours." With that, she proceeded to get down on her knees in front of the lavatory-pan and she pumped a floor cloth up and down, up and down in the pan, until all the water within it had disappeared. "There," she said, "and now you can give the pan a good wipe round with this powder to make sure that it's really clean before you flush it again." She got up off her knees then, panting a bit, before turning to the bath. Oh yes, I thought to myself, trust me to get this job. Why couldn't she just buy a brush anyway? It would save all this getting up and down on your knees. But that would be an unnecessary extravagance for Auntie: I had very soon realised on moving in with the family that thrift was very important to her. "Look after the pennies and the pounds will look after themselves," was one of her favourite quotations. If you could do something manually, then why pay out for an unnecessary implement. Oh well, I consoled myself, at least this job that had been shelved onto me was better than emptying chamber-pots, as I had done at the Owens'.

Marion, though, had the cushy job of dusting the front-room where the piano was. She was having tuition on this instrument, which stood in a dominant position before the large bay window, which afforded the best light and the greatest prominence. She wasn't that keen, though; she hadn't really got an ear for music, but because it had been bought for Marion by her adoring God-mother, Aunty's best friend, she was persuaded by her mother to persevere. "Don't let Auntie Ada down," she had been told.

In my naivety regarding the piano's importance to this tight little circle – Auntie, Marion and her God-mother – I had innocently sat one day, idly tinkering on it in a quiet fashion. To my surprise, the door of the room had suddenly burst open and Auntie blustered in. She then proceeded to cut me down to size by informing me that I was not touch the piano. "That was bought for Marion," I was told, "by Auntie Ada, her God-mother, who wouldn't want anyone else playing it!"

I slipped quietly off the stool and didn't go near the thing again. I had been truly slighted and shocked. Had I been thumping away on the piano, I could have understood this outburst to which I had been subjected, but that had not been the case. It made me realise, however, that I was very low down in the pecking order within the family and should, in future, 'know my place'.

The sequel to the piano incident, I look upon now as being rather petty. Auntie Ada had obviously been informed about my faux-pas before her next weekly visit to the house and was quite clearly bearing it in mind. As she sat down with us at the tea-table that Friday evening, she gazed across at me with a look of disdain on her horsey features. For most of the time, anyway, she looked as if she had a bad smell under her nasally nose and spoke accordingly. This came into full play then as she asked Marion, pointedly, in her usual nasal fashion, "How are you getting on with your piano then, dear? Are you getting plenty of practice in?" She threw a quick, meaningful look in my direction as she said this, leaving me in no doubt as to what she was alluding.

But before any answer came her way, Uncle intervened: "Yes, it's all right, Ada," he said, sharply, "I can assure you that Marion has plenty of time on the piano, don't you worry about that!" Ada might be his wife's best friend, but at times this woman got on his nerves. To blow this small thing out of all proportion, as she was doing, was unacceptable to him, and he conveyed this to her in no uncertain terms. "Point in question finished!" he said with some force.

Auntie Ada squirmed a bit uncomfortably in her chair at this rebuff but, as I looked searchingly at this dour, small-minded woman, who suddenly seemed lost for words, I fully understood then why she was still a spinster: her harsh, tight-lipped looks; her total lack of charisma – what had she to offer anyone? It just amazed me that she was the best friend of Auntie's, but to be married to a person such as this, surely would be catastrophic. She was a real sourpuss, if ever there was one.

THE UNPRODUCTIVE
SCHOOL

Soon after I moved in with the Finches, I changed schools from junior to senior. I was allocated a place in a central school because of my ability with English – a fact which is rather surprising when one considers the almost total lack of teaching in my earlier, formative years, owing to my prolonged periods off ill-health. This decision by the education authorities was deemed to be the most suitable choice for me. I had actually taught myself to read at quite a young age, and during my prior periods of enforced rest in various hospitals while I went through these years of inactivity, this competency of mine proved to be a Godsend which enabled me to tolerate these long hours, as I read book after book. Obviously this was an inherent trait which had stood me in good stead. What a blessing this gift had been to me – the quality of my life would certainly have been poorer without it.

Goodness knows what time I left home in the morning to reach the school, which was situated in neighbouring Harpenden, two bus rides away and then a twenty-minute walk from the town centre; and if it happened to be tipping down with rain, you got very wet before you actually reached the school, and this happened on quite a few occasions. Wellingtons and hooded mackintoshes were imperative for many children who made this long trek each morning.

Sometimes on the way to school I would stop midway between buses to call on a class-mate, who wasn't a special friend of mine, but I had always been curious about her circumstances. She was being brought up by a very old lady whom I had presumed to be her grandmother, and I can only describe the place in which they lived as being very grotty.

Their house was slap-bang on the main road, where I would alight from the bus and make my way to them. Having arrived at the house, I would stand surveying it before I then reached for the knocker. What a shambles! I would think each time I came to this place. The door badly needed a coat of paint; the windows were dusty and dirty, owing to the continuous stream of traffic passing and belting out exhaust fumes; and the small front garden was overrun with weeds. What a mess!

Once inside the house, nothing was any different. The drab shabbiness of the interior equally matched its exterior appearance and, as I stood waiting, I actually shivered: I swear that it was colder inside the house than outside! There appeared to be no heating in the room in which I stood. There was a fireplace in it, immediately in front of me, but it was unlit. My friend and her grandmother were obviously very poor to be living like this, I thought, not realising at that time that this depressing place was just a half-way house where the council had accommodated them until such time that they could move into something better, but I knew that they had been there for quite a long time. How awful! I thought, and not only that, but other people apparently lived in this immodest building, on the second and third floors. My friend and her grandmother merely occupied just the ground floor room, and everyone in the house had to share a bathroom and toilet.

I never did discover, however, what the dire circumstances must have been for these two people to be living in these extremely poor conditions, but they must have been quite desperate at that time, I thought, for them to be living this lifestyle.

My eyes wandered then, as I stood there, to the kitchen, which was to one side of me. I had become conscious of a measure of warmth coming from this direction and, as I glimpsed through its open door, I realised where the warmth was coming from. The gas cooker within it had its oven door wide open and the jets were full on, giving out quite a bit of heat.

I moved unobtrusively toward the kitchen to get a better look at it and I was pleasantly surprised. This was obviously where my friend and her grandmother spent most of their day. In comparison to the bleak room in which I stood, this was a welcoming sight. It wasn't modern by any means but a lot of effort had gone into making the kitchen cosy and habitable. A small table and two chairs stood just a little way from the cooker, I observed, and above the cooker, within easy reach, someone had erected a shelf, which had a small wireless standing on it. Over the sink, hung an oval mirror. A cupboard and pantry stood side by side in there and, in a corner of the kitchen, a small armchair fitted neatly into it. Of course, it would be much cheaper keeping warm in there, I thought, and it even looked as though someone had recently given the kitchen a fresh coat of paint.

As I went to move away, the early-morning sun chose that moment to filter through the window in there, and it settled on several colourful plants which were dotted along the window-sill, above the sink. This, of course, only served to further enhance this little room-within-a room.

I brought my attention back to my friend and watched with interest as her poor hunched-up grandmother crept around her while making sure that her granddaughter had 'this', 'that' and 'the other' to see her through the day before she left home.

I noticed that the old lady wore woollen mittens on her hands, which covered the hands and wrists. Only the base of her thumb and fingers were exposed, thereby allowing freedom of movement within these. She wore several layers of clothing to keep her warm but, periodically, she would dab her nose onto the mittens, as though she had a perpetual cold. "Are you sure you've got everything, then?" she once again asked of her granddaughter.

"Don't fuss, Gran," my friend chastised her grandmother. She threw me an apologetic smile as she said this, but as we said our goodbyes at the door, the two of them threw their arms around one another, while they pecked each other's cheek. "You mind you're a good girl today," Granny told my friend in a mock reprimand.

"Aren't I always good, then?" my friend replied with a cheeky grin, as she bestowed yet another kiss onto her elderly guardian.

As I witnessed this affectionate banter going on between these two, I felt a hint of jealousy surge through me. The love and fondness that existed between them was very palpable at that moment, and I felt a sadness within myself because my friend had something that I hadn't had for a long time. I didn't care then that the grandmother was old and decrepit... I didn't care that she and her granddaughter lived in abject poverty in that drab house... they had one another, didn't they? That was what mattered to me at that moment, and I walked along to the bus-stop with my friend in silence.

In a trice, though, as we entered the bus and joined up with all the others going to the school, I threw off these melancholy feelings and joined in the noisy chatter going on between everyone and when, eventually, we reached our destination in Harpenden, and I spied through the window my two special friends waiting on the pavement for me, I selfishly forgot the other, with the elderly granny, for whom I had waited patiently not so long ago and the unwarranted jealousy I had felt towards her. I stepped briskly off the bus and literally threw my arms around these more-sophisticated friends of mine, who I knew came from quite posh homes.

We walked the, all three of us: Milly, Betty and me, the rest of the way to school, our arms interlinked with each other's, and we chatted away as though we hadn't seen each other for weeks. In my fickleness, I had left the less-important friend behind. A strong bond drew us similar three together, however – we were almost like triplets.

Millie was a stunning-looking girl, with her high cheekbones, limpid eyes and lustrous long hair – always looped back in a ponytail for school. Betty was petite and perky, with an outrageous sense of humour: you could never feel downcast while in her company. We got into all sorts of scrapes at the school, but we always came out laughing.

One particular incident I remember involved a woman teacher at the school who was vehemently disliked by all the pupils and was secretly called 'Pin-bum'. This was because she had a very large posterior, which wobbled as she walked. She had piggy eyes and buck teeth and, when she made an appearance in class first thing in the morning, a deathly silence would prevail as she walked in, in a somewhat menacing manner. She would be carrying a stack of books and, as she reached her desk, she would drop them forcefully onto it with a loud clatter, while she surveyed the class in her no-nonsense way. "That's enough from you, Jennings!" she would shout at a certain unsuspecting boy, even though he hadn't opened his mouth; but as she glared at him, before she commenced the lesson, you could have heard a pin drop!

Her terrified pupils sat quivering in their seats: she started as she obviously intended to go on. But I knew that in these enlightened days, this bully of a teacher would never be allowed to continue. When you can mentally abuse pupils as this woman did, how can you instil any knowledge into them? We were all too afraid to learn anything from her – to just get through her lessons with us without being verbally assaulted was an achievement in itself! How could we possibly learn anything in our terrified state?

I particularly remember one day when Millie, Betty and I really incurred her wrath. She happened to be on dinner duty on this particular day, and she stalked around the tables with her all-seeing eyes bulging from her head. It happened to be sausages on the menu that day and I knew that Betty didn't like sausages.

As she sat immediately opposite me at the table, I indicated to her with me eyes to pass her two sausages under the table to me, and I would eat them: while Pin-bum was on duty, nobody would dare to leave anything on their plate. Unfortunately, as Betty surreptitiously passed the sausages, she managed to drop one on the floor and, like a bolt from the blue, the dragon was onto us. Instantly she summed up the situation, while we could do nothing but sit with guilty and embarrassed expressions on our faces. Like a bull, she bellowed at us: "HOW DARE YOU!"

I had managed to pick the offending sausage up from the floor and sat trying to conceal the greasy thing on my lap, but this wily woman was not to be fooled. She knew just what was going on. She looked at me in a murderous manner and I really thought that she was going to strike me; but she bellowed out once again, while she sustained this frightening look: "HOW DARE YOU TAKE HER SAUSAGES!"

251

She looked around the table to see what effect she was having on the other pupils who, of course, just sat very silent. But then her eyes alighted on Millie, who was sitting right next to me, and her fierce expression changed to one of incredulity. She couldn't believe what she was witnessing. It was the 'How dare you take her sausages!" bit that had sent Millie into paroxysms of laughter, she told us later. But here she was now, her head in her hand and shoulders shaking; and when she could not control this silent fit of laughter any longer, she gave out a loud belly-laugh, with tears streaming from her eyes.

"Oh dear, oh dear," she said, as she dabbed at her eyes and tried to control herself. "Oh dear," she said once more. But the mood had been set and everyone else started laughing, until the table was in uproar.

This had the effect of taking old Pin-bum by complete surprise and for a moment she wasn't sure what to do. She couldn't take the whole school on, she was obviously thinking; but she then pulled herself up to her full height to reassert her authority. "Get out, you three!" she boomed at us, while dragging us from our chairs. "Get to the Headmaster's office!" she ordered, with a nasty expression on her face. She whacked Millie across her head, leaving her lovely hair spread-eagled across her face.

Fortunately, when we went to Mr Webster's office, he wasn't there. This was a bit disappointing for our aggressor. She couldn't stop; she couldn't forget the disorder that we had left behind. "Sit on those chairs!" she bawled. "And when Mr Webster comes back from his lunch break, you can tell him what you've been up to." She then hurried away, leaving us sitting a bit stony-faced, wondering at this terrible crime that we had supposedly committed. But we weren't too bothered, however, about facing the Head, because he was a 'sweetie'. He probably had not a mean bone in his body but, more to the point, was the confusion that the three of us girls felt over the magnitude that had been attached to this minor episode. Was the woman mad!

On reflection, I realise that a measure of sympathy should be felt for this insane woman. Rumour had it that she was stuck at home, caring for her elderly mother. Certainly, she seemed quite poor. I remember that, for the whole of my time at the school, she would wear the same dress every day, and then, presumably, wash it at the weekend to wear once again for the following week. And for the whole duration of our being at the school, this pattern never changed; so perhaps it was pity we should have felt for this unbalanced woman, not scorn.

Mr Webster eventually made his appearance, and he stopped short at the sight of these three woebegone girls sitting outside his office. He peered at us the over the top of his pince-nez glasses. "Well!" he said, in a mock-startled manner, "and to what do I owe this pleasure – three lovely ladies waiting for me?" What brings you here, then? Come into my office and tell me."

Completely disarmed, we accepted Mr Webster's invitation, and we proceeded to tell him of our crime in the dining-room. He listened in a serious manner to our explanation of what we had done. "I attempted to take Betty's sausages and they fell on the floor," I told him.

"Oh, Liz!" he said then, after giving the matter some thought, and all the while looking over his pince-nez glasses. "Oh, Liz – you mustn't," he said. "You just mustn't. What would Betty's mother say if she knew that somebody else was eating her sausages, eh?" I couldn't think of an answer to this, so I just looked down at the floor. "And, Betty," he said, as he turned to her. "Promise me you will eat your own sausages in future, will you?"

"Yes, Mr Webster," Betty simply said.

As he saw us out of the office, he instructed us to go and find Miss Bennet and apologise to her. "Tell her that it won't happen again," he called after us. And this is what we did – and this horrible woman just gave a self-satisfied smirk. She told us that we were nasty pieces of work, and to 'watch out' in future; but what she didn't see, as she turned away from us, was three very-extended tongues sticking out at her departing back. That gave us a lot of satisfaction, I can tell you; and as we made our way home after school, we laughed our heads off. "How DARE you take her sausages!" Millie threw at me in mock derision, as she mimicked this awful teacher. "How DARE you!"

"Anyway, I'm going to tell my Mum," Millie indignantly told us then, "what that horrible woman did to me today – smacking me across the head like that. I'm going to tell her as soon as I get home. She had no right to do that."

We backed her up wholeheartedly. "Yes, Millie," we said. "You do that, and we'll come home with you to help you to tell her." And this is just what we did: Millie had no intention of letting this crime that had been committed against her, go unreported…

The fact that I never learned anything while at this school – or should I say, very little – is hardly surprising when you consider the whole context of the matter. Hugh Myddleton Central had been hurriedly evacuated from London at the start of the War, along with the children, to share a building with Manland School, now called Sir John Lawes, in Harpenden. The London staff were of very poor-quality, mostly elderly people dragged out of retirement owing to the dire situation of all the younger teachers having been called-up to fight in the War, so that we were left with the under-qualified oddballs to instruct us.

One prime example was Mr Moody, old 'Spit and Gob' as the children called him. He would cough his way into class each day, spluttering and gobbing into a large, very off-white, handkerchief. He had no idea how to control the class, which was always in uproar.

At that time, I was sitting next to an obnoxious boy who would insist on calling me 'Boney' – my surname being Bone. "Watch out, Boney!" he would say to me, as I participated with the restt of the class in creating havoc prior to the entry of Mr Moody. "Here he comes, Boney," this dreadful boy would say to me, as we heard old 'Spit and Gob' spluttering his way along the corridor outside, towards the classroom. He would almost nudge me off my seat, as he spoke in this offensive way to me, and I would turn on him and thump him.

"DON'T call me that!" I would shout at him; but he would just laugh. And it wasn't until some years later, when I accidentally bumped into him one day, that he confessed to insulting me in this fashion just to get my attention, as he had always fancied me. What a nutter!

The indiscipline that went on in this decrepit teacher's class during his lessons was unbelievable. He would glare at the offenders through his wonky and ill-fitting glasses, and then launch a continuous stream of pens and books towards the culprits, but all to no avail. These missiles flying around the room, which for most of the time missed the guilty ones anyway, just added to the non-stop hilarity, and only once do I remember any intervention by more-senior staff, who couldn't possibly have failed to hear the bedlam going on in that class, and that was Mr Webster, as he suddenly made his entrance one day, unexpectedly.

A hush had come over the class as the Headmaster had surveyed the pupils, and then his eyes moved to Mr Moody. "Everything all right, is it?" he asked our surprised teacher, who at that precise moment stood with yet another book poised in his hand, all ready to be thrown at another recalcitrant pupil.

"Yes, everything's fine," Mr Moody assured him, and our headmaster was quite happy to leave it at that.

"Oh, that's all right, then," he simply said, as he slipped quickly back out of the door.

Of course, nobody ever learned anything during old Spit and Gob's classes but, by the end of them, we had all had a fantastic, exhilarating time, although, how we didn't all go down with T.B. or some other serious chest infection, our being so exposed to this teacher's coughing and spluttering all the while, I shall never know, but at that perilous time in history, with all the bombing going on just twenty-five miles away from us in London, from where we had all come, perhaps it was considered the lesser of two evils! And the fantastic afternoons of games in the extensive sports field surrounding the school, usually immediately after Mr Moody's lessons, and taken by the one and only young member of staff, a Mr Hicks, when we must have run miles, playing endless games of rounders under his supervision, I'm sure would have contributed to warding off these germs with which we had all been in contact. I still remember even now, after all these years, the excitement and absolute stimulating thrill of whacking the ball viciously with the bat time and time again, before running like hell round and around the vast area of posts that we had all hammered feverishly into the ground before we commenced the game. Oh yes! All that heavy breathing with the continuous running, as we unconsciously exercised our previously-assaulted lungs, must have saved us, I'm sure, from some ghastly chest condition settling within us.

One teaching period at the school that we all looked forward to and really enjoyed was Mr Webster's lesson. I can't remember exactly what his subject was but I do remember that the class always treated him with a reverence that was sadly lacking for others of the staff. Not that this Headmaster was overly-strict or threatening in any way – in fact, he was rather soft – but he had an affinity with his fellow beings, which is not often seen in someone in his position of power.

There was no need for any disrespect towards Mr Webster from the class then and he would quickly walk in on us, only to stop and stare in surprise if someone was being over-exuberant at the time of his entry. "Eric!" he would exclaim quietly, "that's not like you," and the offender would cast his eyes down in an ashamed-fashion; nobody ever had any wish to upset Mr Webster.

"Right then, let us begin," he would say after a moment's silence, when all was forgiven.

The class entered fully into the teachings of this totally-respected Head of the school, even though he had this often repeated habit of harking back to his younger days. "Ah, yes," he divulged to us during one of these episodes, as his eyes suddenly took on a far-away look. "Those were the days – my spell in Mesopotamia, when I was a young army officer! Did you hear, Liz?" he gently chided me when he thought I wasn't giving him enough attention. "I was in charge of a whole battalion out there," he reminisced, the pleasure of these thoughts showing plainly on his face.

"Cor! A whole battalion, did you say, Sir?" one of the boys asked.

"Yes, Thompson, I did say a whole battalion." Mr Webster peered at this boy over his pince-nez glasses, delighted that he had been asked this question. "And do you know, Thompson – that battalion would stop marching on my command. Yes! Just on my command. What do you think about that, then?" Mr Webster, at that moment, was in his element.

"Cor!" The whole class mimicked Thomspon – they loved it when Mr Webster got carried away like this. But a woebegone expression suddenly replaced this exhilarated look on his face, as he then told us in a quick manner, and almost to himself, "Now I can't even get a bus to stop for me!"

"Cor! Sir…" The whole class looked sad at this disclosure from our Head. "Is that why you were late getting to school this morning, Sir?" one of the class asked him.

"Yes, Jenkins: that's why I was late. I put my hand out but the bus just sailed past me. That's what things have come to for me now," he disclosed, a momentary troubled expression showing on his face. "…Anyway, that's enough about me – let's get on with the lesson," he then said, quite chirpily.

The whole class relaxed at this quick change of mood from their Head – of melancholy to cheerfulness. A big burden had been taken off their shoulders, but they mumbled among themselves about the grotty attitude of the bus-driver in not stopping on Mr Webster's command. How dare he? What a rotten man!

THE BATTY FRENCH
TEACHER

These halcyon, but unproductive, years at the school helped me, I think, to sustain a measure of equilibrium in my otherwise unsettled existence outside of it.

There were no demands or pressures for learning and so I attained no achievement in any subject apart from English, for which I had a natural ability but, of course – I had almost forgotten – there was French, which also seemed to come naturally to me. It certainly wasn't because of any effort Madam, our teacher of this subject, made. She seemed to have her mind, for most of the time, on something very different.

"Bonjour, mes enfants," she would call to us as she, in her usual fashion, blustered her way into the classroom: she always seemed to be in a hurry. She would then sling her bulging, shabby briefcase under her desk, as she carried on her conversation with us. "Comment allez-tu?" she would ask us.

"Nous sont tres bon a jour, merci, Madam," we would all reply in unison.

"Il fait beau aujourdhui," she would throw at us then, even if it was raining cats and dogs outside.

"But, Madam, it's raining!" we would tell her, as we all pointed to the windows, where rivulets of water gushed down against the panes outside.

She would look in surprise to where we pointed, then. "Ah! Bon, bon. Tu a regardez." She would say this in a knowing manner, as if she had been trying to catch us out. "C'est bon," she would repeat, "mais nous continuez… et parle-tu en Francais, s'il vous plait." She would proceed then, having sorted this out, to a much more pressing issue, which required no French at all!

"I want you all," she told us, fervently – in English! – "to take these leaflets," (which had been emblazoned across the top of each 'RSPCA'). "I want you to take them home and distribute them." The French lesson had been quite forgotten by now. "Look at this!" and "Look at that! Those poor animals just completely neglected! What do you think of that then, children?"

"Ahhhh…" we would all chorus together, much to Madam's gratification. We didn't at all mind discussing suffering animals instead of struggling with French. And so it went on until:

"Mon Dieu! Regardez l'heure!" She had suddenly noticed the clock, which announced that it was almost time to go home. She rushed to retrieve her briefcase from under her desk and then proceeded to hand out lists of verbs to each one of us. "Learn these for the next lesson," she told us. Needless to say, no-one ever bothered. She would have completely forgotten by the next lesson and, at the end of the year examination, I was the only one to get any worthwhile marks, simply because I had a bit of a flair for this language. But it didn't make me very popular with the others in the class, especially when Madam chastised them with, "If Liz can achieve these good marks, why not the rest of you?" Everyone just scowled at me: I had really let the side down!

True, I never learned much while there, but when I think back now to those carefree school-days at Hugh Myddleton in Harpenden, I consider that I was actually privileged to have been part of this disorganised and sometimes mad place, simply because of a unique sense of belonging. The head of the School, Mr Webster, was far too soft for his position, yet he was held in high esteem by everyone; Madam, the French teacher, was bonkers!; Pin bum was – to quote one of her own idioms – 'a nasty piece of work'; and old Spit and Gob, with his rowdy classes presented, I'm sure, more of a threat than an advantage to his pupils.

Music, with Miss Pickering, was a shambolic yet enlivening session – if only she didn't keep getting upset every time Jennings insisted on singing one too many 'Hallelujahs' during certain parts of a rather long requiem that we were attempting to learn for the School's Christmas concert. In the end, Miss Pickering, in her exasperation, would rush up to him and whack him smartly on top of his head with the music book that she held in her hand. "SHUT-UP!" she would bellow at him and, having done that, she would just simply walk away. We never heard any more out-of-place 'Hallelujahs' from Jennings after that: he just decided to keep his mouth shut whenever he reached those certain parts!

The P.E. Master – the one and only young member of staff – was our saviour, with his almost-daily sessions of rounders outside in the fresh air. And he didn't stand any nonsense. "Hit it! you silly bugger," he wouldn't hesitate to shout at an ineffectual member of the team, until he was given a warning from Mr Webster.

"No, no; we can't have that sort of language on the field," the Head gently reprimanded him. But prior warnings had been given to this brisk, and perhaps mildly uncouth sports master, so that nobody was left in any doubt but that they were to be on their toes to always give of their best. How could the competitive spirit between the teams then, not leave all the players completely exhilarated and exhausted at the end of the game, while patting one another on the back: "Good game, yeah, good game," they would be telling one another, as they walked off the field.

After all these revelations of mine, people will empathise, I think, with my reluctance at the end of each day to return from these happy, but slightly bizarre, school hours, to the ordinary drabness of my living. I would almost count the minutes on my return home to the resumption of being with my friends again... Mr Webster... rounders... and the unfinished requiem for the School Christmas concert. Schooldays at that time for me, were the happiest; if only I could have boarded there, away from the uncertainties and pettiness of my immediate life with a galaxy of different carers and their idiosyncrasies to cope with... if only!

THE SWIMMING
INCIDENT

It was one of those baking hot days, and Auntie shaded her eyes as she stood outside in the blistering sun. She called out to Uncle, who was taking advantage of the more cool part of the garden, where he sat reading the daily newspaper.

"What do you think to the idea of taking the girls swimming after lunch, Bob? You know, the open-air pool along Cottonmill Lane. What do you think, then?"

Marion and I, as we had just finished our apportioned jobs around the home and just sat lazily around, looked apprehensively at one another as Auntie made this request to Uncle. The old pool that she spoke of was primitive in the extreme, and freezing cold always but, because the admission fee was very cheap and the spectator part very pleasant, this was a favourite place for her to take us sometimes.

Uncle had reluctantly agreed; he was very comfortable where he was but he realised, of course, that he would be needed for the provision of driving us to this outdated and unmodernised place, where you couldn't even get a cup of tea. "All right, Lucy," he said. "Yes, all right."

The water, as Marion and I gingerly entered it was, as usual, freezing. No matter that it was a baking hot day outside, submerging ourselves into this ice-cold pool was sheer agony. We stood side by side, shivering violently, and looking towards Auntie and Uncle, as they sat comfortably ensconced in the spectators' area to one side of the pool.

"Go on; get your shoulders under," Auntie called to us. But we ignored her, until she came rushing over, when we did make a feeble attempt to immerse ourselves and go through the motions of swimming. "That's right," she instructed us, as she poised herself right on the edge of the pool, while leaning forward so that we could hear her better as she called to us. "Do your arms, and kick your legs… come on, come on… that's it… that's it!"

It only took some cheeky lad then to surreptitiously walk behind her and poke her in the back, to send her headlong into the water, fully clothed!

As she flailed about, trying to regain her footing, a pool-side attendant jumped in to save her. He dragged her unceremoniously out of the water to safety.

She stood there spluttering and coughing-up water, while the attendant berated her with, "Spectators are not allowed around this area." It was a bit late in the day, I thought, for him to be telling Aunty this. "You should know better," he told her as he walked away, a supercilious look on his face.

Uncle, having seen it all, rushed from the spectators' area where he had been looking after all the clobber, and he draped Auntie in the two large bath towels, which should have been for Marion and me. "Quick, all of you!" he said hurriedly, get in the car. Let's get home." And he shoved us all unceremoniously towards the vehicle which, fortunately, wasn't far away.

There was an embarrassed silence as we headed for safety, with not a word at first being spoken by anyone. But then Auntie gave a shamefaced laugh, as she tried to defuse the situation. "Fancy that cheeky boy pushing me into the water like that, Bob. I'd have boxed his ears if I'd known who he was, what do you think?"

"Well, I'll tell you what I think." Uncle stared straight ahead, tight-lipped, as he drove in the direction of home. "I think you should have known better, Lucy. You were poised, fully-clothed, on the edge of that pool there, shouting out, telling the girls how to swim, when you don't even know how to swim yourself. You were just asking for trouble."

Auntie gave another little laugh. "Well, I can see the funny side of it now," she said, and I laughed with her. Marion, though, looked towards me then and stuck her chin out. "You think you're so clever, don't you!" she spat at me, which had the effect of shutting me up altogether. I had just wanted Auntie to know that it didn't matter that she had made a fool of herself. It was much nicer, I had thought, for the incident to be laughed at to dispel any embarrassment, but obviously I had been wrong. Marion was shivering in the car because of her mother's foolishness, but then, so was I. Her parents didn't rebuke their daughter for her spitefulness to me, and once again I became aware of where I came in the pecking order of this family.

THE VILLAGE

We bustled around, bumping into one another as we hastily tried to make up for lost time, our having lingered for too long over breakfast.

"Come on, come on, you two girls!" Uncle threw at us, as he bundled clothes into a large suitcase, while Auntie cleared up downstairs. It was Saturday, you see – the day that we all went to visit 'Nan', who lived in the little village of Sandridge. There were two buses to be caught, because Uncle didn't, for some reason, use the car for this weekend journey, and here we were, rushing around like chickens with two heads, as we made the supreme effort to get to the first bus on time. If we missed that, we would lose the connecting bus in the town and would therefore have a very long wait.

We caught the bus by the skin of our teeth and fell onto our seats, all of us puffed-out by the effort. Uncle had to struggle to the back of the bus with his heavy case owing to there being no vacant seats at the front. He, with difficulty, attempted then to lift this cumbersome thing onto the overhead rack, when he suddenly became aware of a slipper dangling precariously from it.

"Oh, look at that, Lucy!" he shouted down the bus. "You almost got to Nan's with only one slipper. Look at that," and all the bus laughed as he attempted to either push it in or pull it out. But in the end, we turned up at our destination with the slipper still protruding from the case!

Nan's cottage stood, adjoined to one other, right in the middle of the village, but slap-bang on the edge of the main road, onto which we alighted, as we left the bus.

There were three pubs in this little village, all within striding distance of each other, and one of them reposed in a peaceful manner right alongside the beautiful church, whose small frontage boasted little bench seats, where wanderers could tarry a while and survey the immaculately-kept flower-decked grounds. The pub never impinged itself in any way on the church; in fact, it seemed almost to be a part of it.

Right opposite to Nan's cottage, on the other side of the road, stood a bright and well-kept general store, where you could buy just about anything, from a bag of sugar to a mop-head. There was no need to travel into town – just walk across the road, where all the news and gossip regarding the village also took place in this well-stocked shop. Who had died... Who had just had a new baby, etc., etc., Nan knew it all, and furnished us with the facts almost as soon as we stepped into the cottage. "That young schoolgirl who lives just up the road has got herself pregnant," she told us on one occasion.

More than five decades later, this little village has changed very little. The general store... the three pubs... the lovely church... and the two little cottages standing side-by-side right on the main road – so much busier now, of course! Although the façade of the cottages remains unchanged, amazingly, a very up-to-date feature has been added on a small space immediately adjacent to these old but durable dwellings. Two very-necessary garages have somehow now been squeezed into this small gap; and astonishingly, as a complete sign of the times, a four-wheel-drive vehicle parks in all its grandeur outside one of the garages...

How we all fitted into that little cottage on these weekend visits, I shall never know, because also staying there would be Nan's son – who was Auntie's brother – his wife, and their little girl. The interior of the cottage, though, was surprisingly spacious, and I remember being given a tiny box-room, but where all the others slept, I had no idea.

I know the kitchen and lounge-cum-diner were ample for us all, but there was no bathroom and – horror upon horror! and almost unbelievable when I think about it now – the lavatory was outside in the back garden. It consisted of a wooden hut, which housed the most primitive toiletry requisites that I had ever seen. Once inside the hut, you were faced by a long wooden bench, into which a series of round holes had been cut, and placed strategically under these holes were buckets into which you were required to do the necessary. Each week, the council workmen were required to come round and empty these ghastly, repellent things… Urghhh!

I dreaded using this bog-hole that had spiders running around in it. In my fastidiousness, I would rather have not used it at all. I would emerge from this dark, frightening place like a bolt from the blue, tripping over the underwear still around my ankles. "Oh-o-o-o," I would be silently screaming to myself, as I rushed full-pelt to the safety of the back door, leading into the house.

…Nan, of course, loved these weekends with all her family around her. Her little granddaughter, Jackie, was about three years of age, and one of the loveliest and prettiest little things that I had ever seen. Not only was she very attractive, with long blonde hair and exquisite features, but she also had a lovely temperament. She was completely unspoilt by her no-nonsense parents, even if she was an only child. This stance taken by her parents, was necessary, I think, because of the fact that this lovely little girl was unintentionally spoilt by others around her, so lovely was she.

Her mother would, however, show concern for me, having to contend with Marion, who also was an only child but rather spoilt by **her** parents. "Listeners never hear very good of themselves," Marion had said to me one day, in her high-and-mighty manner, and little Jackie's mother had rushed to my defence. "Don't speak to Liz like that!" she told this toffee-nosed girl, who had obviously decided she didn't really need a sister. And it is only now that I understand the excessive emotion that I displayed during an incident that took place as we travelled back to St Albans the next day; when we once more left the little village behind until the following weekend… and many others to follow.

THE TRIP HOME

We had somehow missed the Sunday afternoon bus from the village that would take us into town to catch the connection home. Uncle stood in sombre mood while grumbling to himself, then. "You'll have to pull your socks up," he said. "You knew what time the bus left the village."As we weren't sure to whom he addressed the remark, we remained silent.

Suddenly, as I stood there listening to Uncle chiding us, I saw a wonderful sight in the distance. At first I couldn't believe what I had seen, but then… yes!… it was one of my long-lost brothers who was walking in our direction. He looked very handsome in his Royal Air Force Officer's uniform. His arm was around his sweetheart's waist, and they gazed into each other's eyes as they conversed with one another.

I had not seen any of my five brothers for a very long time; since the War, in fact, had pulled me from their clutches, and I had been wrenched from them. I had, of necessity, learned to live without my family, pushing them into the recesses of my mind, while I coped with the daunting task of living with strangers. To suddenly be confronted, then, with this wonderful sight of one of my own within reaching distance, proved to be too much for me and I, without thinking, flew towards him, as though my feet had grown wings! I didn't care about what I had left behind: three completely astonished people, their mouths agape at the suddenness of what had just happened. But at the point, when I took off, I had had no inhibitions – to get to my brother was all that mattered to me. "Arthur! Arthur!" I was calling to him, but he didn't hear me.

As I, without warning, came upon him, I threw my arms around his neck, and I cried as I leaned against him. "Arthur," I just said, as I clung to him.

My astonished brother held me aloft then. "Liz!" he said. "It's you." And, "What's the matter?" he asked, as he noticed my tear-filled eyes. "Are you unhappy?" He hadn't at first appreciated this unexpected interruption by his sister to his liaison with his sweetheart, but as he looked searchingly into my face and saw the emotion that I couldn't control, he became concerned and drew me to him. "Let's get back to your foster parents," he said, putting his other arm around my waist then and kissing me.

Auntie and Uncle shook hands stiffly with my brother as he introduced himself. My foster mother reproached me, however, for taking off and leaving them in the sudden manner that I had. "You could have got yourself killed," she berated me. "You actually ran onto the road almost in front of a bus. What possessed you, for goodness sake?"

It was true what she said to me, but my brother intervened with, "Liz didn't mean anything, but she hasn't seen me for a long time," while giving me a reassuring smile.

"Yes, quite so," replied Uncle, a wry expression showing on his face.

My brother became immediately aware of the implication of these three words, and the silent look of disapproval being levelled at him, and the whole meeting became very strained, especially as Auntie glanced past him and fixed her eyes on his girlfriend. Her meaningful look said it all, and it was quite obvious what she was thinking. But my brother quickly interjected with: "Oh yes, I'm here in St Albans while visiting Beth and her family – we're becoming engaged, you see. And maybe before I go back to base, I can come and visit Liz. I don't get many leaves," he finished, lamely.

I had stood in silence through all this conversing between my foster-parents and brother. Of course, I realised that my foster-parents had been correct in their chastising of him, with regard to his never once having visited me, but in my distressed state, as I listened to their accusations regarding this, I just wanted to shout out, "It doesn't matter! It doesn't matter!" I didn't want him to feel guilty or distraught on account of me, because I still loved him as a brother... loved him for the way he had cared for me, along with my other brothers when I was much younger, before the War had torn us asunder. Nothing could take that inborn, family love away... Nothing!

As we finally noticed our bus chugging up the hill towards us, we gave a sigh of relief. It had been a long wait, having missed the village bus, which would have got us into town in time for the connection.

My brother assisted us all onto the bus, but Auntie had to have a final word with him. "Do you know," she said, "that's the first time I've ever known Liz to show any emotion." She jerked her head in my direction. "But we'll discuss that when you come to us.

... A big bunch of flowers was presented to Auntie when my brother made his appearance with Beth the following evening, and now, instead of animosity, a feeling of friendship prevailed as Auntie bustled round to find a presentable vase to put the flowers in. "Oh! They're lovely!" she enthused. "I can't remember the last time anyone bought me some flowers." She threw an accusing look at Uncle, but he laughed this remark off.

"Well, make the most of it, then," he told her, saucily. But the atmosphere was set then for a pleasant intercourse between my brother and foster parents.

This presentation of flowers to Aunty had the effect of completely disarming her from whatever grievances she might have to air against me, and a very-pleasant interlude presented itself. I was chuffed by the fact that Arthur had kept his promise to visit that evening. I remembered how upset I had been at the time when he hadn't kept his promise, a while back.

He had dropped me a quick card then to say that he was on leave and would meet me from school on the Thursday. I was wildly excited on that day: my brother looking so handsome in his officer's uniform coming to meet me. Everyone would see him and I would feel so proud. But he failed to turn up, which plummeted me into the depths of despair. As I travelled home on the bus, I felt lonely and forgotten. I hadn't seen any of my family for months, but once more I had made the supreme effort to bottle-up my anguish: this pain deep inside of me, I set it to one side and just got on with living my sad existence. But here he was; sitting and listening in rapt silence to what was being said to him by a fervent woman, the congenial phase having passed.

My foster-mother was having a field-day then, as she expounded to my brother, while displaying at the same time, a mock solicitous stance. "Your sister," she told him, "seems to have quite a bit of difficulty in relating to us as a family. She seems to be devoid of any affection or feelings, and I find that very difficult to cope with, at times." Then her face brightened. "Now, awr Marion," she enthused, "she soon lets us know how she feels. She could be stamping her foot one minute, and throwing her arms round us the next!" She gave a false laugh as she said this. "We treat Liz, here, as one of the family, you know; so there's really no need for her to be like this."

As she said those insincere words to my brother, it flashed through my mind how unjust these remarks of hers were: "We don't want you touching that piano – that was bought for Marion, by her Godmother!" These words resonated in my mind. And with regard to me showing no feelings, was it any wonder? Of course I kept my emotions rigidly in check. I'd certainly had good practice over the years, having to cope with the idiosyncrasies of several families, and of being the underdog, to boot. Would I have dared 'stamp my foot' while living there? Of course I wouldn't. Oh yes, I had become quite adept at controlling my emotions, but this woman had failed to understand my need for doing this.

As my foster-parent finished her ranting, she looked searchingly round her at her silent audience. She had obviously felt at that moment a bit out on a limb while she looked at these quiet and contemplative people who had allowed her free-rein of her vociferous criticisms of me.

"Well, Bob: what do you think? Ain't that right, then?" She looked at her husband, silently appealing for his support. The mute response, though, to her damning diatribe **of me**, threw her somewhat off balance, then. But, before Uncle could utter a word, my brother decided to intervene. He lay the cup and saucer that had been on his lap to one side, the tea within having gone cold, his attention having been so rigidly focused on this woman who had spoken so insensitively regarding his sister.

"I quite understand what you're saying to us all," he said, while at the same time intimating with his eyes that surely this matter being discussed so openly would have been better to have been spoken of in private. "But has my sister been any trouble while she's been living with you?" He said these words in a point-blank manner.

"Oh, no, no, no," my foster-mother replied, rather hesitantly, having been thrown right off course. "No, no," she repeated.

"So what actually would you say the problem is precisely?" My brother leaned forward as he asked this question. He was using his newly-acquired way of speaking, since he had been recognised as officer material on joining the RAF to fight in the War. He had completely thrown off any suspicion of his East-End background, with its cockney accent; and here was Beth, his fiancée, now hanging onto his every word, as she sat wide-eyed beside him.

My foster-mother became flustered and started to fidget uneasily on being asked this question. But my brother wasn't finished. "You have to remember, Mrs Finch that my sister here has had a lot of trauma in her life… First, she loses her mother at a very young age. She's been half-starved and abused; quite apart from the fact that she has had to spend a lot of time in and out of hospital, owing to her having been rather delicate; although, thank goodness, she seems to be growing out of this now." He looked affectionately at me as he said this, and gave me an encouraging smile.

I remembered, then, his anxiety for me those years back when I had been so very ill in London, before we had all been split up. I was five years of age. He had come into the bedroom where I lay, as everyone else waited for the ambulance to take me to hospital. Arthur had sat holding my hand. "Yer'll be awright, Liz," he had said to me. "Yer'll soon ge' better in 'ospital, you'll see." He had slipped into my hand, then, a small packet of biscuits. "'Ere yer are, Liz. I go' these for yer: they're yer favourites, ain't they?"

As though clutching at a straw, my foster-parent jumped in here. "Oh, yes. Well, she's been well looked after with us," she hastened to assure my brother. "She's certainly well-fed and watered, so to speak." She tittered at this quip of hers. "And we treat her the same as awer Marion," she lied.

"Yes..." my brother still hadn't finished, "but you have got to remember what went on before she came to you, Mrs Finch. Her life has been very unsettled. She has never had the love and security that your own daughter here, has had. He grinned broadly at Marion as he said this, but he continued: "It has been very necessary for my sister, in the past, to hold her emotions in check for quite a while, and you can't really expect her to change at the drop of a hat."

Now, this utterance from my brother, with its intensity, really upset my foster-mother, who couldn't possibly begin to understand just what he may have been getting at. Was it perhaps *her*? she was obviously thinking. She turned quickly then to Uncle who had, like Beth, sat saying nothing. He had clearly, though, been mulling over the somewhat heated discussion that had gone on between his wife and my brother. He answered now in a serious fashion. "I understand what Arthur has been saying, Lucy," he told his wife. "We knew, before Liz came to us, about her unsettled life. You can't expect miracles, my dear. She's never been any trouble, that's for sure. You will just have to accept the situation as it is, and bear in mind what has just been said."

"Yes... but, Bob..." my foster-mother intended to make one last stand. "Bob!" she appealed to him. "When do we ever hear Liz laugh?"

All this time I had sat through this intense discussion about me as though I wasn't there, with everyone talking over my head; but I jumped into the dialogue at this point, much to everyone's surprise. "Oh, I do. I do laugh sometimes," I told them. "What about how I laughed when Auntie was pushed into the swimming pool while she still had all her clothes on? I laughed then, didn't I?"

After a momentary startled look from everyone, as I made this completely unexpected remark, Uncle then burst into laughter. I had sat there saying nothing for all this time, and then this! He looked over at my brother and Beth, as they sat with bemused, questioning expressions on their faces. What was this happening that they knew nothing about, then? they were clearly thinking.

My foster-parent hooted with laughter again, and he gave his knee a resounding slap… "Oh-h-ha-ha-ha." He gave a deep, hearty guffaw as he remembered this incident. "I won't bother to go into details," he told Arthur, as he continued to chortle.

If looks could kill, as the saying goes, Uncle would have been lying dead on the floor, as a result of the one my foster-mother conveyed to him, with an intense, stifled anger. "That's strange, ain't it, Bob…" She spoke through tight lips. "You didn't think at the time that it was so funny, did you! In fact, if I remember rightly, you were rather shirty with me!" She snorted as she said this, while at the same time, she threw me an acid look.

Soon after this unpleasant interlude, that had so spoilt the evening, my brother decided to take his leave. "I do thank you for taking such good care of my sister," he told my foster-parents, as he donned his military outer-garments. "I'm so relieved that she isn't causing you any trouble. I have been at fault for not keeping in regular contact with her, but I intend to put that right for the future."

I once again held my emotions in check, as I kissed him goodbye at the door, even though I felt my heart would burst! I, in fact, never saw Arthur again while I was at the Finches, as he became immersed in his spell of duty with the Royal Air Force. His visit to the house, I'm afraid, had not in the end had the effect of pouring oil on troubled waters, as everyone hoped it would. Unfortunately, it had the opposite effect, which was soon to become evident, almost immediately after his and Beth's departure.

I had become aware, then, as I silently turned back into the house, of angry words being exchanged between my foster-parents: all on account of me, apparently.

"If she's not happy here, then it's best she goes!…" I stopped short on hearing these words from my foster-mother as I re-entered the room, and stood uncertainly at the door. My presence, as I stood there, brought about an abrupt halt to what was being said, and Uncle quietly left the room; but as he passed by me, he gave me a sympathetic, almost apologetic look, which left me in no doubt that, in some way, he had been defending me.

My foster-mother started then to plump up the chair cushions, unnecessarily, in quite an aggressive manner, and she turned to me, while doing this. "Tomorrow, when you leave school," she told me in suppressed fury, "I want you to stop off in the town and go to the billeting office. Tell them…" she continued, "tell them that they need to find you somewhere else to live, because you're not very happy here!"

She seemingly appeared happier once she had said this to me, as though a weight had been taken from her shoulders, and she walked off with a twisted smile on her face, while I stood stunned. I couldn't believe what she had just said to me and, in my confusion, I made my way to the sanctuary of the bedroom. I was lost for words: sad and disillusioned. If only I had kept my mouth shut, I thought, as I sat on the bed… if only.

"Do you really want to go?" I became aware, then, of Marion seating herself beside me on the bed. She looked worried as it came to her that she might be losing her foster-sister, and I turned to her in surprise. It had never occurred to me that she would miss me if I went, but what choice di I have?

The following day seemed to pass in a blur: how could I possibly concentrate on anything at school with this heavy burden resting on my shoulders? What would I say to the staff in the billeting office, on my way home? What could I possibly say? Was I to be foisted onto yet another billet? What terrible thing had I done to deserve this?

With heavy tread, then, I approached the entrance to the building, still in deep concentration, pondering what I should say. I never gave it a thought, then, in my present absent-mindedness, to read the information displayed immediately before me, affixed to the glass door that led into the building. I twisted the knob and shoved at the door, but it wouldn't give! I stood perplexed for a moment before my eyes then observed the notice displayed before me: 'CLOSED ON MONDAYS'. Yes, of course; I should have remembered, I told myself. It had always been closed on Mondays.

As we sat at table that evening, everyone in sombre mood, hardly a word was spoken. My foster-mother bustled about in her usual fashion as she danced attention on Uncle. "Now, come on, Bob. Will you have seconds?" she asked of her husband. But he was saying little, as he studied the plate before him.

I, myself, had sat in contemplative mood. Did I announce to all the fact that the billeting office had been closed that day, or did I just keep my mouth shut? I decided to do the latter, as it gradually became clear to me that my foster-mother had obviously known all along about this; and the self-satisfied looks that she threw at me clearly showed that her punishment of me had been complete. Yes, she had certainly achieved her aim, and from that point on, until my eventual return to London, as the War ended, I kept myself very much under wraps. I withdrew even more into myself; I caused no bother to anyone; I adhered to every rule. But, what little affection I might have harboured within myself, flew straight out of the window. I became, if you like, a bit of a characterless zombie!

Life carried on as normal in the household, once the meeting with my brother and the unfortunate consequence faded away. Uncle cracked his jokes once more at the table and Auntie continued to – as she would put it – 'keep us all well-fed and watered'. Marion carried on as usual and lost her apprehensive look, once it had seemed certain that I would continue living at the house, and I made very sure not to put a foot wrong, even though I was still unable to show any affection to anyone.

The day that I had left my foster-family to return with my father to our much-bombed and scarred home in London, remains cloudy to me. I remember nothing of the transition, my being too emotionally-drained. Was I troubled about the move at this time, or was I not? I cannot say, as I remember none of it, and retain only glimpses of the life that was to come in the following months.

At a later stage, I was to be in touch again with the Finches, but not yet awhile… not until much later, after my ill-fated marriage.

THE HOSTEL IN HOXTON

Before I was moved by the Welfare into the hostel in Hoxton, my life had been a bit of a shambles. I was thirteen years of age when I had been brought back to London to live with my father in rather unsatisfactory conditions. I'm sure that he did his best for me, but always having been a drinker, there was very little that he could offer.

The house in which he lived, in a very poor part of the East-end, was a hovel, with no creature comforts whatsoever. It was as much as my father could do to look after himself, without looking after me, and very soon I was moved to live with a much older sister, Jane, who had a daughter the same age as myself. My mother must have been very young when she had Jane – named after herself – and I had no knowledge of yet another sister, until she suddenly appeared on the scene.

My stay with her was uneventful. She must have known of my previous existence, yet I can't remember her even once being in touch with me during my former, unhappy years. I had recommenced my schooling at Hugh Myddleton Central which had, with its pupils, moved back to London. I felt a bit 'out on a limb' during this phase of my life. I had no affinity with this much-older sister, really, although I'm sure she did her best by me, and I got on well with Penny, her daughter and my niece. But they were strangers to me, really.

On one occasion while at school, I was taken by a teaching assistant to Moorfields Eye Hospital for an operation to have a cyst removed from under my lower lid. Afterwards, I was taken straight back to school, with my eye swathed in bandages, because there would have been nobody at home to look after me. So, when the Headmistress announced to all the pupils the next day, how brave I had been in coming straight back to school, even though I had felt rather faint at the time, I was very tempted to put her right, that it wasn't bravery, but necessity, which drove me back!

Through my foggy rememberings of this stage of my life, one incident is, none the less stamped very clearly on my memory. My much-older-sister requested of her husband, one Saturday, to take us two girls – her daughter and me – in to town to buy new shoes for us both. We were the same age as one another and took the same size in shoes. On arriving home with the shoes, however, my sister was intrigued as to why her daughter's shoes were far superior to the ones that had been bought for me, and questioned her husband regarding this.

"Oh," he replied, in a somewhat flippant manner. "Well, I bought the shoes for Liz off the market, that's why."

My sister looked aghast at him. "Will," she said, "Liz might not be your daughter, but she's my sister, and we get paid for looking after her. Don't treat her like some sort of servant."

It didn't really matter; I had got used to being treated as a nonentity. My brother-in-law wasn't a very nice person, anyway. I sometimes wondered why my sister had married him in the first place, and besides, unbeknown to me at that time, an exciting change was to come about in my life soon after this incident. I was to move with the sister who had been evacuated with me into a hostel in Hoxton. I was to be happy for the first time in a long while!

From the moment that we moved into the hostel, I felt that I belonged. We were all equal there – outcasts from sections of society, if you like. We bonded together, even though we were all of different ages, me being the youngest. I don't remember the day of moving, or why this sudden change had come about, but even today, after all these years, my memories of this phase in my life are of fondness and affection for Miss Jacobs and Mrs Busby, who lived at the Hostel and looked after all of us.

Miss Jacobs was a little formidable in comparison to Mrs Busby, who showered affection on us all, knowing, I think, of the hard times that most of her adopted family – as she used to refer to us – had had. Her beaming at us all, as she poured the tea from a large pot at breakfast time in the dining-room, and then again in the evenings at dinner, was something that money could never buy. She performed her duties with love. How could one not feel safe and secure, then, while being nurtured by this wonderful woman?

Miss Jacobs, as was required, struck a more formal pose. She was in charge of the running and maintenance of the Hostel. She took no nonsense from anyone; in fact, in my mind's eye, even today I see her wandering around, a slightly haughty expression showing on her somewhat haughty features, summing things up – making sure that all was as it should be. Nothing much escaped Miss Jaobs, and I clearly remember one night, as I crept through the front doors five minutes late, she was waiting on the other side of the doors, with key in hand, and she motioned for me to follow her into the office immediately next to the entrance. "You know I don't tolerate lateness, Liz," she berated me and, as I tried to point out it was only five minutes, she brushed it to one side. "You've got to remember," she told me, in her no-nonsense stance, "that if you, why not others!" No more needed to be said. I meekly apologised to Miss Jacobs and made sure that I wasn't late again.

As I crept up the stairs to my bedroom, however, Mrs Busby was coming down. She silently threw her arms around me in a big cuddle, while at the same time, she chastised me, a wicked glint in her eye. "Oh, how naughty you are, Liz!" It occurred to me then, as I quietly laughed with her, how like a mother and father she and Miss Jacobs were to me: one a necessarily-strict parent, and the other, a loving and forgiving being; and I loved them both, for how they were.

Every day at the Hostel was, for me, a treat. I was very young at the time – just fourteen – and had recently left school to work in a City office. Maybe being so young was a good enough reason for Mrs Busby's cosseting of me, although she was affectionate to everybody. The brightness radiating from her face, as she walked briskly along each day, wherever she was – usually with a large bunch of keys jangling from her hand: a key for this room; a key for that cupboard, so many different doors to open and close during the course of the day – but her expression never varied. She radiated happiness and affection to all of us residents, as we went about our daily business.

Absolutely no males, unless they were workmen, entered the Hostel: it was a completely female-dominated domain. This, personally, did not bother me, as plenty of social activity went on there, without the need for the opposite sex.

On one particular day, I remember a group of us decided to put on a show, which consisted of some Irish dancing, taught to us by a cultured young lady, whose fiancé was a newly-qualified doctor at the large hospital nearby, where she herself was a dietician. Most of the time was spent laughing, as this delightful person endeavoured to teach us the intricate steps of the dance. But, in the end, we mastered them to a certain degree and put on quite a good performance. It was with the singing, however, where we came unstuck, when one of the girls, deciding not to wear her glasses, even though she could see practically nothing without them, finished up facing the wrong way as we took a bow at the end.

The laughter then from the audience, outclassed anything that I'd ever heard before. We led this almost-blind singer back to her glasses. "What an idiot I've been!" she exclaimed, as things came back into focus. But we thumped her on the back. "You were the star of the evening!" we told her. And what's more, we meant it!

The day someone suggested attempting a séance, though, I realised before long, we were making a mistake. I had no idea what this constituted and became quite frightened after a while, when strange things started to happen. Most of those around the table were laughing at what was evolving, but I became alarmed. I slid quietly from my chair and went to my room until the séance was finished. I came downstairs later for the nightly drinks of Horlicks or cocoa, which were being poured out by Mrs Busby, who mildly chastised those responsible for their suggestion of this unacceptable pastime. "Look at Liz's white face, she told them, as I walked into the dining-room. "You must never play that again," she finished, in a somewhat authoritative manner.

279

A group of the Hostel girls – August, 1948, whilst I was in hospital. My sister, Barbara, is second from the left in the front row.

On Saturday morning, we were all required to change the bedding in our rooms, and to hoover and dust them. Mrs Busby would be there with her keys, praising us for our efforts as, at the same time, she oversaw all the activity going on. As she stood one morning chatting to us, we all became aware of a lot of shouting coming from one of the Saturday-morning market traders in the street below the Hostel. Mrs Busby dashed to the open window in my room and stuck her head out. "What's the matter?" she called.

The enraged hot-dog stall-holder indicated the open window next to mine. "Someone 'as just thrown a load of long 'air outa tha' window, and it's landed in among me 'ot sausages!" he bellowed. "I've a good mind to come up there an' knock that person's block of! 'ow can I serve these people 'ere with 'ot dogs that's all arrand wiv 'air? It's people like you wot ruins people like us, that's wot!" he finished.

Mrs Busby apologised profusely and, with the young lady responsible, she had no choice but to go and buy those inedible sausages, and to see that it never happened again. The stall-holder wasn't easily-appeased. "I'll knock yer block off next time," he told the chastened young lady, as he handed her the sausages.

During the months that I lived at the Hostel, there were several changes of people in that 'hot-dog tragedy' room next to mine, and one day I became aware of two newcomers sharing the room, another bed having been squeezed into it. This was most unusual to have two in these small rooms, and I was very intrigued.

"Liz, this is Norma, and her mum, who will be occupying the room next to you." Mrs Busby was introducing me to my new neighbours, as we ate in the dining room. I looked with interest at these two new people, and tried not to show the astonishment that I felt as I viewed them.

Norma was a girl of about the same age as myself, and she was quite lovely: dark-haired and with laughing brown eyes – these were the first thing I noticed about her. She shook my hand vigorously, before turning to her mother while at the same time putting her arm round this completely contrasting person's shoulder.

"This is my mum," she announced to me, her eyes momentarily beseeching me to say nothing.

As I made this woman's acquaintance, shock-waves went through me. Had I heard correctly? Surely this woman must be Norma's elderly grandmother, not mother, I thought. But what alarmed me the most, was the almost completely flat nose adorning her elderly features. What on earth had brought that about?

To my credit, I managed to maintain an equilibrium, which reasoned that it was quite acceptable to have a flattened nose like that, but my innermost thoughts jangled away inside me in opposition. I nonetheless chatted away to this person who, as she talked to me, threw continuous loving glances towards her ebullient and protective daughter, who hung on her every word.

I never did discover the circumstances that drove Norma and her mother to seek refuse at the Hostel. They weren't with us for long, but while we had them, they were a joy to behold: Norma laughing and her mother with her. But one day, they were gone as mysteriously as they came, and not a word had been divulged about them. The first I knew of their sudden departure was seeing the extra bed being removed from the bedroom that they had occupied. I would miss them and wished that I had been there to say goodbye before they so secretly left. I pondered afterwards on the circumstances of this mother and daughter. I remembered the fierce protectiveness bestowed by Norma onto her mother who, quite frankly, resembled a prize-fighter, so badly battered was her face. It occurred to me then, as I sat on the bed in my little room weighing things up, that in all probability these two nice people had been victims of domestic violence… a lot of heavy-drinking went on in the East-end of London! There was no doubt in my mind any longer that, yes, Norma and her mother were under government protection from their abuser, being secretly moved from place to place. I remembered how they never went out during all the time they were at the Hostel, how they never talked about their circumstances, and now they had been moved to another place of safety, and I had not had the opportunity to wish them well. One minute they were there, the next they were gone!

As I got off the bed to go down for the evening meal, I felt completely bogged down with sadness. I would have liked to have talked about things relating to the sudden loss of my neighbours – Norma, who had so bravely shielded her mother from any, even unintentional, ridicule, owing to her rather grotesque appearance. She laughed continuously, and also had her mother laughing at anything and everything. That is as I shall always remember her: this very young person, who even though she had this heavy burden on her shoulders, managed to rise above it. She could so easily have been ashamed of her mother's bizarre looks to have become cowed, but she had been too brave for this. Her fighting spirit sustained her. She had been, while at the Hostel, like a mother lion ferociously protecting her cub from imminent danger! How I had wished that I could have remained in touch with this enigmatic couple, but the circumstances surrounding them were too covert. "Sorry, Liz, my sweet, I can't disclose anything." Mrs Busby put her arm around my shoulders then: "Just forget they were here, Darling," she said, quietly and earnestly, to me. So much for my enquiry. I had no choice, then, but to do as Mrs Busby requested. I shelved Norma and her poor mother to the recesses of my mind, but I never totally forgot them.

FIRST LOVE

The day John came bursting into my life was like a shaft of sunlight suddenly bursting through a heavy cloud.

He had been doing a stint in the fashion shop, which traded right next door to the Hostel. This boutique was owned by a vociferous Jew, who never stopped in his endeavour to entice the young ladies from the Hostel into his shop. "Morning girls. How are we terday, then?" This was his greeting each day, as we left the Hostel to travel to our places of work. He was always loitering around in his attempt to engage us in conversation, and would quickly inform us of any new lines that had arrived at the shop. "Let me know if yer ever need ter get anywhere urgently, cos me car's just around the back," he'd tell us in his Cockney way of speaking. As though we would allow this! He was probably completely harmless, but who knows?

It was in a Saturday morning when I had ventured into the shop with a couple of other girls from the Hostel to inspect his latest 'new line', (there's safety in numbers, we had laughingly told one another), when I became aware of John. He was working there each Saturday to earn some pocket-money, while he was at college, he told us. He certainly was an asset to the place, with his good-looks and pleasant manner.

"Na' look a' this," and "look a' that – would suit yer a treat." Our talkative shop-owner never stopped snapping at our heels. "Na' come on, gels, wha'd yer think, then?"

All three of us eventually finished up with a dress each, which John then stowed carefully into three elaborate bags. And that is how I came to meet him.

What fun we had together, even though we had hardly a spare penny between us. But John came from a truly lovely family who welcomed me with open arms: just to be with them was bliss.

One evening, though, as he and I met to go to the pictures, I could see that John was very upset. His eyes looked a bit red, as though he had been crying. As I showed my concern, he divulged to me, in a choking manner, that his little sister, whom I knew to be Downes-Syndrome, had been bought a kitten by their parents. She loved this little thing but, tragically, as she cuddled it later in the day, while her parents were otherwise occupied, she clutched it too tightly and before anyone could do anything, it died! The whole household was grieving, as was John. It made me realise what a wonderful person he was and, to my lasting regret, because of our youth, and what was to happen within a few months, we were destined to part.

JOHN

Life for me, I know, would have been so different, so much more secure, had I stayed with John… but it wasn't to be. My happiness with him was soon to be disrupted.

A bout of influenza while living at the hostel, lay me very low. There were several of us bedridden with it, and Mrs Busby was rushed off her feet going from one to the other, attending our needs. Like the others, I shakily threw off this debilitating virus that had struck us down, but we were all left very weak. It had been a particularly virulent strain that had attacked us and, although we left our beds, we languished around as if all the energy had been sapped out of us.

John

285

"Let's take a picnic to Epping Forest on Sunday morning, now you're feeling better. The fresh-air will do you good." John's enthusiasm rather outstripped mine, as I weakly agreed to this suggestion of his. I was feeling very fragile still, after suffering this potentially-lethal illness, but brushed how I felt to one side, as I convinced myself that the fresh-air that John had mentioned was, indeed, probably what I needed.

Sunday proved to be a beautiful day, as we travelled by bus to the Forest. We had a lovely time as we walked and walked through its beautiful woodlands, while stopping at a little wayside tea-bar to eat our sandwiches.

It was then, as we sat on the grass together, that I became conscious of the pain in my legs. I said nothing at that stage to John, but as we later made our way for the bus to take us home, it became almost impossible for me to walk! In our alarm then, we viewed my legs, which were by then, very swollen.

"Straight to bed, Liz." Mrs Busby took command, as she watched me limp through the doors on our arrival back at the Hostel. "And tomorrow, we will call the doctor," she called after me as, with some difficulty, I negotiated the stairs to my room.

"The hospital it will have to be, I'm afraid." The doctor lost no time in telling us this, after his examination of me. "I believe she has acute nephritis, an aftermath of influenza," he knowledgeably told Mrs Busby.

What a terrible shock! But by this time, my face was swelling up also, and the outcome was that I spent the next three weeks in hospital recovering from this unpleasant and enfeebling illness, brought on by the after-effects of 'flu; this vicious virus, that we now know can be quite deadly.

It was almost worth my enduring being hospitalised, though, I told myself later, for the convalescence which followed. Miss Jacobs had arranged for Mrs Busby to take me, with a group of girls, to a beautiful country-house called Effingham House, in Copthorn, Surrey. It was the middle of October, but we were fortunate in having a beautiful week, weather-wise. We had several holidays at this lovely place, thereafter, all arranged by Miss Jacobs and Mrs Busby, who truly had their residents' welfare at heart.

Effingham House, Copthorne

We were like one big family, all going off together for these lovely, inexpensive holidays. All of us, who had been somewhat lost and disquieted when we first entered the Hostel, embraced one another now in friendship and togetherness, feeling a sense of belonging, which had been missing in most of our lives.

But, after the living at the Hostel for almost a year, my sister, who had initially moved in there with me, but of whom I had seen very little, suddenly announced one day to me at breakfast, "Liz, I think we should move back to St Albans." She had developed itchy feet and was impatient now to go back to where we had formerly been evacuated, and where she had left friends behind. She never had completely settled back in London.

I was in a quandary at this sudden announcement from her. It couldn't have come at a worse time as I, along with everyone else at the Hostel, was in a state of grieving over the recent loss of Mrs Busby, who had been ill one minute, and then had died quite suddenly, the next. The loss of her to everybody was catastrophic and we were all still reeling from the shock of this terrible event in our lives.

Over the next few days, after this announcement from my sister, I wavered from one decision to another. Yes! I would go with her... No! I wouldn't. How could I? It would mean leaving John. It would take me away from the security of living at the Hostel. But there was no Mrs

Busby there now to cosset us. A ray of sunshine had gone from our lives. What should I do? What should I do?

In the end, I reluctantly agreed to go with my sister, not realising at the time that it was completely the wrong decision. But I had lost my anchor at the Hostel. I was confused and grieving. Maybe this was what I needed, I told myself, to get away for a spell. I could always come back if things didn't work out; but this was not to be.

DARKNESS

Once again, the occasion of moving back to the country remains a blur to me. I remember nothing of any goodbyes at the Hostel; nothing of the departure from John. This had always been my way of coping with the sadness of my life – my survival tactic, if you like – and my memory returns only as I recall living with Greta, in her house on a large council estate in St Albans.

Greta was a street-wise, no-holds-barred, ebullient type of person. She was married to Jack who, in complete contrast, was a gentle giant of a man, and they had twin boys.

The estate, to me, was depressing and had only recently been built. It was full of young, hard-up mothers who, with their husbands, struggled to survive on poor wages and nothing much else, and I suspect that this was why Greta took my sister and me in: to supplement her income. I felt really sorry for private dwellers on the other side of the lane to where we now lived. They had become trapped in their lovely, contrasting private houses and bungalows since the building of this ugly estate right opposite them. Who would want to buy these lovely private properties, blighted by these ugly, featureless houses which faced them on the other side of the lane?

The rapid erection of these cheap, featureless council dwellings, built in haste by the government because of the sudden population explosion which followed the cessation of the War, gave a truly bleak outlook in their unattractive sameness, as they stood row upon row along the opposite side of the lane to their alluring neighbours.

One day, I was completely taken aback as I walked from the bus along the lane. A truly bizarre sight met my eyes, and I felt even more sorry for the private home-dwellers on the other side of the lane, as they must have viewed this spectacle which came towards me. A group of people, walking in crocodile-style, was coming in my direction. It was headed by a dark-skinned man, wearing a turban and long, black flowing robes. He was followed by a woman wearing a burka over her face and long black clothing which hardly moved, as she glided along, silently and unobtrusively. She held the hand of a very young child, while three others followed sedately behind her.

A second woman, who was similarly-attired to the first, then came upon the scene, and she was also followed by four children, all of them walking in silent obedience behind the leader with the turban. I stood in amazement as they all passed me, their eyes fixed firmly to the front of them. What on earth were these primitive people doing living here in our liberated country? I thought, as I stood glued to the spot.

It later transpired that this strange man, with his two wives and his brood of children, lived further along the lane, and he had been clever enough to use his religion to persuade the council to knock two houses into one to accommodate his two wives – which, according to him, was permitted by his religion – and his numerous children. Only after all of this had been accomplished, did an eminent follower of his religion speak out that the man was a disgrace to the brotherhood. "Only those who could afford two wives and an abundance of children should go ahead with this commitment," he had declared. "Man should not allow himself to become a burden on the state through dishonesty," he had finished. Well! good for him, I had thought at the time. These wily people, who used their religion for their own selfish advantage were hypocrites! Did our government not have enough to cope with? I remember thinking at the time.

Within a short span of time, something similar happened at our local hospital, where I worked as a receptionist on the main reception. A seemingly very cordial foreign gentleman came to me at the desk to request a change of time in his appointment to see one of the consultants.

"I'm afraid that the time I have on this card," he said, as he held the appointment card towards me, "interferes with my prayer-time." He smiled brightly at me as he said this. I was very apologetic and assure him that I would do the necessary in getting the time altered. But just as he was in the process of walking away, he was waylaid by a young doctor who had been sitting in the large reception area, which also contained the W.R.V.S. tea-bar. He had been availing himself of some refreshment and had heard the request being made. He accosted the complainant in a controlled but angry manner: "Now, you must know as well as I do," he said to the surprised man, who stood wearing his prayer hat, which is usually worn only when going to the mosque, "… you must know that you are excused prayers in the case of medical needs, so why are you bothering this lady with an unnecessary request?" The young doctor, who was obviously of the same religion as the dissatisfied patient, looked over to me after he had said this. "Just keep his appointment as it was." he called to me. "We're much too busy to pander to people."

As he saw this foreign gentleman to the exit, I could see that he was still chiding him, but I did as I had been told, I kept the appointment as it had been. I was annoyed, though, that once again, here had been yet another person using his religion unfairly as a scapegoat, but how I admired his young accuser for taking the matter in hand – he could so easily have just sat and said nothing.

Part of my life while living with Greta and her family on this large, depressing estate, which seemed to be devoid of any character, was deeply unhappy. I, of course, missed living at the Hostel with all of its camaraderie, but it never occurred to me to move back there, which is, of course, what I should have done. I was happy in my job but lacked anybody to confide in. Who could advise me? So I stayed as I was, even though I really missed John.

Friday nights, I remember, at the house, were always reserved for the inviting in of the neighbours from next door, Sharon and Charlie. They played cards, but I always declined, having an abhorrence of this pastime with my having been forced so many times to play with 'Mum', when I was younger.

These Friday nights, however, in the house, were rather hilarious, with Jack, Greta's big, kindly husband, having difficulty controlling his farting! "Oh, Jack!" Greta would shout at him, each time he exploded. "There's no need for that – just control yourself."

"Look, I'm sorry, Janey," his pet name for Greta, "I'll try and control myself," he told her, as everyone, including me, laughed their heads off.

One night, he excused himself. "I'm just going into the kitchen for a drink of water," he told us, and he left the card-playing hastily. He hadn't been gone two minutes, when we all heard the biggest explosion ever. Phff! and then Jack walked back into the room, all innocent-looking and carrying his glass of water.

"JACK!" Greta was telling him, amongst all the laughter. "I'm taking you to the doctor tomorrow, because there's definitely something wrong with you when you can't play a game of cards without farting all the time."

With all the hilarity in the house, however, an undercurrent of drama prevailed. It would appear that Sharon had found herself unintentionally pregnant, but Greta had assured her, in her distress, that she would put matters right for her. "I'll come round tonight when all the children are in bed," she told her friend and neighbour, "and I'll bring one of my long knitting needles with me. I'll soon sort things out for you, don't worry!"

And so the deed was done, but soon after, Sharon had to be taken urgently to the hospital for a blood transfusion, so much haemorrhaging had the abortion brought on. The shock of all this to me was catastrophic, that people indulged in this sort of thing, and I sought solace in a colleague at the hospital. "Oh, yes. I know it goes on." She nodded her head slowly in a sad manner. "I happen to live on the edge of that estate, and only a short while ago I witnessed an abortion performed on one of the young mothers there. It was a little boy; born dead, of course. I would have had him myself, rather than for that to have happened."

I made up my mind there and then, that I must move away from this hell-hole. I could not accept this way of living, and tolerate this low-class, depressing estate, which made me feel miserable each time I came onto it, but I was glad it took a few weeks for me to move, because I was there for Charlie, Sharon's husband, when he came to the hospital one day on a mission to see his elderly mother who was in the geriatric wing. He came to say hello to me on his departure and, as we chatted to one another, Charlie suddenly broke down in tears.

I was completely taken aback – one minute he had been smiling as we had chatted away, and the next, he was sobbing! I rushed to his side to console him, and led him somewhere more private as he released the tears. "What a fool I'm making of myself, Liz," he said, shamefacedly to me, "but it's just things, you know." He cried some more, as I told him that he had nothing to be ashamed of, and that it was probably a good thing that he had released his feelings. I knew as well as he did why he had broken down like that. One minute he was going to have an addition to the family, and the next – nothing.

"You won't mention this to Sharon, will you?" he said, as he wiped his eyes.

"Of course I won't," I assured him. But, yes, I was glad that I would soon be moving. Everything seemed so dismal on that estate. At least, where I was moving to was not way-out-and-beyond as it was there. I would be moving to a more-settled community, where mostly retired people lived; and what's more, it was slap-bang right next to my place of work, and just a little distance from the town. Oh, yes, I'll be much happier, I told myself.

THE DOTTY LANDLADY

I wrinkled my nose with distaste, as I entered the toilet on that first day in my new abode. My eyes straight away took in the squares of newspaper hanging from the wall, immediately by the lavatory pan. Someone had screwed a hole near the edge of the squares of paper and threaded some string through them before adjoining the whole lot to the wall for people to use as toilet paper.

I was appalled at the scrimping of money by the people I now lived with. A proper toilet roll didn't cost that much, surely. I decided to wait until I got to my place of work, rather than wipe my private regions with newspaper, and I would, in the meantime, buy myself a toilet roll for my own use, I told myself.

I had moved in with my brother's in-laws, Mr and Mrs Brimm: the empty-headed one, and the whisky drinker. "We will look after you," I had been told, and an agreement had been made for me to pay an amount each week for my keep. Maybe, I had thought to myself, they would be able now to buy some proper toilet rolls, but they never did. On the rare occasions that I used the toilet while living there, I would sneak in with my own privately-bought paper. There was no way I was going to poison my system with heavy print.

The food that I was given while living with the Brimms was disgusting. It started in the morning with tea and toast, the tea having been watered-down so much, it was a wonder it had the strength to leave the pot.

As I left the house for work after breakfast, I would have a pack of sandwiches put into my hand. "There you are, then. I've made this especially for you for your midday lunch." Mrs Brimm would be grinning from ear to ear, and giving that silly little nervous laugh as she handed the sandwiches to me. I knew, though, what I would be doing with the packed lunch each day as I arrived at my place of work: straight in the rubbish bin. I had discovered that they had been wrapped in blood-stained paper, which had been around the weekend joint of meat, the blood having been dried off so as to enable the grease-proof paper to be used again, namely for my daily sandwiches.

I waited patiently each morning for the W.R.V.S. tea-bar to open, so that I could fill-up with the delicious jam doughnuts that were delivered each day to the hospital. It came as no great surprise to me, then, when Mrs Brimm went down one week with serious food poisoning. The doctor came several times to his stricken patient, and it was some days before she was able to appear, in a very weak state, from the bedroom.

I had taken the opportunity, meanwhile, to make sure that I had some decent tea with my toast in the mornings, but the sandwiches for my midday lunch, I didn't bother with, because the bread would be several days old, and the paper to wrap the sandwiches in was, as usual, blood-stained.

To my amazement, Mrs Brimm was overwhelmed by what had happened to her – what had made her so ill. "I can't understand it," she said, as she had languished in a very fragile state on the settee in the living-room. "I'm always so careful with food," she assured us.

Never mind, I felt like saying, as least I've had some decent cups of tea while you were so ill. But I kept my mouth shut. Nothing would ever be any different in the house, I told myself. The cut-up newspaper in the lavatory to wipe your bottom; the dried out blood-stained paper in the kitchen for wrapping around sandwiches and things; the greasy, several-days-old mutton stew with patches of fat floating on top, which was served up in the evening. All of these health hazards would remain because Mrs Brimm hadn't the common-sense to realise how dangerous they were. It's just a good thing, I told myself, that I was soon to be married and I would be shot of all this, not realising at this time that I would be jumping straight out of the frying pan into the fire.

My fiancé was very young, (as was I), and handsome. We had met at the community's Saturday night 'hop'. His dancing, I had noticed, as I stood with my friends observing the couples as they swirled past, was very suave, and this had been what had first attracted me to him; so that when he made my acquaintance later in the evening, I was quite agreeable to being his partner.

As he walked me home very late that night, he told me that he was in the retail trade, as leading assistant at the large, local 'Co-op'. I was very impressed! It seemed to me then, to be a leader of anything was quite something.

As our courtship proceeded, it seemed that he, like myself, was unhappy at home. In a very short space of time then, we decided to marry. We had no money and we were very young; but we were full of optimism. How foolish we were to plunge ahead, as we had done. The marriage was to be a disaster!

THE WEDDING

The question that I asked Mrs Brimm that evening, had initially evoked a look of intense pleasure but then, just as suddenly, her expression changed and was replaced by a serious, thoughtful, far-away gaze, which directed itself over my shoulder.

It was all very simple: I had just requested permission to get married from the house, but my landlady obviously wanted to make a big thing of it. "Well now." She rubbed her chin as she considered this appeal of mine. "Well, of course, you will have to ask Mr Brimm's permission," she told me. "He is, after all, the head of the house!" At this, she gave me one of her silly little laughs, and I just walked away. "All right," I had said. "I'll do that, Mrs Brimm."

What a stupid woman, I thought to myself, as I made my way to the head of the house, to once again beg permission, this time from her equally-stupid husband, for my request. He had had his tot of whisky, I thought as I sought him out, so he should be quite amenable; but the reaction from him, on me once again making my request, was even worse than that of his wife! He drew heavily on the cigar that he was smoking, and just looked past me, as though I wasn't there. Several minutes passed with nothing being said… I got up from where I sat, to leave him as he pondered on this seemingly difficult thing that I had asked of him. Only then did he demean himself to answer me, when he realised that he had been silent for too long. "Yes, yes," he said quickly, then, as I lingered at the door. "That will be all right; yes, that will be all right."

What a strange couple! In some ways they couldn't stand the sight of one another, she being empty-headed, and he being somewhat academic, but quite difficult to live with. "Why do you stay with him?" I had asked my tearful landlady, when I found her one day sobbing her eyes out in the kitchen. He had been particularly difficult and hurtful to his wife earlier on, and I stood comforting her in her misery.

"Oh, how could I leave him?" she told me, with tear-filled eyes. "My religion doesn't permit it, you see, Liz." The fact that neither of them was remotely interested in religion – even scornful of it, sometimes – didn't come into it.

When, because of my concern, I later discussed it in private with her daughter, she simply, with my brother, laughed her head off. "Religion, did you say!" she chortled, "my mother wouldn't even know the meaning of the word! Oh, ha-ha, that's the best yet. Look, Liz," she finished, "don't concern yourself like that. I can see that you have been upset but, believe me, my mother is quite capable of handling my father. He himself has a lot to put up with sometimes, you know." This didn't completely dissipate my feeling s on the matter, but I decided to take Beth's advice and put the issue aside; after all, I would be leaving this enigmatic couple soon.

The wedding took place on a beautiful September day. Mr and Mrs Brimm – this strange landlord and landlady of mine – were beside themselves with excitement as they bustled around about me, doing this and that in preparation for me to be whisked off to the church.

Mr Brimm was in excellent mood, having had several tots of whisky, and Mrs Brimm giggled away, darting here and there doing unnecessary things.

I didn't bother to look back as I left the house; in fact it was with some relief that I went from this mystifying household with its penny-pinching woman, and strange, moody man, who was happy one minute, but scathing the next. They had certainly put on a good act between the two of them when they had, some weeks earlier, hesitated in my request of them to allow me to be married from their house. It must have been a crafty pact of their twisted mentalities to intimidate a young, naive person, such as myself, I thought later, as I witnessed their obvious enjoyment of the whole affair – a rarity in their mundane lives.

'Extraordinary' would have been the word for me to use regarding the wedding itself, with yet another recently-discovered sister of mine turning up in an unbelievably over-elaborate hat, whose appearance was really quite laughable and caused quite a lot of head-turning. My prospective mother-in-law who, as with the rest of the entourage, showed an unexpected elegance, had, behind the scenes, anxiously hidden a bag of cigarettes, which were to be displayed on each table at the reception and which, to her annoyance, she had to quickly retrieve at the end, as nobody had availed themselves of even one of them.

Mr Brimm, in his half-cut state, laughed loudly all through the reception at anything and everything, and my father sat with impatience, just waiting to get away to the nearest pub for a booze-up to properly – in his eyes – celebrate his daughter's wedding. "Come on, Joe, Arthur, Jim, Charlie!" he had called out loudly at the end to my brothers. "Let's find somewhere to really celebrate!" And even though my brothers declined, he rushed off anyway, leaving a table full of church-going relatives looking quite shocked at his departure.

Not even a goodbye from him to me; and his former promise made to us in one of his more rational moments before the wedding, to settle-up money-wise with his share of expenses, just went with him to the pub! Was this charade of a wedding to be a forerunner of my mode of future living within the marital state? Indeed it was, but that's another story!